In the "neighborhood" of the Americas, Canada alone has maintained consistently cordial relations with Cuba, in spite of considerable pressure from the United States. In the first book-length study of the subject, John M. Kirk and Peter McKenna explore this unusual dynamic, focusing mainly on the period since 1959.

They begin with the evolution of the Canadian-Cuban relationship, which was initially founded on pragmatic economic and commercial considerations. Cuba has always been one of Canada's major trading partners in Latin America, and it is the second most popular vacation resort for Canadians. Subsequent chapters, ordered historically, explore each Canadian prime minister's response to the revolutionary government in Havana. Changing personalities and ideologies in that office have had a significant impact on Canada's Cuba policy. The authors also look at the relationship from the Cuban point of view: they have drawn on privileged interview and archival material from Cuba, including never-before-seen diplomatic records from Cuba's Foreign Ministry, to create a thoroughly rounded portrait.

In what is perhaps a controversial stance, the authors seek to use Canada's Cuba policy as a lesson in good neighborliness for the United States, and they dedicate their book to "all those who struggle for the introduction of common sense, dignity, and justice into U.S.-Cuban relations."

Canada-Cuba Relations

Canada-Cuba Relations

The Other Good Neighbor Policy

John M. Kirk
and Peter McKenna

University Press of Florida
Gainesville Tallahassee Tampa Boca Raton
Pensacola Orlando Miami Jacksonville

02 01 00 99 98 97 6 5 4 3 2 1

LIBRARY OF CONGRESS CATALOGING-IN-PUBLICATION DATA
Kirk, John M., 1951–
Canada-Cuba relations: the other good neighbor policy /
John M. Kirk and Peter McKenna.
p. cm.
Includes bibliographical references and index.
ISBN 0-8130-1520-0 (alk. paper)
1. Canada—Foreign relations—Cuba. 2. Cuba—Foreign relations—
Canada. 3. Canada—Foreign relations—1945–. I. McKenna, Peter,
1961–. II. Title.
F1029.5.C9K57 1997
327.7107291—dc21 96-51464

The University Press of Florida is the scholarly publishing agency for
the State University System of Florida, comprised of Florida A & M
University, Florida Atlantic University, Florida International University, Florida State University, University of Central Florida, University
of Florida, University of North Florida, University of South Florida,
and University of West Florida.

University Press of Florida
15 Northwest 15th Street
Gainesville, FL 32611

For all those who struggle for the
introduction of common sense, dignity,
and justice into U.S.-Cuban relations.
As the Canadian-Cuban relationship shows,
mutual respect and fairness can work wonders.

Americans should never underestimate the constant pressure on Canada which the mere presence of the United States has produced. We're different people from you and we're different people because of you. . . . Living next to you is in some ways like sleeping with an elephant. No matter how friendly and even-tempered is the beast, if I can call it that, one is affected by every twitch and grunt.

Pierre Elliot Trudeau, 1969

Yet despite these differences, they have been our best friends—the most firm and loyal, the most independent. . . . I have always given Canadian-Cuban relations as an example to follow. What a pity that, instead of having the United States so close by, and Canada so far away, it wasn't the other way around.

Fidel Castro, 1994

I think of all the things that have ever been done in my country, this [Helms-Burton law] is the stupidest. . . . I think what is being done now is an insult to Canadians.

Jimmy Carter, 1996

Contents

Tables

Preface

The seed for this book was planted at a LASA conference several years ago when Rafael Hernández, of Havana's Centro de Estudios sobre América dragooned one of the authors into substituting on a panel on Cuban foreign relations when a participant didn't show up. The rest, as they say, is history. The topic came into clearer focus after John Kirk accompanied Premier John Savage of Nova Scotia as his counselor-interpreter on two successful commercial delegations to Cuba in 1994 and 1996.

Since then Kirk has acted in a variety of other functions that have helped provide further understanding of this dynamic: as a consultant for various Canadian companies with investments in and exports to Cuba; preparing a report on Canadian research priorities in Cuba for the International Development Research Centre; giving evidence on Cuba to foreign affairs committees of the Canadian Parliament; and working for a variety of nongovernmental organizations under the umbrella group of the Cuba-Canada Interagency Project. The specific topic of bilateral relations was then placed into the framework of Canada's fast-developing ties with Latin America by Peter McKenna.

We owe our gratitude to many people who have offered their insights into this topic, one that has become timely in the wake of Cuba's economic liberalization on the one hand, and Washington's repeated attempts to see the Castro government removed on the other.

An earlier version of this manuscript was read by Wayne Smith, of the Center for International Policy in Washington. Smith, both as a former diplomat (he headed the U.S. Special Interests Section in Havana during the Carter years) and as a scholar of U.S.-Cuban relations for many decades, provided valuable insights into diplomatic niceties of the trilateral relationship. Louis Pérez of the University of North Carolina at Chapel Hill, undoubtedly the leading scholar of Cuban history, encouraged the authors to step outside the original bilateral parameters to examine the role of powerful catalyst that Washington plays in Canada-Cuba relations, a fact that became increasingly important in the wake of the 1996 Helms-Burton legislation. Finally Michael Erisman, of Indiana State University, author of several works on Cuban foreign policy, provided a most useful background on Cuba's international relations against which the Canada–Cuba–United States triangle was set.

The bulk of the historical research of this work was carried out in Havana and Ottawa. Both the Department of External Affairs in Canada and its Cuban counterpart, the Ministerio de Relaciones Exteriores, graciously allowed extensive access to their archives. We owe a particular debt of gratitude to Carlos Alzugaray, who went above and beyond the call of duty to make sure that documentation from the ministry's archives was made available. His counterpart in the Historical Division in Ottawa was Ted Kelly, whose professionalism and untiring cooperation with both authors are much appreciated.

Diplomats are often the butt of much criticism—indeed Peter Ustinov once defined them as "nothing but a head-waiter who's allowed to sit down occasionally." In the case of Canadian-Cuban relations, however, there have been some fine representatives of the diplomatic craft in both countries—and it has been our pleasure to have met with them on many occasions. From the Cuban side, three outstanding ambassadors deserve recognition: José Fernández de Cossío, Carlos Castillo, and Bienvenido García Negrín. Fernández de Cossío read and offered several useful criticisms on the manuscript. The firm footing of bilateral relations is due largely to his untiring work during the Trudeau years. Castillo was ambassador to Canada during the Mulroney years, not an easy time, yet he worked assiduously and with great skill to develop the relationship. His successor, García Negrín, the current ambassador, has maintained this tradition.

They have been supported by a number of extremely competent professionals. Among those who have been particularly helpful to the course of this material are Aurora Gramatges, for many years the first secretary in the Ottawa embassy and a walking encyclopedia on Canada-Cuba relations; Lourdes Urrutia, the former Cuban consul in Montreal; Carlos Fernández de Cossío, head of the North American bureau of MINREX, who knows Canada well, having spent much of his formative youth—and learning how to play hockey—in Ottawa, where his father was ambassador; and Dagoberto Rodríguez, Rubén Ramos, Mario Medina, Deborah Ojeda, Jorge Ferrer, Miguel Alfonso, José Cabañas, and Mario García, all of whom have treated this project with great respect and cooperation. To them all, our heartfelt gratitude.

We owe a debt of gratitude to some other Cubans who assisted us in understanding the commercial aspect of the bilateral relations. Ramón Castro, both in Canada and Cuba, has been generous and supportive in appreciating the agricultural ties that bind the two countries (as can be seen from the descendants of Canadian Holstein cattle that dot the Cuban countryside). Raúl Domínguez and Mayra Gil, representatives of the Cuban Fishing Fleet in Canada, as well as Jesús Benjamín (the experienced and wise deputy minister of the Cuban Fishing Industry), have often provided invaluable insights into the excellent fishing relations between the two countries.

Colleagues in the Ministry of Foreign Trade in Havana who have also worked hard in providing assistance on trade matters are two superb specialists on things Canadian, Marilú de la Luz B'Hamel and Obdulia Barreiro. Their colleague in Montreal, Cuban trade commissioner Alberto Río, and his successor, Héctor Pérez, have also been extremely helpful to this project. Old friends Ineloy and René Rey are also to be recognized for their support since our paths first crossed more than twenty years ago.

On the Canadian side there are also many diplomats who have provided invaluable advice. For some twenty years embassy personnel in Havana have been contacted for a variety of research projects and in general have been unfailingly polite and cooperative. Of particular importance is Mark Entwistle, who has been Canadian ambassador to Cuba since 1994. A tireless and extremely talented negotiator, he is undoubtedly the most dynamic and successful ambassador to Cuba during the revolutionary period. He, more than any other individual, is the reason for the successful relationship currently enjoyed by both countries. Others from the Canadian embassy who have been helpful are Nobina Robinson and Roberta Cross. A particular debt of gratitude is owed to David Morrison, who for several years was first secretary and who possessed a first-rate understanding of things Cuban.

On a more general level, the authors are grateful to a variety of current and past members of the Department of Foreign Affairs and International Trade, who have provided comments on the broad topic of Canadian policy toward Latin America. These include Harold Hickman, John Graham, Richard Gorham, Paul Durand, Karen MacDonald, Peter Boehm, Brian Dickson, Alfred Pick, and Doug George. Thanks are also in order for Tommy Bruce, Elizabeth Spehar, Gabriel Silva, Rafael Pardo, and César Gaviria, all of the Organization of American States. Their ideas and insights have strengthened the intellectual content of our study.

Others who have been helpful in understanding the dynamic are Jim Sutherland and Stephen Free, who direct an impressive development assistance program in Cuba for CIDA, and former ambassadors Jim Hyndman and Ken Williams, who provided helpful insights into the Cuba policy of the Trudeau years. Of great assistance too has been Ross Snyder, who heads the Cuba desk in Foreign Affairs and whose understanding of the bilateral relations has always been fair and balanced.

A variety of other friends from diverse backgrounds have also been involved in numerous discussions about Cuban matters. While we apologize for any omissions, we would like to thank Arch Ritter, who has pioneered Cuban studies in Canada for so long; his colleague at Carleton University, David Pollock, who read the manuscript and made helpful suggestions; Roderick and Jean Barman and Sandor Halebsky of UBC; Ivan Head, formerly senior foreign policy advisor of Pierre Trudeau and now professor of law at UBC; Doug Lewis of the Canadian Council for the Americas; Minor Sinclair and Martha Thompson who direct some first-rate projects for OXFAM-Canada in Cuba; my colleague at Dalhousie Julia Sagebien, who has written extensively about bilateral commercial ties; Ian Delaney, Patrice Merrin Best, and Carolyn Hunt of Sherritt International, who have borne the brunt of unfair attacks against them resulting from the Helms-Burton legislation; Mark Drake of the Canadian Exporters' Association; Bob Whitney of McGill University, the author of a superb doctoral thesis on pre-revolutionary Cuba; Sheila Katz of the Canadian Labour Congress and Chris Rosene and Mark Fried of the Cuba-Canada Interagency Project; Senator Heath McQuarrie for his decency in pursuing the development of bilateral ties many years ago; colleagues at FOCAL (Juanita Montalvo, Hal Klepak, and Wendy Drukier); Wanda Hebb, our efficient secretary who helped us survive the perils of word processing; and Noni and Doug MacDonald, for their research support and friendship in Ottawa during many trips there.

Finally we would like to thank our families for their support in our academic endeavors these many years—Austin and Angelina McKenna, and the Kirk clan, Margo, Lisa, Michael, and Emily.

Needless to say, we accept full responsibility for views expressed in this book and for the accuracy of translation into English of original Spanish material. It is a timely topic—presenting as it does an implied comparison with U.S. policy toward Cuba. Precisely because of the emotions resulting from an analysis of contemporary Cuba, it is inevitable that there will be criticism from some quarters. Be that as it may, we believe that the message of bilateral relations between Canada and Cuba *should* be told: it *is* possible to have a mutually beneficial relationship, as can be seen here—and as President Franklin Roosevelt outlined in his inaugural presidential address. We hope that this study will act as a catalyst to all those seeking to examine the real Cuba, warts and all, and that it can lead to an examination as to how this approach can be applied elsewhere.

Introduction

Let us imagine this scenario: Newt Gingrich flew to Cuba in October 1995, to deliver $3 million in medical aid; Ricardo Alarcón, president of the National Assembly, was invited to Washington in 1995, where a dinner in his honor was hosted by Gingrich and the U.S. Congress; in January 1997 Secretary of State Albright flew to Havana to discuss foreign relations with Fidel Castro; while expressing concern over Cuba's human rights policy, the Senate Foreign Relations Committee recommended in a special report on U.S.-Caribbean relations a fast-track approach to trade with Cuba; the president of the National Bank of Cuba and the minister for foreign relations were invited to Washington by the government; Vice-President Lage addressed a group of business representatives in New York; after a long hiatus, development assistance to Cuba was renewed by the Congress; Jimmy Carter flew to Cuba in September 1995, heading an influential group of potential investors in its economy; President Clinton called openly for the United States to "turn the page" in its relations with Cuba; by 1996, more than a hundred U.S. universities had established relations with their Cuban counterparts; during the winter direct flights from more than a hundred U.S. cities took 1.5 million Americans to Cuba to vacation; off the eastern seaboard 100 Cuban factory trawlers fished in U.S. waters; the governors (or deputy governors) of seventeen states had headed commercial delegations to Cuba over two years to drum up business.

Virtually all of this challenges the imagination of the U.S. body politic in the late 1990s, bogged down in the Cold War rhetoric and climate of mutual animosity that has plagued U.S.-Cuban relations for almost four decades. The Trading with the Enemy Act (the title says it all), assassination attempts on Cuba's president in the 1960s, the funding and training of an exile army to overthrow the Cuban government in 1961, pressure on U.S. allies to break diplomatic and economic relations with Havana (seen most clearly in the Torricelli bill of 1992 and the Helms-Burton law of 1996), a vocal exile minority, threats and counterthreats during this time, and, finally, nine presidents vowing to set foot in a free and independent Cuba have all created a psychological black hole that makes it difficult to imagine anything other than the status quo. Put simply, any of these approaches to revamping bilateral policy are absolutely unthinkable in the mid-1990s, and any U.S. politician advocating such policies would probably be committing political suicide.

Yet at the same time all of these developments reflect what Canada has in fact done in the last few years in its bilateral policy toward Cuba. While some editorial license has been taken (multiplying some of the numbers by a factor of ten—the approximate differential in population size—in the case of university connections, number of fishing vessels, and tourists to Cuba), the rest is a fair reflection of the Canadian approach to the "Cuban question." In the fall of 1995, Speaker of the House of Commons Gilbert Parent did travel to Cuba with medical aid, Alarcón was invited to Ottawa for a formal state dinner, Minister of Foreign Affairs Lloyd Axworthy did meet with President Castro in Havana to discuss human rights and international relations, the Canadian Senate Foreign Relations Committee did advocate a strong Canadian trade interest in Cuba, Bank President Soberón and Foreign Relations Minister Robaina were both invited to Ottawa by the Canadian government in 1995 (and Minister of Foreign Investment Meléndez and Vice-President Lage also visited Canada that year), former Prime Minister Trudeau did return (as he has on several occasions) with a Canadian business delegation, and a third of Canadian premiers have traveled to Cuba in the last two years. Perhaps just as important, during that period influential Canadian politicians (the prime minister, minister of foreign relations, secretary of state for Latin America, and minister of international trade) have all decried U.S. policy toward Cuba, stating that "the 1990s are not the 1960s" and urging Washington to "turn the page." In early 1997, Minister of Foreign Affairs Axworthy, returned to Canada with a wide-ranging bilateral accord on human rights, ministerial cooperation, and exchanges.

And this from a people who share so much in common with their neighbors across the 49th parallel. The proverbial "world's largest undefended border," close political ties, and defense alliances (NATO and NORAD) all illustrate the common front in foreign policy shared by Washington and Ottawa. The United States is also the single largest market for goods produced in Canada—fully 80 percent of Canadian exports go there—and under NAFTA steady growth in this trend is indicated. Culturally we are also similar: Canadian hockey players dominate U.S. teams, while American baseball players dominate the rosters in Canada. Canadian cultural figures (from Michael J. Fox to Céline Dion) head south to be discovered, and thus garner lucrative contracts, as do Canadian journalists (Peter Jennings and Robert MacNeil). Far more pervasive, though, is the wave of popular culture flooding northward. We speak the same language, revere the same heroes and heroines, drive the same automobiles, and do not feel particularly threatened by the other's presence.

Yet in our policy toward Cuba we have each pursued a radically different approach, in no small degree because Canada has never held any pretensions to being a superpower, nor does it have a vocal and powerful Cuban exile population. As a result, aided in part by its geographical distance from Cuba, it has never in any way felt threatened or pressured by the Castro government. Similarly, Havana has adopted a respectful stance toward Ottawa, and the level of political dialogue has generally been remarkably civilized, even when there have been fundamental disagreements, such as over Cuba's role in Angola. For, while the Canadian government harbors reservations about Cuban human rights policies, it has expressed those concerns in a thoughtful, nonthreatening fashion. Engagement, civility, and respect have constituted the lowest common denominator, and the ensuing dialogue and negotiations generally have worked.

In sum, while it is a relationship that is not particularly important to Canada, which exports to the United States in one day more than it does in a year to Cuba, it is nevertheless one that has been built on a foundation of dialogue and respect. It is not particularly lucrative for either side (some $500 million in bilateral trade in 1996), but it is one in which steady commercial connections have been maintained since the eighteenth century, when vessels from the Maritime provinces of Canada traded salt cod and lumber for rum and sugar. (Unless otherwise stated, all references to dollars are to Canadian currency.)

A subtheme of this book springs from the Canadian-Cuban and Canadian-American relationship, since the strictly bilateral Ottawa-Havana axis is often affected by Washington's concerns and pressures, at times converting it into a trilateral relationship. Indeed, with some consistency the United States has taken the natural affinity between the two North American neighbors as the justification for seeking to bring Ottawa to its side. In most cases this has backfired, as can be seen most recently in a fierce rejection by Canada of the Helms-Burton law. Nevertheless, it is a common feature of the relationship.

The closeness of Canadian-Cuban relations is partly a function of a shared or common foreign policy "problem" in the sense that both countries have had to deal with the myriad challenges posed by their superpower neighbor. Both countries are significantly affected by the United States in a variety of crucial domestic and foreign policy areas. Clearly, Canadian and Cuban sovereignty—political, diplomatic, economic, or cultural—has been directly challenged, albeit to different degrees, by the superpower reach of the United States. Over the years, the political leaders in Ottawa and Havana have been engaged in devising political and economic strategies to bolster or strengthen the sovereignty or independence of each country vis-à-vis Washington. And from a security or territorial standpoint, both countries, and their respective populations, have maintained a deep-seated concern about the potential implications of U.S. "manifest destiny." Not surprisingly, then, both Canada and Cuba have been able to locate a nationalistic common ground upon which to build a mutually beneficial bilateral relationship.

Without any question, both Ottawa and Havana have had to resign themselves to the reality that they were, and continue to be, disconcertingly vulnerable to the twitches of the United States. Neither country could expect its behavior—either domestic or external—to be truly independent of Washington. In some ways, then, Canada's and Cuba's clear vulnerability to or dependence on the United States was a fact that they shared and one that represented an area of common concern and interest.

Having in common this shared hegemon, and the difficulties that it has entailed for each, has served to move Canada and Cuba closer to each other. Indeed, this common concern, which has resulted in periodic discussions on how best to cope with this inescapable reality, has provided an interesting basis for building a stronger bilateral relationship. For instance, it has helped not only to create a common bond between the two societies but also to set in place a positive tone for the relationship—perhaps even to diminish somewhat the differences and disagreements between the two countries. Rather than simply focus on the various problems of the bilateral relationship, it gave political leaders and government officials in each country a point of discussion on which both could agree.

Over time, it became increasingly obvious that both countries could derive mutual benefit if they could find a way to work together to confront this shared reality. Certainly both have seen their favorable environment for political dialogue, along with the continuation and deepening of their relationship, as a way to fortify their sovereignty and independence. This has manifested itself in a host of economic, political, cultural, and diplomatic exchanges. Put simply, the Canadian-Cuban dynamic, as seen from Ottawa and Havana, is an expression of each country's national independence and is designed in part to send this message to their own citizenry, to the United States, and to the rest of the world.

At a time when U.S. policy toward Cuba is again floundering, it is perhaps appropriate to examine the Canadian-Cuban relationship as a point of comparison. Most of what is noted here will not be applicable to Washington's approach to dealing with the "Cuban question." There is too much acrimonious history that has evolved on both sides of the Florida Straits, too much invective that has been hurled in both directions. That said, it is important to take stock of the style and content of the Canadian policy, given the fundamental similarities between U.S. and Canadian foreign policy goals, not to mention the deeply rooted cultural relationship that binds us. There might, in short, be something for Washington to learn from the manner in which Canada—for better or worse—has managed the Cuba file.

As will become clear, there have been many errors of judgment and a host of faux pas committed by both Canadian and Cuban diplomats and politicians. Yet through it all, based perhaps on a mixture of the proverbial Canadian compromise and on the Cuban need for commercial ties in the capitalist world, a tone of respect accompanied by fairly cordial relations has evolved. Fidel Castro has referred on many occasions to the relationship between Canada and Cuba, despite their radically different political ideologies and systems of government, as the model to be emulated in all of Havana's external relationships. And he is probably right, for it has served both countries well—in terms of domestic politics as well as international relations and commerce.

We seek to piece together both the nature of this bilateral relationship and the stages of its evolution. Following the first chapter, designed to set the historical scene, our approach has been to concentrate on the nature of the strategy toward Cuba adopted by each prime minister since the Cuban revolutionary victory in 1959. We have followed this model because foreign policy in Canada is largely set by the prime minister, supported by the cabinet of ministers, and then passed to the Foreign Affairs ministry where it is officially implemented.

Our analysis of thousands of diplomatic dispatches and cabinet documents, both in Havana and Ottawa, and of interviews and meetings with dozens of Canadian and Cuban politicians (former ministers, diplomats, and business leaders in Canada and their Cuban counterparts, including Foreign Relations Minister Robaina, President of the National Assembly Alarcón, and President Castro) has showed us that at times there have been serious problems in the bilateral relationship, with errors on both sides. Yet the historical record has shown that despite many of these errors, and despite the fact too that some diplomats and members of the security service—in both Canada and Cuba—have still not come to terms with the end of the Cold War, common sense and respect have generally prevailed.

Franklin D. Roosevelt, in his inaugural speech of March 4, 1933, noted a new direction to be followed by Washington toward Latin America: "In the field of world policy, I would dedicate this nation to the policy of the Good Neighbor, the neighbor who resolutely respects himself, and, because he does so, respects the rights of others; the neighbor who respects his obligations and respects the sanctity of agreements in and with a world of neighbors. We now realize as we have never realized before our interdependence on each other; that we cannot merely take, but must also give." Canada is a little distant in geographical terms from Cuba, yet we are neighbors nevertheless — and it is a relationship that has served us both well, largely because it has been a relationship, to use Roosevelt's words, of both give and take. As the new millennium approaches, and as incipient democracies struggle to develop in Latin America, with the Organization of American States attempting to impose a new, and pertinent, direction for the hemisphere, it is clear that the potential for change in the South is steadily taking shape. It is also clear that, in the era of the single superpower, new challenges await the United States.

Within that context of the awakening of Latin America and the unipolar world, the role of Cuba will be important. A natural leader in the Caribbean, highly respected in Latin America (in no small measure because of its leadership in social indices throughout the continent), Cuba has taken enormous steps in recent years in adapting to the post-USSR era. The flood of foreign investment (notwithstanding U.S. legislation to prevent it) and a radical policy of economic liberalization have changed Cuba forever: Cuba is now indeed open for business. In international relations, the pariah of the 1970s has been replaced by a country that is a threat to nobody and instead is eagerly seeking foreign investment around the globe. The vote in the UN General Assembly in November 1996 supporting Cuba's motion to condemn the U.S. embargo was an overwhelming 137 votes to 3 (with only the United States, Israel, and Uzbekhistan voting against). This vote and the scheduled visit of Pope John Paul in October 1997 speak volumes about the changing global perspective on the new Cuba. In addition, the international protest against the Helms-Burton legislation in 1996 and 1997 from the European Community, the Organization of American States, the Non-Aligned Movement, CARICOM, Japan, China, and Washington's two NAFTA partners, Mexico and Canada, reveals beyond the shadow of a doubt the international displeasure with Washington's approach to Cuba.

It is clearly time, then, for Washington to adopt a more pertinent and pragmatic approach to Cuba — which the rest of the world learned some time ago. Over the years it has proved difficult for U.S. policymakers to come to terms with this reality, but now they have virtually no international support for the traditional policy of squeezing the Cuban economy — and waiting for an old man to die. It clearly is time for Washington to accept the new reality and to consider an alternative approach; certainly the international community has. This does not have to be a particularly painful exercise—for Havana is clearly keen to make a deal, and the United States has already shown its pragmatism by normalizing relations with Vietnam, where some 58,000 Americans lost their lives.

Perhaps there is also something to be gained by examining the Canadian-Cuban dynamic (which in 1995 celebrated the fiftieth anniversary of the foundation of official diplomatic relations with Cuba). Certainly it has shown that, despite ideological differences, a modus vivendi can be worked out—and one that often leads to fruitful and mutually advantageous relations. This, then, is not a blueprint to be followed to the letter, but it is nevertheless an outline or sketch of an approach that, for whatever reason, has worked. Maybe some of the message is applicable to Washington? Certainly the old policies have not been particularly helpful, and a study of what U.S. neighbors to the north have done—successfully—might be worth examining. We would like to think that Franklin Roosevelt would certainly agree.

1

Setting the Historical Scene
Salt Fish and Lumber for Sugar and Rum

*Relations between Canada and Cuba have always
been primarily commercial and financial.*
Department of External Affairs instructions to E. H. Coleman

Writing to E. H. Coleman on March 11, 1949, an official from the Department of External Affairs in Ottawa bluntly expressed the basis for the bilateral relationship. The occasion was the appointment of Coleman as the third Canadian head of mission in Havana. The letter was accompanied by a detailed report of Canada's role within the inter-American community, information on its trade with Cuba, and on historical ties between the two countries. In the midst of the lengthy report, however, there remained one central piece of advice, namely, that the new ambassador was above all to develop the economic aspects of the appointment. He was told, "since Canada's ties with Cuba are primarily commercial," he would have but two "main duties": to protect Canadian commercial interests (chiefly banking and insurance) and to broaden Canadian trade opportunities in Cuba in an effort to offset the effect of the preferential tariff arrangements with the United States which in past years considerably handicapped Canadian exports to Cuba.[1]

The External Affairs representative was of course correct in emphasizing the official perspective on the underlying basis for bilateral relations, since the commercial relationship was of paramount importance for Ottawa. (As early as 1910, a trade commissioner had been posted in Cuba to promote Canadian products, one of the earliest such appointments.) However, there were also political concerns at play in the bilateral relationship that sometimes were (cautiously) developed by both Ottawa and Havana as they sought to evolve from the hemispheric dominance of the United States and pursue a more independent foreign policy. Moreover, a case can be made to show that in Canada during the nineteenth century popular sentiment toward Cuba was several steps ahead of official policy, a situation that has also been true of the revolutionary period. These related political concerns will be touched on in later chapters, when Canadian independence vis-à-vis the United States became significantly more important in dealing with Cuba. In fact, the nature and extent of post-1959 Canadian-Cuban ties cannot be grasped fully without viewing that relationship through the Canada-U.S. prism.

The advice to Coleman concerning the head of mission's principal responsibilities might at first jar because of its bluntness, yet it is a fitting illustration of the underlying basis of Canada's longstanding interest in Cuba. Regardless of the nature of the regime in power, and despite intense lobbying from Washington, or for that matter virtually any other consideration, the prime concern for Ottawa has traditionally been how to sell more Canadian products to Cuba—salt cod and potatoes in the nineteenth century, spare parts and wheat today. Political concerns have hardly affected this relationship: "business is business" seems to have been the slogan as much during the colonial regime and the U.S. military occupation (1898–1902) as it was during the presidencies of leaders as different as Ramón Grau San Martín, Carlos Prío, Fulgencio Batista, or Fidel Castro.

This introductory chapter seeks to set the historical stage for the remaining sections of the book, which examine in more detail the importance of this bilateral relationship during specific historical periods. The thesis of this preliminary section is that throughout the history of this relationship, trade has been a leading factor in first establishing, then strengthening Canadian-Cuban ties. Moreover, until the post–World War II period, when geopolitical factors began to exercise a greater influence, it can be argued that it was the principal element of the relationship, and that bilateral ties have been at their strongest during times of rising exports. (Conversely, when the Cuban export market was viewed as offering poor prospects for Canada, Ottawa tended to ignore the island.)

Historians have often waxed eloquent, for instance, about the early contacts of "Canadians" in Cuba, and invariably the names of Samuel de Champlain and Pierre Le Moyne, Sieur d'Iberville, are mentioned. Champlain, the founder of New France, apparently visited Cuba in 1601 and spent four months there, traveling and writing a thorough series of reports on the colony. In 1706 Pierre Le Moyne arrived in Havana to enlist the support of Spanish authorities to attack English settlements along the southeastern coast of North America. Unfortunately he died in Havana shortly after landing and was buried there. (To this day there is a plaque in his honor in Old Havana, and for several years, in a sign of Canadian-Cuban friendship, the Canadian embassy would lay a wreath at that plaque whenever vessels of the Canadian navy were in port.)

It is also important to bear in mind the role played by Canadian individuals and groups during the 1868–78 and 1895–98 struggles for independence from Spain. In both cases volunteers went to Cuba to fight against the Spanish forces following the formation of active solidarity organizations, particularly in Montreal and Halifax. Furthermore, given the restrictions of U.S. legislation on filibustering expeditions, many Americans came north to join Canadians traveling to Cuba. By comparison, in the 1895–98 War, many Canadians joined U.S. forces that flooded to Cuba in the wake of the destruction of the U.S. warship *Maine* in 1898. One Torontonian revered as a hero of the struggle for Cuban independence was William Ryan, whose portrait still hangs on the walls of the former governor's mansion in Havana's Plaza de Armas. For several years he transported volunteers to Cuba and in 1871 was involved in defeating Spanish forces at Camagüey — for which the leader of the insurgent forces, Carlos Manuel de Céspedes, appointed him brigadier general. Two years later he was captured by the Spanish and executed for his actions. In the 1895–98 War, two French-Canadians, Jacques Chapleau and Georges Charette, also played a significant role: Chapleau commanded a successful rebel regiment, eventually being killed in combat, while Charette played a leading role in blocking Santiago harbor by sinking a large vessel — the "Merrimac" — near the channel entrance.

These distant links, while seemingly limited in scope, have nevertheless served as the historical basis for the relationship and are clearly of some significance in the Latin cultural psyche. They are not particularly profound, but they do constitute historical connections and are replete with political symbolism that has been employed by both governments.

Important though these early contacts may be, their symbolic value in connecting Canada and Cuba pales in comparison with the importance of trade between the two countries, which really started in the late eighteenth century after the foundation of Halifax. The prime focus of trade was of course the West Indies, yet Cuba, particularly the eastern city of Santiago, was soon added to the ports of call for vessels from the Maritimes. Salt fish (particularly the abundant cod), potatoes (both table and seed), and lumber were traded in exchange for sugar, rum, and exotic fruits, a trade that continued unabated, if in a somewhat erratic fashion, for many subsequent decades. The Fisheries Museum in Lunenburg, Nova Scotia, still has a variety of stencils bearing the names of companies in Santiago and Havana that imported salt fish, which was the basis of the Nova Scotian economy for several centuries.

This rather loose pattern of maritime trade received a major boost in 1866 with the arrival in Havana of a delegation from the Fathers of (Canadian) Confederation. Fearful that the United States would soon abrogate the 1854 Reciprocity Treaty with British North America (as it was then known), the Canadians formed the Confederate Council for Trade and traveled to Mexico, Brazil, and the Caribbean. In essence they were seeking new markets for their lumber, fish, and grain—a particularly pressing matter since their market in the United States was now in some peril. A month in Cuba convinced them that they had found a natural trading partner, although their task was made more difficult by three concerns: a high tariff on imported sugar to Canada, the traditional role of the United States as intermediary in Cuban exports to what at the time were known as "the British Provinces," and the higher cost of Canadian produce when compared with the United States.[2]

The commissioners of course offered Canada as an alternative source for trade with Cuba, but their best intentions were bedeviled by the fact that Canada was still a colony of the United Kingdom, and as such had remarkably little latitude in determining its own trade or foreign policy. (This point should be emphasized if one is to understand fully the limitations on Canada's attempts to develop bilateral ties with Cuba at this time. As an illustration of this dependency, it should be borne in mind that until 1945 all diplomatic and consular concerns of Canada in Cuba were dealt with by the U.K. Legation in Havana, and that even for some time afterwards, British diplomats there continued to look after Canadian consular questions outside Havana as well as all shipping matters.) Accordingly, despite the best of intentions, Canadian officials were impotent to introduce amending legislation that would have significantly favored the commercial growth that they clearly desired and recommended. A decade later a further attempt was made to improve trade relations, when Sir Alexander Galt traveled to the Caribbean. Prime Minister Alexander Mackenzie, who wrote to Galt on February 2, 1876, was clearly aware of the importance of increasing trade with Cuba, advising him to consider in particular trade with that country and the Dominican Republic: "[I am] inform[ed] that you propose visiting some portion of the West Indian islands very soon. I have for a long time been considering how we could extend our trade in that direction. . . . The Cuban and St. Domingo trade is in its magnitude far more important than any other, and in many respects the trade of these large islands is different from the trade of the other islands. My own impression is we would do better with them than with the others."[3]

Unfortunately, the best wishes of Mackenzie came to naught, largely because of difficulties in the sugar market: on the one hand London feared for the effect on the British West Indies of Canadian purchases of sugar, while on the other Madrid found it much easier and quicker to sell excess

Cuban sugar to the United States—just 100 miles away. To emphasize the difference in buying power between the two markets, a useful point of contrast can be drawn from trade figures in the years preceding the 1895–98 Spanish-American-Cuban War. In 1892, for instance, of the total Cuban sugar production of 802,471 tons, Canada purchased some 2,056 tons, a miniscule amount when compared to the 666,677 tons destined for the United States. By 1895, Canadian imports had risen significantly to 28,372 tons yet were still dwarfed by the 769,000 tons going to U.S. refiners.[4] Clearly from the historical Cuban perspective, the market offered by Canada was comparatively small and would remain so for most of the twentieth century. The United States has always been an obstacle, in geopolitical and economic terms, to closer Canadian-Cuban ties. The three countries thus saw their economies closely intertwined long before the embargo on revolutionary Cuba was imposed almost a century later. And Canada found itself with not only niche market possibilities but also great difficulties in competing with the far larger United States.

The defeat of Spain in 1898 was a major catalyst to the opening up of the Cuban market. The military intervention of the United States in 1898 and the subsequent occupation of the island by U.S. forces changed Cuban history irrevocably. The Cubans, who had fought for three decades against the Spanish, found themselves no better off, as the U.S. military administration swiftly disbanded the Cuban rebel army, imposing their own form of government on Cuba. Very clearly it provided a stability (under U.S. tutelage) that Cuba had not enjoyed since the outbreak of resistance to Spanish control in the 1868–78 war, although this was done despite Cuban protestations at the heavy-handed paternalism. Moreover, the devastation resulting from the 1895–98 struggle for independence, the massive loss in human life, and the virtual destruction of the sugar harvest had all left Cuba economically bankrupt and politically exhausted. As a result, with the overthrow of the Spanish system that, with minor modifications, had remained in place on the "ever faithful Island" for three and a half centuries, there was obviously an enormous administrative gap to be filled, a role that the United States keenly rushed in to assume.

Among the most colorful of the Canadian businessmen who came to Cuba at the turn of the century was William Cornelius Van Horne, described accurately by Peter McFarlane as "the classic Victorian-Age capitalist."[5] Born in Illinois in 1843, he became a legend in Canada for his ruthless drive to finish the transcontinental railway for the Canadian Pacific Railroad company (CPR). He subsequently became president of the corporation, earned a knighthood because of his railway prowess, and was awarded Canadian citizenship. In one of his many business ventures (this time in pulp and paper investments in Quebec and New Brunswick), his partner was General Russel A. Alger, President McKinley's secretary of war from 1897 to 1899. It was Alger who, recognizing Van Horne's business acumen and profound entrepreneurial zeal, invited him to accompany Alger and Elihu Root (secretary of war from 1899 to 1909) on a tour around the island in search of promising business ventures.[6] With traveling companions of this stature (and political clout) it was clear that Van Horne's commercial ventures would be viewed favorably during the U.S. military occupation of Cuba between 1898 and 1902. His own entrepreneurial brilliance and track record in Canada with the CPR, together with the clear market for a greatly expanded railway network in Cuba and these political connections in Washington, augured well for his business interests in the Cuba of the early twentieth century. It is also important to recognize that he cultivated the friendship of Gonzalo de Quesada, a leader in the revolutionary struggle against Spain and companion of José Martí, the spiritual leader of the 1895–98 war. De Quesada became Cuban ambassador to Washington after the defeat of Spanish forces and was often a guest at the New Brunswick estate of Van Horne.

At first Van Horne was interested in electrifying Havana's tramway system, a project in which Edwin and William Hanson of Montreal were rivals for the contract. Later, however, having lost out in the scramble among several competing interests, he realized that a far more financially rewarding project would be to establish a nationwide railway system in Cuba. Following some thorough research and effective lobbying in Washington concerning the advisability of the project, he helped found the Cuba Company, which was incorporated in New Jersey in 1900.[7] By 1902 the first section of the line was complete, and he continued adding to the system for a further ten years, also purchasing lucrative business interests in the tramway system and sugar mills.

Financial Pioneers: Banks and Insurance

Peter McFarlane's eminently readable *Northern Shadows* has as its central connecting thread the concept that Canadian investors in Latin America often took advantage of the sound investment climate that had resulted from the intervention of the United States to establish their own profitable business ventures there. Harold Boyer reaches a similar conclusion when analyzing the post-1898 period in Cuban history.[8] Certainly the case of Van Horne would seem to bear out their thesis, particularly if one takes into account the extremely useful political backing afforded by influential supporters such as Alger and Root. Less dramatic—if equally convincing evidence for this argument comes also from the development of the banking and insurance industries, which also arrived in Cuba around this time. In all these cases it was clear that the United States wanted to "modernize" Cuba (on Washington's terms), opening the doors to North American investment, and making it a useful commercial partner. In this process Canadian interests invested in some remarkably profitable business ventures, taking advantage of the rapidly growing U.S. commercial presence and the political stability that resulted from the military intervention.

The pioneer in what was soon to become a successful international business venture was the Merchant's Bank of Halifax (which in 1902 changed its name to the Royal Bank). Following an enthusiastic campaign by Edson Pease, manager of the Montreal branch who was clearly aware of Van Horne's promising interests in Cuba, the bank's directors (albeit somewhat reluctantly) approved their first overseas branch. Significantly, the joint manager of the Havana office was J. A. Springer, the former U.S. vice-consul, thus guaranteeing yet again good political connections with the U.S. military government of the island. The bank's fortunes grew, as well as its reputation and the number of Cuban branches, with subsequent openings in Santiago (1903) and Camagüey (1904). In addition, in 1904 the Royal agreed to become the agent of the Cuban government in paying off veterans of the Liberation War, distributing in total some $60 million, a not insubstantial sum at the time. The Royal Bank's involvement in the disbursement of these pensions proved to be a most successful move, not only because many of the former soldiers then decided to open accounts in the various branches of the bank but also because subsequently the Cuban government itself decided to deposit large funds in the bank.

The Royal Bank was the preeminent Canadian commercial success story in Cuba in the first half of the twentieth century.[9] Its first branch opened in Havana on March 8, 1899. Because of U.S. banking legislation, which only in 1913 permitted U.S. banks with federal charters to establish foreign branches, it had virtually no competition. It increased its role quickly—to five branches by 1904, eleven by 1908, twenty-seven by 1918—and by the mid-1920s had an astonishing sixty-five branches in Cuba. Business boomed, and by 1913 deposits outweighed loans by a full 40 percent. In 1919 it opened a new seven-story head office in Havana, clearly reflecting its status as one of the commercial leaders of the island. Its customers were among the political and commercial elite of Cuba: the Bacardí family, whose son José Bacardí worked in the Santiago branch; Van Horne's various commercial and railroad interests, which the Royal Bank followed as the railroad was built increasingly toward Santiago; the Swift and Armour meatpacking companies; Minor C. Keith, of United Fruit Company fame; the Romeo y Julieta cigar-makers; the Havana Telephone and Havana Docks companies; and Presidents José Miguel Gómez and Gerardo Machado.

Another Canadian bank, the Bank of Nova Scotia, entered the Cuban market in 1906 but did not possess the same branch system as the Royal. They competed with each other in the Caribbean, and by 1926 there were 114 branches of Canadian banks in Cuba and the West Indies, but an overwhelming seventy-two belonged to the Royal.

The importance of the banks grew further in the early 1920s, although the development could have not been foreseen. Bilateral trade had increased substantially between Canada and Cuba, with Canadian exports rising almost fourfold—from $578,013 at the turn of the century to $2,096,778, and imports from $343,374 to $1,770,874.[10] This in part helped to explain the growth of the Royal's rising stature, although far more important was the astronomic rise—shortly followed by a calamitous fall—in the price of sugar following World War I. The price of sugar had increased throughout the war (largely because of the impact on European beet production), increasing from 2.27 cents per pound in July 1914 to 23.5 cents in May of 1920. Understandably the bank managers, witnessing an unprecedented economic boom, approved increasing credit to landowners, whose apparent wealth developed rapidly. The fortunes of the Royal, paralleling what was happening to the national economy as a whole, also soared, leading to the opening of no less than twenty new branches between 1919 and the mid-1920s.

Unfortunately, this unprecedented growth was not to last for long, and the price of sugar fell as rapidly as it had risen, falling to 4.38 cents per pound in late 1920, and even lower—1.8 cents—in December 1921. Put simply, it absolutely devastated the sugar industry in Cuba, wiping out the fortunes of many thousands of the banks' borrowers, who were subsequently faced with no other option but to foreclose their mills and land, which of course passed to their creditors. In this way the Royal Bank lost most of the money that it had loaned to its customers but ended up by gaining sixteen sugar mills and 300,000 acres of land.

The arrival of Gerardo Machado as president of Cuba in 1925 augured well for the stability of the Royal Bank, at which he kept his own personal account, and whose manager became a close personal friend. Indeed in 1925, when a run on the Royal Bank occurred following rumors that the bank would be trapped in a debt moratorium, Machado personally intervened outside the main Havana branch to shore up the bank's assets by ordering the treasury to deposit its own funds. The manifest support of the dictator was not without difficulties for the bank, however, for the opponents of Machado targeted it and placed a bomb in the Havana headquarters.

The 1920 crash in sugar prices had a devastating effect on the Royal Bank. Deposits plunged from $73 million in October 1920 to $32 million the following July, and—with great trepidation and reluctance—the bank took possession of land that had been put up as collateral for sugar loans. Clearly by 1930, with under three decades of financial involvement in Cuba, the Royal Bank had reached its pinnacle of influence, which in both political and economic terms was quite substantial. Throughout the 1930s the Royal (and the Bank of Nova Scotia, which found itself in a similar situation) began to liquidate its control over the vast majority of its landholdings and sugar interest, and in addition reduced the number of branches from a high of sixty-five to just thirty-eight in 1930. The impact of the depression also had a negative impact on the Canadian banks. The main Havana branch, for example, saw its lending (which had reached $43 million in 1926) shrink to just $5.2 million a decade later; in 1932 the branch actually posted an operating loss.

Clearly the bloom was now off the rose, and the banks began the process of reducing their role in Cuba, looking elsewhere for more lucrative markets. Yet they still enjoyed a preeminent role in prerevolutionary society. Throughout the rest of this period the Canadian banks maintained a commanding presence in the banking industry, accounting for 28 percent of total deposits in commercial banks in January 1948, second only to U.S. (36 percent) and Cuban interests (35 percent). According to a 1950 study prepared by the World Bank, the Royal Bank held more deposits than any other commercial bank, with the Bank of Nova Scotia in fourth place.

A similar, if less dramatic, story emerges from a study of Canadian life insurance companies in Cuba. Again the insurance companies began to make inroads into the Cuban market early in the twentieth century. A confidential memorandum for the governor-general by the American Division of the Department of External Affairs on June 21, 1957, for example, noted the "preponderant" role of Canadian life insurance companies since the 1890s, adding that between 75 and 80 percent of all life insurance in force had been underwritten by Canadian companies. A similar picture is painted by Boyer, who shows that, despite there being some sixty companies in Cuba selling life insurance in the mid-1950s, including five Canadian interests, Sun Life, Manufacturer's Trust, Imperial Life, and Confederation Life, these four companies alone had sold two-thirds of the total annual premiums. For such white collar investors from Canada, then, business was definitely booming, while at the same time these companies built up a reputation for fairness among the Cuban populace.

An Overview of Prerevolutionary Commercial Relations

While the growth of Canadian banking and insurance companies was steady throughout the twentieth century, this was an exceptional facet of the bilateral commercial relationship. In part because of the lack of U.S. competition (given effective legislation in the United States concerning the banking industry) for fifteen years after the defeat of the Spanish, but also because of the reputation of dependability developed by the Canadians, the growth of these particular businesses was remarkably consistent.

It is to the credit of Canadian and Cuban exporters that steady bilateral commercial growth did continue despite the normal peaks and valleys of economic crises and international political calamities (for example, until the late 1920s, 70 percent of all fish imported to Santiago and 10 percent to the Havana market came from Canada). Boyer tracks the development of this trade in some detail, providing figures for Canada's exports and imports from 1902 to 1933 (see table 1.1).

Two specific trends can be seen from these statistics: first, the balance of trade was clearly in Canada's favor, since there were only seven years in this entire period when Canada bought from Cuba more than it sold, and second, World War I had an extremely positive impact on bilateral trade. These figures show that despite comparatively high tariffs limiting the flow of exports to the other's country, there was a solid (if small-scale) basis for ongoing trade—albeit one that revolved around a limited number of exports: sugar and, to a lesser extent, rum and fruit from Cuba, with potatoes, wheat flower, cod, processed milk, and whiskey coming from Canada.[11]

The Machado dictatorship in the 1930s coincided with the impact of the depression on Cuba—a combination that left a trail of commercial and human devastation in its wake. The subsequent drop in income from sugar exports (from $270 million in 1925 to $45 million in 1932) understandably resulted in a noticeable reduction in Cuban imports. Added to this were domestic political obstacles in Canada placed by powerful business groups lobbying to protect the nascent sugar beet industry. The result was a cooling of economic relations that lasted until 1940. Then once again, as had been the case in the First World War, the European conflict led to a significant increase in the amount of bilateral trade.

Between 1935 and 1940, Canadian exports to Cuba fluctuated around $1.4 million per year, with imports around $600,000. A combination of the depression's aftermath, closer U.S.-Cuban commercial ties, and a series of countervailing duties all militated against the development of bilateral

Table 1.1. Canada's exports to/imports from Cuba, 1902–33 (in thousands of $U.S.)

Year	Exports	Imports
1902	265	396
1903	256	396
1904	772	433
1905	1,227	485
1906	1,330	788
1907	1,364	807
1908	1,457	556
1909	1,385	839
1910	1,871	1,259
1911	1,514	1,281
1912	1,531	2,041
1913	1,754	2,785
1914	1,465	1,332
1915	1,123	1,453
1916	3,766	861
1917	4,651	1,361
1918	4,791	2,339
1919	7,670	3,841
1920	5,720	17,474
1921	5,030	2,319
1922	3,758	4,907
1923	2,678	5,596
1924	5,489	3,338
1925	8,619	6,455
1926	7,070	4,584
1927	6,032	4,651
1928	4,833	5,043
1929	4,284	3,564
1930	3,363	2,768
1931	1,637	1,041
1932	1,048	741
1933	989	872

Source: Boyer, "Canada and Cuba," 76.

trade. The onset of World War II, however—particularly with the destruction of the European sugar beet industry and the fact that Canada was cut off from traditional Commonwealth sources—meant that there was once again a guaranteed market for Cuban sugar, and the industry flourished.

Bilateral Commercial Relations after World War II

The outbreak of World War II was actually good news for the Cuban economy. The world badly needed sugar, and as the largest supplier, Cuba stood to gain. The same also proved true for Cuba with the onset of the Korean War. It is therefore no surprise that the trade figures compiled by the Department of External Affairs in Ottawa in 1949 indicate the rapid growth in bilateral trade between 1937 and 1947 (see table 1.2).

The war years were thus a major impetus for developing bilateral trade relations, although for the first time in their history, the deficit in the balance of trade clearly favored Cuba (as can be seen from table 1.2).

A dramatically new stage in these relations was initiated by the 1947 General Agreement on Tariffs and Trade (GATT), drawn up in Geneva and signed by both Cuba and Canada. Duties were subsequently lowered on a host of products by both countries, and trade again flourished. A few examples of the benefits of this agreement are worth indicating: Canada now supplied 28 percent of total fish imports to Cuba and, by 1949, was also supplying more than $3 million worth of flour to the Cuban market. Little wonder then that, by 1950, Cuba was Canada's second-best market in Latin America, surpassed only by Brazil. That said, however, Canada's trade with Latin America has traditionally been of relatively minor importance. In the specific case of Cuba, then, while trade had posted significant gains in the postwar period, the value of Canadian exports to Cuba never represented more than 2 percent of national foreign trade. In sum, it showed solid potential for export growth in the Latin American market, although this was a comparatively small priority for Canadian exporters.

A study of the annual reports submitted by Canadian trade commissioners in Havana to the Department of External Affairs during the period 1948–58 shows clearly the ebb and flow of Canadian-Cuban commercial relations during the postwar years. The 1948 report, for example, was extremely bullish, noting that "Canada's exports to Cuba in 1948 showed a remarkable increase over the previous year and established an all-time high with a total of $10,986,791 over $7,501,550 the year before, or an increase of 46.5 percent."[12] Largely responsible for this development was the substantial increase in Canadian exports of cod (up by $906,000), flour (up by $351,000), seed potatoes (up by $341,000), and brewers' malt (up by $319,000). A sombre note was sounded, however, by R. G. C. Smith, commercial secretary of the Canadian Legation, in an accompanying report titled "Conditions in Cuba." He praised the commercial gains made in 1948, but noted:

The interest in Canada as a source of supply has fallen off precipitously as United States exporters have once more become in a position to export in quantity to their traditional market. The psychological as well as the actual effect of the U.S. preferential tariff is a severe handicap, and while the aforementioned factors [the GATT agreement in Geneva and the steamship connection with Canada] are of undoubted assistance, the market is a buyers' market in most articles with all the elements of severe competition that this entails.[13]

By 1949 Canadian exports had again increased sharply—this time by 31 percent to $14,391,000, with the largest gains being made by flour and table potatoes. Again, however, U.S. preferential tariffs were singled out as being the major factor inhibiting the growth of further Canadian exports, although the growing competition afforded by Japan and West Germany in the Cuban market was also indicated, and would be referred to in several later financial reports. The value of Canadian exports continued to edge upwards—more than $18 million by 1950 and $20 million in 1951. The breakdown of Canadian exports again revolved around raw materials. Indeed, according to the annual report of the Canadian commercial secretary,[14] in 1952 just over 75 percent of Canadian exports were made up of only fifteen products (see table 1.3).

When looked at from the perspective of Canadian exports to Cuba, the early 1950s were a heady time. The significant trade deficit in Cuba's favor

Table 1.2. Canadian exports to/imports from Cuba, 1937–47 (in thousands of $Canadian)

Year	Exports	Imports
1937	1,868	835
1938	1,185	439
1939	1,497	888
1940	1,858	1,430
1941	2,528	4,329
1942	2,117	5,912
1943	2,415	8,551
1944	3,725	4,229
1945	4,534	7,511
1946	5,269	13,227
1947	7,501	23,751

Source: Instructions to Dr. E. H. Coleman from Department of External Affairs, March 11, 1949, 8.

Table 1.3. Leading Canadian exports to Cuba, 1952 (in $Canadian)

Newsprint	$2,863,252
Wheat	2,588,047
Wheat flour	2,202,468
Dried salted codfish	2,111,668
Malt	1,448,511
Machinery and parts	1,017,172
Copper tubing	887,112
Seed potatoes	821,327
Copper wire (insulated)	708,047
Copper wire (bare)	436,543
Medical preparations	305,437
Electric motors and parts	236,066
Calcium compounds	204,776
Sardines	190,834
Drugs and chemicals	139,357

Source: "Annual Report of the Havana Office: 1952," National Archives of Canada.

of the mid-1940s had disappeared completely, with a return to predominance of Canadian exports. There had been a twentyfold increase in such exports from 1939 to 1952, quite remarkable given the preferential tariff treatment granted the United States by Cuba.

It is clear from a study of official Cuban trade figures (table 1.4) in the late 1950s that the value of sugar exports outweighed all other items combined. During the period under study it was never worth less than 60 percent of the value of all Cuban exports, and in the last two years before the revolution accounted for fully 80 percent of the total of Cuban exports to Canada.

The picture thus emerges of a fairly active trade relationship, in clearly defined products, at the time. Yet, active though Canadian-Cuban relations were, they represented but a small fraction of the U.S.-Cuban trade, and Smith's words of 1948 rang ominously true as the late 1950s developed. The Cuban market was virtually free of import restrictions, although Canadian exporters were, of course, faced with greater transportation difficulties and costs. Moreover, preferential treatment continued to be given U.S. products by various tariff arrangements, while Canadian businesses also were burdened by the greater value of the Canadian dollar. The nascent development of local industry in Cuba was also a problem, as it increasingly produced manufactured goods such as cement, wire and cable, clothing, and pharmaceuticals that competed with Canadian products. Last

Table 1.4. Comparative value of Cuban exports, 1955–58 (in pesos)

Class of goods	1955	1956	1957	1958
Animals and by-product	21,839	12,364	7,373	956
Mineral products and stones	180,642	20	5	99,974
Metals and manufactured goods	4,121	9,335	3,563	12,103
Forestry products	200,985	691,715	12,528	1,103,056
Food products	167,479	294,542	209,385	139,126
Sugar and derivatives	5,859,536	6,680,597	10,695,131	13,742,403
Chemical/pharmaceutical products; perfume	280	318	302	216
Miscellaneous	1,096,681	2,092,744	838,057	338,424

Source: "Estudio comparativo por clases arancelarias del valor de las mercancías exportadas por la República de Cuba con destino a Canadá durante los años 1955-1958," Archives of the Ministry of Foreign Relations, Havana, n.d., n.p.

but not least, the traditional U.S. role in Cuba, constituting a psychological and political dominance on the island, should not be discounted because Cubans had become extremely familiar with, and accepting of, U.S. products.

The 1950s were thus a time of steady, if unspectacular, development of bilateral commercial ties, reaching their apex in the early years of the decade and then slowly declining. In part this gradual decline after 1953 was due to Cuba's clear decision to pursue more aggressively the larger U.S. market, but it was also due to Canadian manufacturing interests being steadily edged out by their U.S. competitors. As a result, control by the United States of the Cuban economy rapidly expanded, with Canada still providing valuable raw materials and food, yet slowly seeing its trade with Cuba decline. Writing to External Affairs on April 2, 1953, Canadian Ambassador Harry Scott explained graphically the close nature of Cuban-U.S. ties and the extremely powerful influence in Cuba wielded by Washington. Sixty percent of Cuba's exports were to the United States, with no less than 80 percent of its imports coming from there. Some 5,000 U.S. citizens were permanent residents (compared with just 250 Canadians), and no less than 38 officers worked in the U.S. Embassy (out of a total of 115 foreign diplomats representing 29 countries):

> In other words, Cuba speaks English—with an American accent. By far the most popular game is baseball, in which Cubans become good enough to play in the major leagues. The Cubans read news supplied from the United States, see American films in the theater and go to Florida and New York on their holidays. If they have enough money

they send their children to school in the United States and invest their savings in Florida real estate or hoard them in New York banks as insurance against a financial collapse in Cuba. . . . Finally, when Batista seized power a year ago the vital question as regards Cuba's relations with other countries was the attitude of the United States. When they recognized Batista, his government breathed an almost audible sigh of relief. It was now over the shoals into the calm waters of international respectability.[15]

The Development of Diplomatic Ties between Havana and Ottawa

Commercial relations were clearly the major raison d'être of bilateral relations. This was accurately summed up by the advice to Ambassador Coleman in 1949 with which the chapter began, and can be seen from the Cuban side in the fact that Havana's first emissary had been based, as early as 1903, in Yarmouth, Nova Scotia, so that he could provide an effective liaison with local salt cod producers. An interesting parallel can be drawn with Ottawa's strategy since six years later (in 1909) the Canadian Department of Trade and Commerce opened an office in Havana with the primary objective of encouraging the development of bilateral trade.

From the overthrow of the Spanish control of the island, all diplomatic and consular matters related to Canada had been handled by the United Kingdom Legation. In 1945, however, it was apparent that Canada should no longer maintain its status as a "Dominion" of Great Britain, and that as a result it should become a nation fully competent to direct its own foreign policy. Moreover, given the growth of the Cuban market during the post–World War II boom, Canadian business interests also felt the need to develop their own commercial ties. The decision in 1950 by Canada and Cuba to upgrade their legations in Havana and Ottawa to embassy status was the logical outcome of these mutually beneficial ties.

It is worth noting in passing, however, that political elements also played a role in the decision to upgrade diplomatic relations. For Canada, which clearly emerged a more mature, self-confident country after World War II, it was merely one more step in showing its independent status as a world nation after centuries of British tutelage. Cuba, though, had been keener on upgrading diplomatic relations during the war, and in October 1942 Batista announced that, to further the war effort, his government would establish diplomatic relations with Canada and Russia. (One historian has indicated three main reasons for this: Havana wanted more recognition for its role in the struggle against Hitler, it was piqued that Ottawa had established relations with other countries in the region and hence wanted to encourage Canada to improve relations with Cuba, and it wanted to use such a development to offset growing "anti-gringo" sentiment in Cuba, due in no small measure to an overpowering U.S. economic presence.)[16]

In the final analysis, however, the upgrading of bilateral relations (from trade commissioners to consuls appointed in 1945 to the eventual naming of ambassadors in 1950) was clearly a somewhat tardy recognition of the booming trade potential. It is important to note, though, that this process had been one of unusual spurts and delays. In 1927, for instance, the Cuban Congress had passed a bill upgrading the Cuban diplomatic presence in Canada and seeking a more comprehensive bilateral trade agreement. This initiative was not well received in Ottawa, long accustomed to the cool proprieties of British formal diplomacy and to the prominent place of the British Empire, on which the "sun never set." The arrival in Ottawa shortly afterwards of A. P. Sainz—a relative of President Machado—to lobby for such a development hardly improved the situation either. The Cuban government was keen to formalize and strengthen diplomatic relations immediately, yet Ottawa was clearly not ready. Canadian diplomats interpreted the Cuban move as rather impetuous and untimely, and accordingly snubbed this particular action.

On May 8, 1945, Joseph Emile Vaillancourt presented his credentials in Havana, the first Canadian diplomat to Cuba. Vaillancourt was appointed with the rank of minister, but it was only five years later that Herbert Coleman would see his position upgraded to that of ambassador. From the Canadian perspective, there was a relatively unbroken ambassadorial presence following Ambassador Coleman's position. During the prerevolutionary years the Cuban side, however, was plagued by government indecision and ill planning, best seen in the impulsive conduct of Sainz. Also indicative of the manner in which bilateral relations evolved at this time was the case of Mariano Brull, who, prior to the August 1950 decision to raise both legations to embassies, had served Cuba in Ottawa as Cuban minister from 1945 to 1949.

A study of official correspondence reveals a steady stream of diplomatic initiatives taken by Canada in the wake of World War II. Clearly infused with a new nationwide self-confidence after the war, Canada pushed ahead on the international front. Even earlier, between 1941 and 1945, Canada had already appointed four ambassadors or ministers to Latin America and was now in an expansive mood—including an invigorated interest in Cuba. Yet it was now Havana's time to play coy. Brull's mail to Havana reveals his concern at a lack of response from his government to the Canadian determination in postwar times to promote the existing diplomatic missions to the rank of embassies. He explained as early as September 12, 1947, how Prime Minister Saint-Laurent had noted that the Canadian government "would look with the greatest pleasure upon any development that would upgrade our diplomatic missions to the rank of embassies."[17] Further dispatches to Havana show his increasing frustration with the Cuban government's indecision over this matter. In early 1949, for instance, he noted Canada's growing interest in Latin America, as witnessed by the opening of several embassies, and commented: "All of this indicates that the Canadian government—which has opened embassies in Latin American countries where they have less interests than in our own, will not wait for a response from our government . . . that they might interpret as a delaying tactic."[18]

Brull was at his most persuasive in a further dispatch to Havana the previous month. Commercial relations were developing smoothly, while mutual respect and consideration were the order of the day in all diplomatic dealings, he noted. Yet he was clearly frustrated at the lack of importance being accorded Canadian matters by Havana. He categorized Cuban policy as being "more or less abstentionist on matters that were possible initiatives of mutual interest." He then outlined several steps taken by Canada to develop the bilateral relationship and concluded that Cuba almost always reacted slowly to Canadian positions—and then without much interest or conviction: "In summary the balance sheet of our combined activities shows that in essence the Canadians have consistently taken the initiative. Moreover many of those initiatives have not been realized largely because of our position—with the exception of the abolition of the need for a tourist visa."[19] Clearly the need existed for the basis of the diplomatic arrangement to go beyond the straight exchange of salt cod for sugar, but it was abundantly apparent that political considerations would continue to be downplayed as long as the commercial question remained healthy.

"Our Man in Havana": Canadian Diplomats on the 1956–59 Revolution

Given the importance of the Cuban market for exporters, and the interest in both capitals to develop the relationship, it is useful to analyze the confidential dispatches sent by diplomats in the field back to their respective Ministry of External Relations. The value of hindsight reveals the strengths and weaknesses both of their diplomatic representatives and of their own governments' reactions to rapidly developing political events. These reports from the field show priorities established by the ambassadors and their staff, while also providing a clear picture of how professional diplomats viewed events unfolding in their host country. The reports are also useful in assessing the goals and values promoted by their home base, especially in situations where clear-cut crises occurred and diplomats (as well as their respective ministers) were forced to make important value decisions. In light of all of the above, it is extremely helpful to be able to piece together political reporting and reactions at a crucial time in Cuba's development. And, while the documentation for this prerevolutionary period in Havana's Ministry of External Relations is somewhat limited, we are fortunate that in Ottawa the official records are well maintained and available to the public.

So how did Canada view political developments in Cuba at this time? What priorities—other than selling Canadian merchandise—did it have? For the last few years of the Batista dictatorship, the picture presented by dispatches from our ambassador in Havana was quite consistent. A detailed study of such reports by Canadian diplomats understandably reveals their concern about the impact on this profitable trade relationship that the insurrection might cause and hence their desire to maintain the political status quo as much as possible. While critical of Batista's corruption, they were also not supportive of the insurrection. In addition, there was a paternalistic attitude toward the Cuban government, combined with a basic support for U.S. initiatives in the country—clearly the most promising means of stabilizing the political situation and maintaining that solid investment climate from which Canadian interests benefited. The position toward Batista gradually evolved, however, from an initial interpretation of him as a buffoon to subsequent criticism of his human rights policies. This, however, was modified by concern about commercial relations and potential instability that might result if the insurgency were to succeed. Moreover, the portrayal of rebel leader Fidel Castro is also interesting, presenting as it does a rather stereotypical and limited view of the insurgents, particularly regarding their motivations and level of popular support. A study of official diplomatic reports (several hundred were examined in the National Archives in Ottawa) of these developments reveals an interpretation that was often superficial, and occasionally badly flawed. It may also show that diplomats are only human too and, perhaps depending excessively on pro-Batista sources, were simply unprepared for the advent of social revolution in what had traditionally been an enclave of U.S.-protected stability.

It must be remembered also that to a large extent the tone for the official Canadian interpretation of this period was set by ground rules issued from Ottawa. The Letter of Instructions sent to Ambassador Harry Scott (who presented his credentials on January 15, 1952, and remained as head of mission until November of 1956) made much of this quite clear. With the best intentions in the world, Ottawa clearly regarded itself as being morally superior to Havana's corrupt and inefficient public administration, and in a rather patronizing fashion requested that the ambassador use his good offices to make Cuban officials aware of the value of learning from Canada's approach: "It is felt that the tactful presentation and publicizing of Canada's record of public stability and sound public administration, for instance, might have some slight effect in providing more balance in the policies of the Cuban Government and more efficiency in its administration."[20]

The attitude concerning the Canadian view of the U.S. position in Cuba was predictably rather complex. Surprising by its absence in prerevolutionary assessments of Washington's role is any reference to nascent economic nationalism in Cuba (a particularly important factor in Cuban politics, which could have resulted in an advantage for Canadian businesses). Attention is paid, however, to the fact that "care should be taken to avoid giving colour to any belief that the Canadian embassy is unduly susceptible to the external influence of the United Kingdom, the United States, or any other country" (p. 10). This was especially desirable, the ambassador was informed, because "it is very probable that the Cuban government and people still do not have too clear a conception of our independent national status" (ibid.). While Canada should seek to be regarded as wholly independent, the ambassador was left in no doubt concerning Ottawa's view of the U.S. political and economic role on the island: "Any efforts which the United States may make to bring more political and economic stability to Cuba should be viewed with sympathy; it is obvious that any increase in the standard of living and well-being of the Cuban population is bound to benefit that country in its trading relations with other countries, including Canada" (p. 9).

The portrayal of Fulgencio Batista showed an interesting evolution in official reports from Canadian diplomats. At first he was regarded by Ambassador Scott as an ineffectual, almost comic-opera leader. Despite abundant evidence to the contrary, the Canadian ambassador persisted in giving him the benefit of the doubt. "On the whole, the President has shown himself to be even-tempered and conciliatory," he noted in February 1956.[21] Even more spirited was his defense of Batista the following month: "The benevolence of President Batista is not to be questioned. He may be lining his pockets at Cuba's expense but it is traditional for Cuban presidents to do so and it is in part made necessary by the uncertainty of political life here. But as a dictator he is a failure, if the standard is Hitler or Mussolini. Public protests against the regime are possible; an opposition is in existence and is weak only because of fundamental weaknesses in the personalities of the opposition."[22]

A year later there had been some evolution in the interpretation of the new ambassador (Hector Allard presented his credentials on January 29, 1957, remaining in Havana until June 23, 1959). In a confidential report to Ottawa dated March 26, 1957, Allard outlined clearly both his own dilemma in interpreting the role of Batista and the traditional Canadian acceptance of the Cuban president. "A review of the political reports submitted during the last twelve months reveals this Embassy's acceptance of the Batista Government. We have been occasionally in two minds about this since there are many manifestations of a strong-man government which are repulsive to minds raised in the atmosphere of Canadian democracy," he commented.[23]

It is interesting to note, however, that while Ambassador Allard and his colleagues were concerned with the flagrant abuses of human rights in Cuba at the time, on balance they still supported the government of Fulgencio Batista. They did this fundamentally on commercial grounds since, to use the ambassador's words, "from the economic point of view Batista has offered the best hope of salvation for this country" (p. 3). He had, noted the ambassador, provided a sound investment climate, so successful that since 1952 some $600 million of foreign capital had been invested, as well as bringing about significant improvement for labor and improving the communications system. As a result, the Canadian ambassador concluded: "In this context, Batista has offered the stability demanded by foreign investors and despite the depreciation of his position resulting from the activities of Carlos Prío Socarrás and Fidel Castro he is still the best hope for the future" (p. 3).

With the value of historical hindsight it is painfully clear that Ambassador Allard, despite wrestling frequently with his conscience, was gravely misreading the situation, since whatever Batista might have been he was obviously not "the best hope for the future." The level of repression was so widespread, the revulsion against Batista so deeply felt, and—despite the apparent economic growth in Havana—the support for the rebels so firmly rooted, that the ambassador (like his predecessor) was simply incorrect in his assessment of the situation. The political reporting from the Havana embassy was, then, at times incorrect: too often the desire for economic stability and a sound investment climate got in the way of a more dispassionate analysis.

This can be seen in several common themes sprinkled through official dispatches from Havana. Mention was made earlier of what one Canadian ambassador interpreted as the benevolent and necessary U.S. presence in Cuba as a means of assuring stability and of Fulgencio Batista as the "best bet" for Cuban development. Similar misinterpretations took place in the portrayal of Fidel Castro and of the strength of the rebel movement. Take for instance two reports by Canadian chargé d'affaires G. A. Browne. In the first, written in December 1956, he scorned the alleged prowess of rebel leader Castro while outlining the apparently unassailable strength of the government:

> The certainty is that Fidel Castro is not a military genius and, as for his overall strategy, the only reasonable speculation is that he is either mad or that he has been badly let down by his supporters. . . . It seems likely that these two alternatives may be interdependent, with megalomania in the driving seat.
>
> In any event, the breakdown of the Movement has made the position of the Government virtually impregnable.[24]

Writing in 1957 the same chargé criticized the viability of the July 26 guerrilla movement, noting that it was "to say the least, an inactive one."[25] Browne reserved his strongest criticism, however, for a potential political role for the insurgent leader: "The first major doubt is the importance of Fidel Castro as a political figure once he ceases to be an armed revolutionary hiding out in the Sierra and by virtue of this position the recipient of Cuban hopes for a release from the burden of the present Government. Affiliated to the Ortodoxos and freed from the glamor and mystery of his present existence he may fizzle as a political leader" (pp. 2–3).

A similar position was taken by Ambassador Allard in his secret dispatch to the secretary of state for external affairs of May 9, 1958. This, it should be remembered, was only seven months before Batista fled the country. Allard spoke about the level of repression by the secret police but concentrated his situation on the power struggle between Batista and Fidel Castro:

> Concerning Batista's position, it seems to be as strong, if not stronger than ever. . . . Many observers feel that Castro has shot his bolt. He has obviously committed a number of very bad psychological mistakes which clearly show a complete lack of political sense. . . . Even if Castro does not show great political intuition, he probably knows better than anyone else that at the present time his popularity has reached its lowest ebb.
>
> He must also know that with the full powers which Batista has now been granted by a submissive Congress, he can do everything he wishes.[26]

The level of political analysis and reporting could have been improved and can only have helped to contribute to a climate of uncertainty in Ottawa when the Canadian embassy staff's predictions foundered.

Coming to Terms with the Prerevolutionary Dynamic

This introductory chapter is designed, by means of a historical overview, to set the scene for the subsequent analysis of the core of our study, namely, the unique dynamic that has permeated bilateral relations between Canada and Cuba from 1959 to the present. It has covered, albeit rather superficially, a space of several hundred years, although its main focus is on the second half of the twentieth century period.

An analysis of this material, if it is to serve as a means of better understanding the following chapters, should provide an assessment of the common denominator of this extensive and multifaceted prerevolutionary relationship. More specifically, it should help the reader to understand better the integral nature of Canadian-Cuban relations as Cuba stood poised on the verge of revolutionary change. A related question concerns what this implied for the future of the bilateral relationship with Canada as Cuba chose to pursue a development path that would lead it to a headlong clash with its traditional major trading partner and political backer, the United States. The implications that this dynamic implied for Canada, which had in Washington its own largest trading partner and major external influence, also need to be addressed for obvious reasons. In sum, if we are to tie the many loose threads of this chapter together, we need both to define the basic nature of Canadian-Cuban relations in late 1958 and—perhaps more important—to appreciate what this projected for the future.

The basis of relations between Havana and Ottawa had been one of steadily growing trade. Since the origins of the salt cod industry, the Caribbean had been a steady market of Maritime fish brokers and would continue to be so 200 years later. But trade does not revolve around historical sentiment, and it was immediately clear to Canadian exporters that Cuba was potentially fertile ground for their trade. The steady growth of foreign investment in Cuba, apparent wealth to be found in the Havana market, and stability for entrepreneurs all constituted an exciting prospect for Canadian entrepreneurs. Havana was a bustling market, and Canada, of course, needed Cuban sugar. Their trading relationship had been a complementary one for two centuries and in the economic boom times of the 1950s continued to be so. As the Canadian commercial secretary noted in his statement of business conditions of January 30, 1959, goods from Canada had consistently been hindered by Cuban tariffs that favored U.S. products. Now, however, with none-too-subtle hints of economic nationalism in the air, trade with Cuba could improve: "Canadians are warmly regarded by the new revolutionary government and by the Cuban people, at a time when both the United States and Britain are under a cloud here due to support given the previous regime and, in the case of the United States, for press criticism of the war criminal trials. Our market for codfish in Oriente remains secure, and the new industries require increasing supplies of imported raw materials and industrial equipment. The new government has announced plans for increased spending on public works and residential construction, and will take steps to encourage still more industrial expansion. This program, designed to relieve unemployment and buoy up the economy, may give rise to a higher level of imports and more opportunities for Canadian exporters."[27]

If commercial ties were developing on a very solid basis, and promised to continue doing so, it is fair to say that diplomatic relations between Havana and Ottawa were a little less firm. This was not due to any ongoing friction or areas of major concern; rather, both countries simply took the other (now, as two centuries earlier) primarily as a commercial partner and thus recognized the need for diplomatic niceties to reflect the importance of the recently upgraded ties. That said, Ottawa certainly looked askance at the rapid political polarization taking place in Cuba and was understandably concerned as to the future of the new government in power.

Admittedly, there were reasonably strong historical ties uniting the two countries, which, in theory at least, would provide some basis for an ongoing relationship. One could point, for example, to the number of Canadian volunteers in the wars for Cuban independence, the special ties that Machado had felt for Canada in the 1930s, or the fact that Cuba had joined the war effort against the Axis powers. Yet all of that had little hard political value in the relationship as it stood in 1958.

One element of what would soon become an extremely emotional equation (and where political and economic relations overlapped) of course concerned the role of the United States. Mention was made earlier of potential economic gains at Washington's expense that Canada could make in revolutionary Cuba, especially with the United States rapidly disengaging (and being disengaged) from the Cuban market. The potential advantages for Canadian entrepreneurs to fill the ensuing trade gap, particularly in the sale of manufactured goods, were obvious. Yet it is also true that Canada has traditionally relied on U.S. international leadership, as well as Washington's interpretation of foreign relations, and was, of course, largely dependent on the United States as its principal trading partner. The result was that Canadian politicians and bureaucrats traditionally were prepared to accept the U.S. position on international politics. Such a willingness to accept the Washington perspective can be seen in a memorandum on Cuba prepared for the governor-general of Canada in 1957 by the Department of External Affairs that revealed an extraordinarily shallow, and indeed basically incorrect, assessment of the U.S. political role in Cuba: "From 1925 to 1933 Cuba was under the dictatorship of Gerardo Machado. He was overthrown under discreet United States pressure. . . . United States policy in Cuba has frequently been regarded with suspicion and resentment by Cubans, but the record of United States dealings with Cuba, as we have seen, finally belied the charges of imperialism. The northern republic did set Cuba free in 1898, withdrew in 1902, and made the withdrawal final by abrogation of the Platt Amendment in 1934. But under the superior economic power of the United States, the inherited inequities of the island were fixed more firmly upon her."[28]

Ottawa's traditional economic dependence on Washington, and extremely close diplomatic ties, could accordingly be expected to play a significant role in any future developments in its bilateral relationship with Havana. The varied elements were thus in play in the late 1950s as Batista's regime continued to stumble: traditional commercial ties between Canada and Cuba, a "hands-off" diplomatic policy tradition carefully cultivated by Ottawa, the potential for U.S. pressure on its trusted ally, and poor political analysis being sent by staff in the Havana embassy.[29] It was still unclear, however, precisely what would be the outcome as a young, bearded revolutionary marched into power, while in Canada an elderly and crusty nationalist, John Diefenbaker, was elected prime minister. What would happen in the next few years, for better or worse, would come to form the basis of what was an extremely unlikely relationship.

2

The Origins of the "Special Relationship"
The Diefenbaker Years

The title of the article in Canada's *Maclean's* magazine of April 6, 1963 — published days before the electoral loss of the prime minister — said it all: "Public opinion in Cuba: Diefenbaker si! Pearson no!" Cubans clearly felt that they possessed a friend in Prime Minister John George Diefenbaker, and as veteran journalist Knowlton Nash noted: "If Cubans could vote in Canada on April 8, John Diefenbaker would win the election by a landslide. To the Cubans the Prime Minister has lately become a hero. They envision him, like Castro, fighting off the grasping Yankee imperialists."[1] The irony of this situation could not have been lost on Canada's thirteenth prime minister, who harbored grave doubts about the Castro regime — almost as serious as those he felt about the Kennedy administration, whose term in the White House coincided in part with his own tenure. It was to be the dynamic of Canadian-U.S. relations, prodded in no small measure by their two political leaders, who detested each other with a passion bordering on obsession, which would act as the backdrop for the "Cuban question" and Canada's handling of it. In addition, during this time the value of bilateral commercial relations would be overtaken by political concerns as the prime catalyst in defining the nature of the Canadian-Cuban dynamic.

The most important factor in the modern development of the Havana-Ottawa relationship was without doubt the moral support of Diefenbaker (caused in no small degree by his ongoing personal feud with Kennedy) at a time when Cuba had remarkably few friends in the West. The commercial nature of the relationship during this time never lived up to its full potential. As a result, it was the political factor that counted — with Diefenbaker clearly showing that he would not be pushed around by Washington on the Cuban question. This chapter seeks to explain the nature of this development, and to examine Diefenbaker's rationale for taking such great political risks in seeking to maintain diplomatic relations with Cuba at a time when U.S. pressure encouraged virtually all its allies to break ties with Havana. While it was not given much attention in Diefenbaker's autobiography, his position on Cuba, which in essence was also an important facet of his position on Canadian policy toward the United States, goes to the very core of his political philosophy. Ultimately, in the wake of the October 1962 Missile Crisis, it was an integral factor in his 1963 electoral defeat.

Even after his loss to Lester Pearson in 1963 the "special relationship" between Canada and Cuba would remain reasonably firm—in no small measure because of the foundation laid during the 1959–63 period by John Diefenbaker. To Washington's chagrin, Ottawa basically maintained the status quo; the continuation of that policy could be seen thirty years later when once again in Canada the Mulroney government was an extremely strong pro-Washington administration, but one that still refused to accept totally the official U.S. position on revolutionary Cuba. Without any doubt, then, the Diefenbaker government's decision to maintain diplomatic relations with Havana during such a turbulent period was crucially important for Fidel Castro. This of course raises the question: precisely what caused Canada's Conservative prime minister to resist substantial pressure from the U.S. government and to ignore highly critical reports from his own embassy staff in Havana? The importance of Diefenbaker's stand on Cuba should not be underestimated, for in essence Canada simply refused to go along with the clamor of opposition, generated by Washington, that sought to isolate Cuba from the Western world. In fact, along with Mexico, Canada was the only nation of the Americas not to break relations with Cuba in the early 1960s.

This chapter also charts the beginnings of this unusual bilateral relationship between two highly unlikely governments and two even more dissimilar political leaders. If the foundation of modern ties can be traced to these two governments, what were the crucial factors that fostered such a development? Perhaps more important, why did Diefenbaker maintain this diplomatic relationship—which could only bring him political embarrassment? On the other side of the ledger, what benefits accrued to Canada from Ottawa's maintenance of relations with Havana? And to Cuba? Finally, how can one characterize the 1959–63 period in regard to the nature of bilateral ties?

Coming to Grips with the Diefenbaker Enigma

John F. Kennedy would probably never have believed it, but Diefenbaker was fervently and rabidly anticommunist. A strong supporter of the British Commonwealth, a lifelong monarchist, and an unswerving NATO loyalist, he held strong partisan feelings on the Cold War. Enormously suspicious of Soviet intentions to expand communism and profoundly concerned at the possibility that Beijing might manufacture its own atomic bomb, he steadfastly argued for a strong Western alliance to counteract potential expansionist tactics by the communist powers.

In addition to his strong anticommunism, one can detect in Diefenbaker's writings an unusual cocktail of opposition to the Canadian elite. He was from a poor Prairie family and had experienced firsthand the ravages of the depression. Moreover, it is also necessary to analyze the manner in which Diefenbaker personally set the foreign policy agenda, since he expressed contempt for many members of the Department of External Affairs. A study of reports by its members who had worked with Diefenbaker all agree on one thing: he held an unhealthy aversion (if not downright hostility) both to diplomats and their function, while in the main they too were distrustful of him—hardly a sound combination for formulating the nation's foreign policy. Despite the fact that on many occasions their policies coincided, neither could ever fully reconcile the policies with the actors themselves, much less the manner in which the policy was developed. One interesting insight into this mutual dislike was recounted by a journalist, who mentioned an incident shortly after Diefenbaker became prime minister in 1957: "One of the problems in deciding the nuclear issue—to have or not to have—was Diefenbaker's distrust of the External Affairs department. He was given a very good reason in 1957 on his first day in office; when he asked to see some foreign policy documents he was told they were secret and that he couldn't have them. Diefenbaker's aides had to go to the just-ousted Prime Minister St. Laurent, to get approval for the new Prime Minister to see government papers."[2]

John Diefenbaker's greatest political foe was the distinguished diplomat Lester Pearson, leader of the Liberal Party, who would defeat him in the 1963 election. Pearson, who as secretary of state for external affairs had received the Nobel Peace Prize in 1956 for his role in settling the Suez Crisis, had enjoyed an exemplary career as a senior statesman, not just in Canada but also on the world stage. In this sterling diplomatic career he had been ambassador to the United States, Canadian representative at the League of Nations, external affairs minister for many years (he was first appointed in 1948), chairman of the Council of NATO, president of the UN General Assembly, and twice had been proposed for the position of secretary-general of the United Nations (on both occasions the Soviet veto ended his aspirations). This wealth of experience in international fora, his long tenure in the Department of External Affairs, and his solid political connections with the influential policymakers in the civil service made him an outstanding member of the ruling political class in the closed world of Ottawa politics. In short, he was everything that Diefenbaker despised, rejected, and, quite possibly, secretly envied.

This frustration at Pearson's influence over External Affairs personnel translated into an extremely profound aversion to them by Diefenbaker. Norman Robertson, for instance, the department's powerful undersecretary of state—another career diplomat—was consulted formally only twice by Diefenbaker during the entire six years of Conservative rule. When visiting foreign leaders came to Ottawa, the prime minister deliberately sought to exclude Robertson, the second most important specialist in international relations, from attending meetings, understandably leading to great frustration among the External Affairs ranks. Basil Robinson, who was trusted by Diefenbaker, acted as the prime minister's assistant in foreign policy matters and was the main link between him and department officials. His insightful study, *Diefenbaker's World,* documents the prime minister's prejudices about the work done by External Affairs officials and, in particular, his fundamental rejection of advice from his mandarins in the department.

Diefenbaker clearly thought that Robertson, like virtually all the power brokers in the department, had worked so long for Pearson that he must have been influenced by the former secretary of state, and that therefore this loyalty to the former leader would of necessity cloud his judgment in providing sound advice. He therefore considered Robertson a major political enemy in a department that, in his opinion, was packed with them. He devised a term for these mandarins—"Pearsonalities"—and lost little occasion to pour scorn on them: "They don't do enough to keep themselves warm," he once noted. Scornful of External Affairs officials' approach to drafting speeches,[3] he deliberately sought to exclude them, to the extent that often senior spokespersons would be excluded from receptions arranged for visiting dignitaries.

During his term as prime minister, Diefenbaker was faced with a major dilemma. He could see the value of using international politics as a tool for increasing his domestic political standing (and was fully aware of the nation-building aura that surrounded Pearson's much-prized Nobel award), yet he was extremely suspicious of the influence of the opposition Liberals within External Affairs. Pearson's popularity and influence were well known after such a distinguished career in the international arena, while Diefenbaker's predecessor St. Laurent had also served in his time as foreign minister. Reluctant to approach External Affairs officials for advice, Diefenbaker preferred to rely heavily on his own political instincts, deferring rarely to the official foreign policy advisors.

The lowest common denominator of this extreme, and rather bizarre, mixture of circumstances is that John G. Diefenbaker himself wanted to formulate the national foreign policy, both for the nation's good and to shore up his own political fortunes. Genuinely a supporter of the marginalized sectors of society, he clearly identified with their situation and together with them tilted his lance at the all-powerful Establishment, which sought to preserve its power and privilege. A self-seeking rebel, fiercely partisan, and unashamedly nationalistic, he sought to reduce international politics to a personalistic equation with which he felt most comfortable—and which he believed would ultimately win him votes. In many ways an angry, almost paranoid political leader, he consistently scorned advice from the professional diplomats, trusting instead his own finely tuned political instincts while losing no opportunity to turn international policy to domestic advantage. An opportunity soon presented itself in the U.S. policy toward Cuba, with which Diefenbaker disagreed. Here was a chance to make political points on the international and domestic political scene, and Diefenbaker happily grasped the nettle of opportunity.

The Canada-United States Paradox

Probably no other single factor influenced Diefenbaker's view of the Cuban question more than the stand of the Kennedy administration toward the Castro revolution. Strange though it may seem, the person to whom Fidel Castro should be most grateful for Canada's decision to maintain diplomatic relations with Cuba was the late U.S. president, who quickly became the cause of John Diefenbaker's frustration at U.S. meddling in Canadian politics. The relationship with Dwight Eisenhower, by comparison, had been an extremely harmonious and productive one, in no small measure because, in Diefenbaker's words: "Canada was not treated as a forty-ninth state composed of Mounted Police, eskimos and summer vacationers."[4] Of course, there were significant differences of opinion—on defense, the appropriate approach to the Cold War, bilateral trade, and even Cuba—yet these were always handled in a respectful and open manner by the two leaders.

Always on a familiar basis, "Ike" and "John" as they called each other (as opposed to the "Mr. President" and "Mr. Prime Minister" of the Kennedy years) genuinely liked each other. They had much in common, ranging from a fascination with fishing to their similar humble, western farming backgrounds. They were also approximately the same age, possessed a shared interest in basic populist politics, had vivid memories of the devastating impact of the depression, and shared simple, middle-brow tastes. Perhaps most important, in addition to sharing similar generational interests with the U.S. president, Diefenbaker believed, as he often boasted, that he could always phone up "Ike" and have any problem between the two countries speedily resolved. That personal relationship would be sorely missed when John F. Kennedy assumed the presidency in January 1961.

For the Canadian prime minister, Kennedy was all that he was not: rich, handsome, young, sophisticated, and a part of the eastern Establishment. Not for him were the days of the depression, the uphill struggle for respectability, the lack of political roots, and the need to win popular acclaim. There can hardly have been two political neighbors more unlikely to have interests in common or to be able to speak the same language of politics. For Diefenbaker, the young, brash president was all the evils of his political foe Pearson incarnate, except that in addition he was both ignorant of Canada (which Diefenbaker loved with an incredible fervor) and not unduly concerned with that ignorance. The fact that for many years Pearson had been a friend of Kennedy's before becoming prime minister also accentuated Diefenbaker's dislike. Clearly there would be problems with their relationship.

An appropriate question to raise at this point concerns the impact that this mutual aversion would have on Canada's relationship with Cuba. Can one say, for example, that Diefenbaker's profound dislike of the U.S. president affected his own views of the Cuban situation? From a reading of his major speeches on Cuba, interviews on the subject, and—most important— observations of his advisors, it appears clear that Kennedy's frustration with Cuba did, in fact, have a negative influence on the prime minister. When combined with a distinctive approach to international relations, a traditional tenet of Canadian diplomacy that international commerce should not necessarily be impeded by ideological differences, a fear of pushing the Cubans into the arms of the Soviets, and the fact that Canada had no major political axes to grind with Castro's Cuba, the deeply rooted aversion to Kennedy quickly convinced Diefenbaker that he should not be dragged "on side" by the charismatic U.S. president. Perhaps more than any other single factor, though, the bitter personal distaste that Diefenbaker felt for his U.S. counterpart was the dominant reason in his decision to oppose Kennedy's designs on Cuba, particularly when he started to pressure Canada to support Washington's position.

Four basic themes can be identified in Diefenbaker's aversion to John Kennedy: the president's blatant ignorance of, and disinterest in, Canada; his government's growing attempts to "push" Canada into supporting the U.S. position on a variety of policies ranging from the Cuban question to the acquisition of nuclear arms; the comfortable relationship that Kennedy had, by contrast, with the Liberal leader, Lester Pearson; and the lack of personal chemistry between the two men, who, apart from fishing, had little in common. Together these concerns combined to make a working relationship between the two leaders absolutely impossible, with the result that Canadian-U.S. relations plummeted to an all-time low.[5] With regard to Canada's position on the Cuban revolution, the steadily deteriorating ties between Washington and Havana had a major impact on Diefenbaker. Frustrated at what he perceived to be U.S. bullying, his government overcame its concern about the leftward tilt of the revolution and increasingly warmed to the Cuban government.

Nothing frustrated Diefenbaker as much about the Kennedy style as what the prime minister perceived to be his lack of respect for Canada, and his apparent taking of its policies for granted. Since Diefenbaker modeled himself on his hero, the great nationalist Sir John A. Macdonald (he even surrounded himself with memorabilia from Canada's first prime minister) and regarded himself as the greatest champion of Canadian nationalism since Macdonald, Kennedy's manifest lack of interest in Canada was scarcely likely to endear him to Diefenbaker. Often Diefenbaker's indignation at U.S. insensitivity to Canada revolved around comparatively minor issues, such as the insistence of Kennedy on using American security forces (and rejecting the security offered by the Royal Canadian Mounted Police) on his May 16–18, 1961, visit to Ottawa. The lack of awareness of Canada exhibited by Kennedy and his top aides really was very apparent: his secretary of state, Dean Rusk, for instance, infuriated Diefenbaker when he remarked that he knew Canada quite well since he had been there on two or three fishing trips. "Is that all he thinks we are good for?" stormed the prime minister, who on another occasion described Kennedy as being "pathologically ignorant" about Canada.[6]

If Kennedy's ignorance of Canada frustrated Diefenbaker, he was also profoundly angered by U.S. attempts to manipulate Canadian foreign policy to suit Washington. For Diefenbaker, nowhere was this seen more clearly than in the episode that subsequently became known as that of the "Rostow memo." This one sheet of paper, an aide-mémoire prepared for President Kennedy on his May 1961 trip to Ottawa by Walt W. Rostow, policy planning director of the State Department, presented Kennedy with a list of objectives that the United States sought to gain from those meetings. Following the meeting it was apparently left behind. Discovered shortly afterwards and handed to the prime minister (who did not follow the normal diplomatic courtesy of returning it), the memo was seized upon eagerly by

Diefenbaker. He subsequently used it in an election campaign as proof of the need for an even greater Canadian nationalism in the face of the U.S. onslaught. The secret memo was straightforward:

What We Want from Ottawa Trip

1. To push the Canadians towards an increased commitment to the Alliance for Progress. . . .
2. To push them towards a decision to join the O.A.S.
3. To push them towards a larger contribution for the India consortium foreign aid generally. . . . Like the rest of us, they have their political problems with foreign aid, but we might be able to push them in the right direction.
4. We want their active support at Geneva and beyond for a more effective monitoring of the borders of Laos and Vietnam.[7]

Diefenbaker's aide, Basil Robinson, recounts his meeting with the prime minister shortly after the document had been found. For someone as sensitive on matters of Canadian nationalism as Diefenbaker (and with such a strong personal aversion to John Kennedy), the document was proof positive of U.S. meddling in Canadian affairs: "The Prime Minister brought the paper out, remarking on the repeated use of the word 'push.' To him this personified the attitude of the Americans: they thought nothing of pushing Canada around. He seemed to be regarding the paper as a sort of trophy."[8] It was this same visceral reaction to the U.S. government's continually "pushing" Canadian policy, as Diefenbaker saw it, that only strengthened the prime minister's resolve to resist Washington's pressure on Cuba.

The mutual personal aversion between Kennedy and Diefenbaker has been commented on in some detail by Canadian journalist Knowlton Nash, who was in the unusual position of knowing both men well on a personal level. They were both simply too dissimilar, too arrogant, and too nationalistic to be able to develop any basis for meaningful communication, he notes with some insight. Their personal relationship had always been poor, but when Diefenbaker decided to use the Rostow memorandum as evidence of an attempt by the United States to bully Canada, thereby gaining valuable points in an increasingly nationalistic electoral campaign, Kennedy exploded: "The president's reaction was the strongest of all. 'Jeezus Christ!' he exploded when he heard of it. Kennedy talked about 'cutting his balls off' in an expletive-filled roar of vituperation; he called Diefenbaker 'a prick,' 'a fucker,' 'a shit,' and other salty characterizations."[9]

Washington apparently expected unquestioning acquiescence from Canada on a whole host of questions, yet Diefenbaker—in an increasingly feisty mood of confrontation—wrapped himself in a cloak of nationalism and refused to be bullied. One of the increasingly significant bones of contention between the two countries became the question of Cuba, on which the Kennedy administration, still smarting from the disastrous Bay of Pigs invasion of April 1961, was particularly fixated.[10] Yet Diefenbaker refused to be intimidated by the steady crescendo of pressure for Canada to toe the ideological line, until eventually his determination would be sorely tested during the October 1962 Missile Crisis and would ultimately lead to his political downfall.

The Evolution of Bilateral Relations with Revolutionary Cuba

In essence the Canadian government's policy toward Cuba was much the same as that followed toward Communist China. Diefenbaker might not have liked many aspects of the Cuban revolution and was clearly uncertain about the role of Fidel Castro, but in the final analysis he was prepared to follow the dictates of Canadian foreign policy traditions and accept the established government of Cuba, warts and all. A diary entry of his ambassador in Washington, veteran diplomat Charles Ritchie, is an articulate summary of Ottawa's position:

> Do we consider what has happened in Cuba as a popular social revolution and not a Russian-inspired Communist take-over? . . . It is unthinkable that anything similar to the developments in Cuba should occur in Canada, but if it did, should we not regard this as our own business and resent intervention? In general in our dealings with Communist countries we have tended to be against the policies of economic strangulation (even more against military intervention). . . . Presumably this is the philosophy behind our trade with China. Of course, our economic interests are the concrete reasons for the policy, but in the background is a philosophical difference as to how best to deal with Communist countries, and our position, though obscurely defined, is basically different from that of the United States.[11]

Diefenbaker followed this approach consistently in all dealings with Cuba, even during the October 1962 Missile Crisis when to do so went patently against the mainstream of popular feeling in Canada and ultimately led to his defeat. In part it was fueled by the prime minister's pursuit of what Ritchie terms "economic interests," although by 1961 it was obvious that the Cuban government was simply unable to expand its imports from Canada. But Diefenbaker's stance on Cuba always went beyond representing just an avenue for increased trade and instead came to represent an extremely complex enigma. Not only did it involve his personally difficult relationship with John Kennedy, but it also included a desire to enhance his nationalistic domestic policy by taking advantage of Cuban-U.S. tension. Moreover, there was also the Canadian foreign policy basis of recognizing countries despite differing ideologies. Finally, despite his ambivalence toward Fidel Castro personally and strong rejection of communism, there was also something of a psychological identification with the "little guy" as represented symbolically by the nationalistic policies of the revolutionary government. During the 1959–63 period Diefenbaker consistently maintained this as the official Canadian position and, in so doing, laid the foundation for the continued bilateral relationship.

During these years a handful of themes occur that deserve to be dealt with in some detail. Because we have had (screened) access to the archives both of the Department of External Affairs in Ottawa and the Ministry of External Relations in Havana, it is extremely useful to compare their interpretation of the bilateral relationship—a process that often yields an invaluable mirror image of controversial material. The major concerns that reoccur with some regularity in the diplomatic correspondence and analysis are trade matters, differences in Canadian and U.S. perspectives on the "Cuban question" (accompanied by a steady stream of pressure from Washington to express virtually constant concern at Ottawa's stance on the matter), an ongoing questioning—both in Havana and Ottawa—as to why Canada should maintain diplomatic relations, a consistently negative flow of diplomatic dispatches from the Canadian embassy in Havana on developments there, and a set of apparently ambiguous policies followed by Ottawa in dealing with the revolutionary government. The result of this complex brew of conflicting goals, economic and political pressures, growing U.S. concern, and Diefenbaker's own ambivalence was, not surprisingly, a situation in which various Canadian ambassadors in Havana regarded Cuban cordiality as being wholly opportunistic and insincere, while their Cuban counterparts in Ottawa were increasingly concerned about the Canadian position on Cuba.

The Trade Question

Following the October 1960 imposition of an economic embargo against Cuba, the dominant image of the Canadian role in Cuba held by U.S. policymakers was of a greedy, grasping nation that sought to undermine the West's unified front against totalitarian dictatorship by continuing to deal with communist troublemakers in Havana.[12] Throughout the Diefenbaker years this interpretation continued to be the norm, especially after the 1962 meeting of the Organization of American States (OAS) held in Punta del Este that "excluded" Cuba from the OAS. From Washington's perspective, Canada refused to be a team player, preferring instead to take advantage of the United States, which had broken off relations with the Castro government. This apparent lack of scruples shown both by Ottawa politicians and money-grubbing business people placed Canada in an unusual situation in its dealings with Latin America, leading one observer to note that "for once the roles were reversed and the pejorative dollar sign was pinned on Canada."[13] The same commentator emphasized the point by presenting a cartoon of Santa Claus wearing a hat on which "Canadian Business" was written and having dollar signs for eyes. On his lap sat Fidel Castro, chomping a cigar, with a rifle, pistol, and dagger prominently displayed, while Santa asked him, "And what would you like for Christmas?" Should there have been any doubt concerning the allegedly mercenary position held by the Canadian business sector, the article was accompanied by an ironic ditty ("Ye Mariners of Canada"), the first verse of which poked fun at the modern-day buccaneers who sought to make a quick profit from Cuba after the United States had declared its economic embargo:

> Ye Mariners of Canada
> That serve your nation well
> And bear Canadian export goods
> To *Barbudo* Fidel.
> Oh, many a fast buck you will make
> Although your pace is slow
> As ye creep
> Through the Deep
> While the Caribbean winds do blow
> While the tempest rages loud and long
> And the stormy winds do blow.[14]

Within two months of the embargo being declared by the Kennedy administration, an eleven-man trade mission from Cuba, headed by Economic Affairs Minister Regino Boti, arrived in Ottawa to discuss how bilateral trade between Canada and Cuba could be significantly improved. The Cubans sought to increase trade tenfold, they claimed, so that they could fill the void left in the wake of the embargo—something that understandably appealed to Canadian businesspeople. The minister of trade and commerce, the late George Hees, waxed eloquent at the prospect of the free-spending Cubans doing business in Canada, commenting gleefully: "You can't do business with better businessmen anywhere. They're wonderful customers."[15] Understandably, Washington was less than overjoyed, and soon was pressing the Canadian government for clarification on its position.

Within a few days a much-chastened Hees appeared on "Front Page Challenge," a popular Canadian Broadcasting Corporation current affairs television program, apologizing for the insensitivity of his remarks and noting his personal lack of sympathy with the Castro regime and its treatment of religious groups in Cuba. Writing to Minister of External Relations Raúl Roa, on January 16, 1961, the Cuban ambassador to Canada explained the reason for this amazing about-face by the Canadian minister. He had just had a private interview with Howard Green (Canadian secretary of state for external affairs), at which Green outlined "the enormous pressure that the government was under from the United States because of the warm reception given the Cuban delegation in Canada" and which had led to the "rectification" by Hees.[16]

Given increasing U.S. discomfort at the confusing signals being given by the Diefenbaker government, the need obviously existed for Ottawa to clear the diplomatic air, explaining exactly what its trade policy to Cuba was. This came about in a major address given by the prime minister in the House of Commons on December 12, 1960. Diefenbaker went to great pains to show that Canada was not being opportunistic in continuing to deal with Cuba. Clearly annoyed by continued sniping from the United States (one newspaper there had even gone so far as to suggest that "Canada's national anthem be changed to 'Red Sales in the Sunset'"),[17] Diefenbaker attempted to set the political record straight. It was common knowledge, he stated, that Canadian commerce with Cuba was slight (in total it was less than the medical supplies and humanitarian aid traded by the United States at that time), yet, despite that economic fact, the pressure from Washington was unrelenting.

It is important to remember that both Howard Green and Norman Robertson (secretary of state and under-secretary, respectively, for external affairs) were convinced that the U.S. policy toward Castro's Cuba was short-sighted and wrong and in the long run would likely bring about the opposite of their stated goal, namely, to weaken relations between Havana and Moscow. Their advice had helped to strengthen the prime minister's convictions about trading with Havana—particularly important since Diefenbaker clearly held ambivalent views about Cuba. In the end, a position was articulated by the government that would allow free passage of Canadian exports to the island (with the exception of those deemed of "strategic" importance, such as arms, munitions, or other goods that could be used by the security forces) but would not allow U.S.-manufactured goods to be reexported through Canada. In essence he sought:

> to maintain the kind of relations with Cuba which are usual with the recognized government of another country.
>
> It is, of course, not our purpose to exploit the situation arising from the United States embargo, and we have no intention of encouraging what would in fact be bootlegging of goods of United States origin.[18]

It was a position to which Diefenbaker would adhere faithfully, noting on January 31, 1962: "So long as our trade with Cuba was in non-strategic materials there was no reason whatever to interfere with it. . . . No consideration was being given to a change in policy."[19]

The actual Canadian trade policy was far less interesting than the enormous controversy surrounding it. There was, of course, a great deal of interest in Cuba in buying Canadian products (witness the Boti trade mission) and thus filling the trade void. Commenting on the daily chaotic scene at the embassy in late 1960, the Canadian ambassador noted: "The commercial side is bursting at the seams with visitors. Our library is filled daily with earnest Cuban gentlemen, and the occasional lady, diligently going through the Canadian Trade Index and similar publications to find firms whose lists may, or may not, have items which they may, or may not, be able to persuade BANCEC (Bank for Foreign Trade) to permit them to order."[20] In actual fact, however, the promise of a tenfold increase in Canadian exports that had so enthused Minister Hees failed to materialize. Exports did double to approximately $30 million in 1961 but fell to $10 million in 1962 and $15 million in 1963—hardly the windfall profits so bitterly denounced by U.S. businesspeople.

Far less spectacular than the controversy swirling around Canada's "bootlegging" (real or imaginary), but nevertheless very important for Ottawa, was the ability of the embassy to protect the economic interests of Canadian citizens. The significance of this, of course, was that U.S. businesses were all rapidly nationalized and the land held by the Cuban wealthy quickly expropriated in the name of the revolution. Cuban sugar baron Julio Lobo even approached the Canadian embassy to lease—for a token rate—his own mansion, so that it, along with a priceless collection of art, would not be taken over by the revolutionary government. Yet Canadian companies and individuals were respected in a manner that was totally different: corporate interests were sold to the Cuban government, while often exceptions were made to existing legislation to protect individual Canadian landholders.

There is no doubt that Canadian companies were given preferential treatment by the revolutionary government. All foreign banks except the Royal
Bank and the Bank of Nova Scotia were nationalized in October 1960.
They too would close after it became obvious that they would be unable to
compete with Che Guevara's Banco Nacional de Cuba. The Royal Bank
eventually sold its interests to the Central Bank for $US8.8 million in De-
cember 1960. Bank employees were guaranteed employment in the Cuban
banking system, and a representative office was maintained in Havana,
providing the revolutionary government with a financial link abroad. The
significance of the exceptional treatment given Canadian interests can be
gauged from the ambassador's dispatch of October 18, 1960:

> One of these [new laws] nationalized 382 firms, mostly big ones, in-
> cluding the remaining 105 sugarmills, the breweries, department stores,
> textile factories, etc. The other law, No. 891, declared banking a state
> function and nationalized *all* the remaining banks *except* the two
> Canadian banks. Article 16 of the law reads 'this law shall not be
> applied to the Canadian banks established in Cuba called the Royal
> Bank of Canada and the Bank of Nova Scotia.' . . . In the TV inter-
> view Castro was asked about the Canadian banks. . . . He said that
> the two Canadian banks, *through their Head Offices,* were rendering
> important services to the Revolution, and therefore were excluded
> from nationalization, confiscation or intervention.[21]

As a further indication of the exceptional treatment meted out to Canadian interests, in essence because the revolutionary government needed to
retain a link with the West and obtain badly needed spare parts for Cuban
machinery, one can cite Havana's approach to other businesses. The case
of one small company, Exquisite Form Brassière of Canada Ltd., is instructive in this regard. After it was expropriated on October 25, 1960, by Cuban authorities, a protest was lodged by the embassy in Havana on the
basis that, given the Canadian ownership of the Cuban subsidiary, the appropriate legislation — aimed at U.S.-owned companies — did not apply. An
internal memo of the Cuban External Relations Ministry issued soon afterwards in response to the Canadian protest noted significantly that "we
should bear in mind the excellent political, social, and economic relations
between Canada and the Cuban revolutionary government."[22]

A similar policy of exceptionalism was widely followed by Cuba in dealing with individual Canadian landowners. The case of Sydney Young, a
longtime resident of Bartle in the province of Oriente (and a Canadian
citizen), is indicative of the treatment given Canadian landowners. He possessed an estate of approximately 11 *caballerías* (1 *caballería* equals about

33 acres), which had been expropriated according to the regulations of the Second Agrarian Reform. A rather loose loophole existed in Article 3 of the legislation, according to which "certain estates could be exempted." Accordingly, on October 8, 1963, the Canadian embassy in Havana, bearing in mind the "good disposition of the Ministry of External Relations, shown on earlier occasions," respectfully asked the Cuban authorities "to cooperate in protecting the interests of Canadian citizens," by providing an exemption from this legislation. The Cuban reply, dated June 23, 1964,[23] did precisely that: once again preferential treatment was accorded Canadian interests.

This approach by the revolutionary government was well received in Ottawa and especially appreciated by Diefenbaker. But there were also advantages for the Cuban government. In the first place, it needed to have a channel to the external financial world, and with the expropriation of the U.S. banks and rapidly deteriorating diplomatic relationship with Washington, the need became even greater. The Canadian banks afforded that possibility. In addition, the Royal Bank was of service in resolving the sticky issue of what to do about the 1,200 Cuban exile prisoners caught following the abortive Bay of Pigs invasion in April 1961. Washington, despite abundant evidence to the contrary, continued to deny any role in this episode and therefore could not negotiate for the exiles' release. Nor did the U.S. banks have any legal standing in Cuba and therefore could not help resolve the problem. Eventually the Royal Bank offered its good services, accepting nearly $60 million in medicine and food through a variety of banking mechanisms. The Royal Bank even waived all fees for the transaction (some $70,000)—a fitting gesture in response to a policy of exceptionalism.

Washington Maintains the Pressure

Because of the very definite attempt shown by the Cuban government to come to an accommodation in dealing with expropriated Canadian property in stark contrast to the manner in which U.S. claims were dealt with, it is understandable that Washington's policymakers would be disappointed that efforts were being made by Cuban authorities to undermine their own attempt to build a united front against Havana. When added to the Diefenbaker government's consistent refusal to suspend trade with revolutionary Cuba, this exceptional treatment, which for obvious reasons the Canadian government was pleased to accept, made it seem clear to the Kennedy administration that Canada could not be trusted to toe the official line laid out by Washington and break with Cuba, or at least suspend bilateral trade. An unsigned note from the Canadian embassy in Washington to Ottawa in early 1961 gave some hint of the degree of pressure being felt by diplomats there: "As you know, there has been a great deal of confusion about Canada's policy [toward Cuba] and we are fighting a rear-guard action in trying to put the fire out."[24]

It was clear to Canadian diplomats that the Cuban question was fast assuming an emotional dimension that blinded, or at the very least blinkered, a rational response from the Kennedy administration. Accordingly, Canada found itself in an unfortunate "no man's land" between, on the one hand, its traditional allies in Washington and, on the other, the socialist government of Fidel Castro. Both Havana and Washington had already entered an upward spiral of shrill denunciation and threats, and it was obvious that both resolutely adhered to the position that other countries had to line up on one side or the other. Canada, however, refused to be coopted by this Manichean formula, and Ottawa tried consistently—albeit with limited success—to explain its very precise approach to Cuba in the midst of a crescendo of distrust and invective that continued to block common sense from prevailing.

Unfortunately for Ottawa, the Kennedy administration was not interested in Canada's claims that it was indeed an ally of the United States yet, at the same time, was in favor of maintaining diplomatic and commercial relations with Cuba. This formulation simply did not compute in Washington, where the intense personal dislike between Kennedy and Diefenbaker, combined with U.S. suspicions about Canada's "windfall profits" in Cuba, made for growing difficulties with Ottawa. Little wonder then that Assistant Under-Secretary of State Ed Ritchie should write to his colleague in the Canadian embassy in Washington that "there has been almost no subject during recent months on which we have had to proceed more carefully than on the question of Cuba. We have been painfully aware of the desirability of clearing up any misunderstandings in the United States."[25]

A campaign of explaining Canada's position, however, was disastrously unsuccessful, with both U.S. policymakers and the public at large. The U.S. ambassador to Cuba, Philip Bonsal, recounted to his Canadian counterpart (and longtime friend) in October 1960 that he personally regretted and deplored "the present position in which Canada appears as a friend of the Castro government."[26] The U.S. ambassador to Mexico, meeting with the Canadian chargé d'affaires, also expressed concern at Canada's continuing to trade with Cuba: "His tone was mild," noted the Canadian diplomat, "but there was a definite indication that the United States felt we had let them down, with a faint hint of back-stabbing."[27] The U.S. ambassador had recently been in southern Ontario, where he had engaged Canadians in conversation over the Cuban question, and had been struck by their conviction that "U.S. high-handedness and lack of understanding" had been responsible for the current crisis in U.S.-Cuban relations. The Canadian diplomat concluded his dispatch by noting that such feelings as Ambassador Hill's were probably widespread:

> Mr. Hill clearly belongs to the old hands-across-the-undefended-border school of U.S.-Canadian relations. While this is touching to many of us, with its pleasant recollections of a less complicated world, it hardly seems to meet the requirements of the day. However, one may suspect from Mr. Hill's reaction that Americans are generally united in thinking that Cuba is poison, and likely to suspect anyone who has trade or truck with it. (2)

The view in Washington certainly was that Cuba was "poison," and consequently Canada's efforts to bridge the consistently widening gulf were regarded with an ever-deepening suspicion. In July 1960, for example, at a meeting in Montebello, Quebec between Canada's minister of national defence and his U.S. counterpart, the issue of Cuba was discussed in some detail. The U.S. delegation gave their assessment of the Castro government, only to be followed by Under-Secretary of State Norman Robertson and Secretary of State for External Affairs Howard Green, who took issue with the U.S. interpretation. Basil Robinson noted that in giving their response "the Canadians spoke with such force and candor that the Americans present were shocked at the extent of the division between the Canadian analysis and their own."[28]

Inevitably this disagreement between governments soon spilled over into more popular and politicized fora. Representatives of the U.S. Congress criticized Canadian pursuit of the "fast buck," and urged their constituents to lobby the Canadian government. Some trade unions with head offices in the United States also sought the support of their Canadian members. Mainstream publications similarly underlined Canada's lack of political solidarity, while emphasizing its mercenary commerce with Cuba. "Trading with the enemy" was clearly an emotional issue and, it was implied, all U.S. allies should follow Washington's lead (even if the U.S. Embassy in Ottawa did insist on bending the rules itself by having a generous supply of Cuban cigars for John Kennedy's ill-fated visit to Canada's capital in May of 1961).

In the United States a campaign was started to lobby against U.S. citizens taking their vacations in Canada. Busloads of demonstrators from New York were driven to Washington where they protested in front of the Canadian embassy. Particularly in southern Florida, anti-Canadian feelings flourished. Writing on January 24, 1961, Canadian Ambassador to

Cuba Allan Anderson mentioned that his principal clerk had recently spent a weekend in Key West, where he had encountered a "very definite coolness when it was found that he was a Canadian."[29] Accompanying his report was a memo from his commercial counselor, Parlour, who commented on the disturbing treatment received by his wife on her recent trip to Miami:

> In Miami she found that when it was known she came from Cuba there was a strict, and even hostile attitude on the part of the United States Immigration, Customs and Health officials and Pan-American personnel. She was given a thorough questioning both on arrival and departure from Miami airport. She was forced to have a vaccination.
> . . .
> On the street of Miami she was stopped by a policeman for jaywalking who gave her a severe and unnecessary calling down, questioned her at length, examined her passport, accused her of illegal entry into the United States and threatened to place her under arrest.

The Diefenbakers themselves were indirectly affected by the growth of anti-Canadian sentiment in Florida. They had planned to vacation there in January of 1961 but, on advice from Canadian Ambassador Arnold Heeney in Washington and Royal Canadian Mounted Police (RCMP) officials, were advised against traveling to Florida "on the ground that it was the hotbed of anti-Castro Cubans and therefore a potentially uncomfortable place for him to stay in view of the recent controversy over Canadian policy towards Cuba."[30] They changed their plans, vacationing instead in Jamaica.

The early 1960s thus saw a growth in anti-Canadian sentiment in the United States, due to Ottawa's policy on Cuba. Meanwhile some of the most disturbing facets of this pressure on Canada were the increasing complaints, petitions, and threats against Canadian diplomats. On January 19, 1961, for example, Ambassador Anderson forwarded to Ottawa a threat delivered to the Canadian embassy from a group calling itself the "Movimiento Revolucionario del Pueblo," which, he stated, was believed to be behind several recent terrorist attacks. The letter from the MRP, translated into English, was clear in its intent:

> For some weeks we Cubans have been extremely worried by the way in which your country is cooperating with Fidel Castro's evil Communist regime which is now scourging our country.
> Hardly a day passes when the underground movement fails to report on some commercial transaction between Canada and Cuba . . . these transactions represent a life line permitting it to continue in

power unlawfully when it is costing so many tears and so much Cuban blood. . . .

Should you continue to help the Communist Castro regime we shall be obliged to fight you with all our strength . . . :

1. Any unpaid balance due to Canada at the time of Liberation will not be recognised by the next government as this will be considered invalid.

2. We shall carry out acts of terrorism against Canadian residents in Cuba, beginning with the Embassy officials.[31]

It was clear that, despite continuing attempts by the Diefenbaker government to explain its position on the Cuban question to the United States, apparently nobody there was listening. The growth of anti-Canadian sentiment was rapid, causing much concern and consternation in Ottawa. The visceral anti-Castro feeling that was prevalent in the United States, and of course was only made more acute after the April 1961 Bay of Pigs invasion, simply became more and more embittered, and the Canadian position suffered as a result of its attempt to maintain diplomatic relations with both countries.

The increasing criticism of Canada's lack of official support for the U.S. stance on Cuba was both unfortunate and unfair. Canadian Ambassador Heeney was officially summoned to the State Department to hear U.S. concerns about Ottawa's position, and Kennedy advisor Arthur Schlesinger subsequently asked Heeney, in what the veteran diplomat termed a tone of "unrestrained sarcasm," whether Ottawa had decided to "put Castro and Kennedy on the same footing."[32] This ongoing criticism reflected the Kennedy administration's concern that a trusted ally would dare to pursue an independent policy that tended—in a minor way at least—to contradict that taken by the North American superpower.

The irony of this particular concern—that Canada was undermining U.S. hegemony in an important fashion—was that the Diefenbaker government was in fact fairly understanding and appreciative of Kennedy's position, as well as being openly critical of Havana's conduct. Arthur Schlesinger might rail at Ottawa's lack of solidarity with Washington and apparent effrontery in pursuing a nonaligned foreign policy, yet the Department of External Affairs personnel, and Diefenbaker himself, made no bones about their distaste for some important aspects of the Castro revolution. Typical of the ambivalent personal feelings of the prime minister himself was his decision not to receive Fidel Castro in April 1959 when the Cuban leader made an unofficial visit to Montreal. Moreover, again as the official records in Havana illustrate, the Canadian government outlined with total clarity to the

Cuban government that it was first and foremost an ally of the United States. Ottawa might have a fundamental difference of opinion with Washington over the appropriate manner of dealing with the revolutionary government of Cuba, yet in official meetings with Cuban Ambassador to Canada Américo Cruz, External Affairs officials made it perfectly clear that Canadian sympathies lay with the United States and the NATO alliance.

The official Canadian stance was at some variance with what Washington claimed it to be. Clearly partial in the conflict and also openly critical of Cuba's conduct in antagonizing Washington, the Department of External Affairs officially notified Havana that the Cuban government should not count automatically on Canadian support for the revolutionary process. It was implied that continued diplomatic relations would be contingent on Havana's not alienating NATO members. The Canadian alliance with the United States was clearly the predominant feature of Ottawa's foreign policy. At the same time—much to Washington's chagrin—it continued to respect Cuba as a sovereign and equal nation with which it had basic differences, yet nevertheless enjoyed a normal diplomatic relationship. This was the policy that Ottawa continued to enunciate to the State Department in Washington and that Diefenbaker sought with so little success to explain to Kennedy.

The official Canadian position on Cuba, contrary to the popular image projected in both Havana and Washington, revealed major differences of opinion with the Cuban government. Writing less than two weeks after the Bay of Pigs invasion, and following a meeting with the under-secretary of state for external affairs and the directors of the Latin American Division, Ambassador Cruz was told some unsettling details of Canada's policy on Cuba. While accepting that the invasion had been organized and financed by the United States despite protestations to the contrary from representatives of the Kennedy administration, the Canadian officials told Cruz that "if there were to be another invasion . . . Canada—as a member of the United Nations—would accept whatever decision were taken by the U.N."[33] Moreover, in that case Canada "would not condemn the U.S. government— as it had not done in the April 1961 invasion." Concerning U.S.-Cuban relations, the Canadian officials not only stated their belief that Cuba "has done nothing to improve the international context by arriving at an agreement with the United States" but also noted that "at every opportunity the Cuban government has been too aggressive" and should "initiate a rapprochement with the United States." Finally, reported Ambassador Cruz, the Canadians understood U.S. concerns that "Cuba will become a base for International Communism to attack the United States" and accordingly recommended that Cuba "should break the union which it has forged with the socialist countries."

There was thus an uneasy relationship between Havana and Ottawa during the early 1960s—nothing like the cozy friendship that U.S. policymakers believed to exist, or at least sought to make the North American public believe. Ottawa had consistently shown its concerns about the Castro government to Ambassador Cruz, who had dutifully passed these along to Havana while explaining his own lack of trust in Canadian intentions. For their part, Canadian diplomats in Havana continued to provide their own increasingly negative interpretations of Castro's Cuba and to imply the need for a shift in direction by Canada.

Reports from the Embassies

To this point we have examined the approach of the prime minister, the opinions of the Kennedy administration, and, to a lesser extent, those of the upper levels of the bureaucracy. One final piece of the Canadian-Cuban jigsaw puzzle needs to be analyzed, however, since the views of the ambassadors in both Ottawa and Havana were extremely important in providing a window on actions taking place in the other's capital, as well as offering summaries of official views of host governments, and—perhaps most important of all—a personal interpretation of the significance of this process.

The Cuban embassy in Ottawa at the time was remarkably consistent in its portrayal of the bilateral relationship. Ambassador Cruz had good personal relations with members of the Latin American Division of the Department of External Affairs and, from his reports, also seemed to enjoy both a good working relationship with the secretary and under-secretary of state for external affairs and fairly good access to the prime minister. From an assessment of his reports on the state of Canadian-Cuban relations, several key themes occur with some consistency.

The first of these was the clear difference of emphasis put on the nature of Canadian relations with Cuba between his own confidential reports to Havana and what the Castro government itself claimed that nature to be. For strategic reasons, Havana clearly wanted to emphasize to the world that, notwithstanding the blockade imposed by Washington, it was surviving and developing without too much hardship, due in part to a good working relationship with Canada. The Canadian banks were helping Havana in external financial matters, manufactured goods from Canada were filling the vacuum left in the wake of the U.S. withdrawal, and Cuba was extremely appreciative of Diefenbaker's independent nationalistic stance despite ongoing U.S. pressure. The image projected by Havana of Canada's role, then, was that it constituted a most valuable and vital alternative strategy for the revolutionary government's political and economic survival. Meanwhile in Havana, Canadian diplomats reported to Ottawa that, in the increasingly polarized nature of Cuban politics, the Cuban government continually emphasized the level of commitment by Canada to the revolutionary process. As Comandante Guillermo Jiménez, director of regional policy in the Ministry of External Relations noted: "Cuba's relations with Canada are the best possible example of how two countries with such different social systems can coexist in peace."[34] This was a theme to which President Fidel Castro himself has referred on several occasions.

Both Cruz and his predecessor, Luis Baralt, commented on the cordial treatment they received from the Canadian government—even when there were fundamental policy disagreements. Baralt (who later defected) waxed eloquent on the exceptional courtesy extended to him when he first came to Canada, and at the attention paid him by John Diefenbaker.[35] Cruz was more circumspect and balanced in his assessment. Writing on June 6, 1961, for example, even when notifying Havana of two major disappointments (Cubana cargo flights had been denied landing rights in Toronto and a shipment of U.S.-made spare parts destined for Cuba had been seized in Montreal), Cruz noted that "in both cases the attitude of the Canadian Ministry of External Affairs had been most cooperative." Relations between the two countries, he noted, "continue to be cordial, and have not changed in the least."[36]

At the same time he continually advised his ministry that Canada's approach to the Cuban revolution, diplomatic cordiality apart, was essentially one of critical coexistence (with the emphasis on "critical"). His reports to Havana frequently emphasized the fact that Cuba should not delude itself about Canadian altruism, in no small measure because of the intense pressure that Washington continued to bring to bear on the Diefenbaker government. He often expressed surprise that Ottawa had to date been able to withstand this inexorable pressure, given U.S. domination of the economy. Typical of many of his reports on this matter was a letter to Minister of External Relations Raúl Roa on May 15, 1961. He had summarized the comments of Howard Green (Roa's Canadian counterpart) following the abortive Bay of Pigs invasion and concluded:

> In general terms the Minister's declarations have been beneficial to us, although in my opinion they also contain an extremely negative

point, since they accept aggression against our country if this is supported or authorized by the OAS. . . .

But really it's not so strange for Canada to adopt such a position when on more than one occasion the Under-Secretary of State for External Relations and even the Prime Minister have told me that Canada will remain on the side of the United States. . . .

In Havana the Ministry will surely believe that I am too pessimistic with regards the topic of Cuban-Canadian relations—and I personally dare to add that at times I have been mistaken about the nature of Canadian friendship. However, I believe myself to be extremely realistic. I have always maintained the thesis that this country will maintain its trade with Cuba as long as it does not prejudice its external relations with the United States. And Canada will maintain a cordial position towards Cuba since we have been especially accommodating to them throughout the revolutionary process, and have acted with exceptional deference in resolving all bilateral problems that have arisen.[37]

Havana might well emphasize abroad the special relationship it enjoyed with Canada, and Diefenbaker might well be known in Cuba as a man who had stood up to "imperialismo yanqui," yet for Ambassador Cruz there was little doubt that the Canadian government policy was anything but firm. He suggested to Havana that to a large degree Canada continued to deal with Cuba out of self-interest. "They need to sell because of the poor economic situation here, and the enormous number of unemployed," he noted on January 24, 1961.[38]

If we try to synthesize the views of Ambassador Cruz it is clear that he possessed a brutally realistic view of the Canadian position on Cuba. Impressed with the cordial, attentive treatment he consistently received from the Canadian government, he was nevertheless extremely aware that behind this facade of diplomatic courtesy there remained grave doubts concerning his government. He was less appreciative of Diefenbaker's nationalistic sensitivities than one would have imagined and seemed unaware of the intense mutual dislike shared by Diefenbaker and Kennedy—a most surprising lapse that the Cubans might well have wanted to exploit. His relations with the opposition Liberals and the social democratic party, the CCF, seem to have been very limited, and he had little time for either party. In a report of April 25, 1961, for instance, he noted the reaction from both parties after he had requested support for Cuba in the wake of the U.S.-sponsored Bay of Pigs invasion: The CCF leader, Hazen Argue, apparently admitted to the ambassador that his party could give no support "because Cuba is considered communist, and therefore politically it would be disastrous for the CCF to pursue a common cause with Cuba."[39] He was even more disdainful of the Liberal Party, which he termed "eminently pro-Yankee. Its leader, Mr. Pearson, was Minister of External Affairs during the Liberal government, and does not hide the fact that Canadian policy should be in agreement with that of the United States."[40] Fearful of a shift in Canadian policy toward Cuba if Pearson were elected, he misread their intentions.

In sum, Canadian-Cuban relations at this time—from the ambassador's perspective—were not all they appeared to be. True, the Canadian government observed diplomatic protocol and was at all times respectful to Sr. Cruz. Bilateral trade had shown some dramatic increases initially but had steadily declined due to Cuban shortages of hard currency. The Bay of Pigs invasion, organized by the CIA, was in many ways a watershed for the ambassador's understanding of official Canadian policy because it showed him that, despite Ottawa's rejection to date of U.S. pressure, when the diplomatic chips were down, Canada would nevertheless align itself with its NATO and NORAD partners. When appeals for humanitarian assistance fell on deaf ears, for instance, and the Canadian government had not acceded to Cuba's request to provide a plane to fly antitetanus vaccines and medicines bought in Canada by Cuba to victims of the invasion, Cruz was disappointed. At the very least he had expected some gesture of people-to-people support and was disturbed to be told by the under-secretary of state that since no government aircraft were available, he should appeal to the Red Cross. This seemed merely to confirm his own nagging doubts concerning the degree of Canadian interest in Cuba. Writing to Raúl Roa, the Cuban foreign minister, on August 29, 1962, he expressed succinctly his feelings on the current state of bilateral relations:

> It is clear that our relations, on the official and formal level, are indeed correct—and Mr. Pick [head of the Latin American Division] has accepted an invitation to dine at my house next week. But I continue to believe that our relations will remain fixed at that level, and will not improve—despite our efforts to do so. . . . As long as Cuba complies with Canada in everything—as we have done until now—everything will move along without problems, but precisely the opposite will occur if we behave differently.[41]

This suspicion of hidden Canadian motives had a fascinating reflection in diplomatic reports sent by Cruz's Canadian counterpart in Havana. The two most active ambassadors of this period were Allan Anderson, who presented his credentials on October 9, 1959, and remained in his post until May 23, 1961, and George P. Kidd, whose mission lasted from July 5, 1961, until January 4, 1964. They followed Hector Allard, who had taken up his post in January 1957, remaining in Havana until June 23, 1959. All three had a strong fundamental dislike for developments in revolutionary Cuba and made that disapproval show in their numerous diplomatic dispatches. By far the most perceptive analysis came from Ambassador Kidd, whose periodic reports and monthly reports were generally incisive and solid interpretations of events unfolding in a society unlike any they had seen before. By contrast Anderson, who had worked in the main office of the Royal Bank in Havana in 1926, found it difficult to reconcile his experiences in Cuba some 35 years earlier with the rapid social polarization taking place in the early 1960s.

While there is much of value in their dispatches and analysis, there is also much that could only have helped to muddy the diplomatic waters back in Ottawa. Some of their reporting could be interpreted as being quite undiplomatic and possibly offensive. Consider, for example, Allard's describing the Cuban leader as "an unpredictable, unreliable, wandering plotter,"[42] or his statement that Castro has "become obsessed with his own importance and infallibility. He has become suspicious of everything foreign, irascible, unapproachable and irresponsible."[43] Allan Anderson's reports in particular are riddled with erratic and occasionally inappropriate observations. He had little positive to say about the revolutionary government, and even those remarks were often couched in derogatory references. "Perhaps an asset, certainly a surprising phenomenon, is the new honesty of government officials. . . . However, those observers who have known Cuba and the Cubans for a long time are not convinced that this is a permanent conversion," he noted drily in early 1960.[44] He also passed along hearsay, although he did not claim necessarily to share those views. Among these observations, albeit accompanied by a disclaimer as to their validity, was that the revolutionary hero Camilo Cienfuegos—whom he compares to the cartoon character Li'l Abner—whose plane had mysteriously disappeared off the Cuban coast was murdered "probably by Raúl Castro."[45] In the same letter he refers again to Fidel Castro's younger brother in disrespectful terms ("Raúl is a queer fellow in more than one sense of the word. . . . He still wears his hair in a pony-tail two feet long, which nobody else does, but he has no beard. Why? Because he is unable to grow a beard," [3]). He talks about a "messianic complex" held by Fidel Castro,[46] and states boldly that "the people now in power are unpredictable and unscrupulous."[47] At least a dozen or so more examples of such observations on Fidel Castro (the particular butt of his ire), the growing communist influence, government leaders, and the changing nature of Cuban society can be encountered in a cursory reading of his reports.

Just as Ambassador Cruz occasionally misread the political situation in Canada, so too did his Canadian counterparts misjudge the reality on which they were reporting, in no small measure because they were unprepared for the radical changes so rapidly introduced in revolutionary Cuba. One example of many will perhaps suffice to illustrate this phenomenon. In late December 1960, Ambassador Anderson set out for the famed holiday resort, Varadero, to get a solid understanding of the revolutionary process. He noted in his dispatch that "on many occasions in the past residents of Cuba have commented to me that foreign representatives cannot get a true understanding of Cuba without travelling outside Havana."[48] Yet instead of going to Oriente province (the poorest area of Cuba), to the western tobacco-growing areas in Pinar del Río, or to industrial Cienfuegos, the ambassador, seeking to "take the pulse" of the rapidly changing situation, instead chose to go to an atypical holiday resort gearing up for New Year's celebrations.

It is clear that diplomats, like anybody else, are complex human beings, beset with doubts and prejudices as well as honesty and benevolence, who often interpret current political developments through a filter of past experiences, their own particular background, and personal ideology and values. Often lacking a cultural sensitivity concerning the land in which they have been sent to undertake their diplomatic mission (and often not even speaking the target language), they can easily misjudge the reality on which they are reporting. This was as true a fact for Allan Anderson as it was for Américo Cruz, with the difference that the Cuban ambassador was not burdened with memories of a Canada of some 35 years earlier. Anderson, by contrast, did remember (and with great fondness) the "good old days," with the result that for him the changes happening in revolutionary Cuba were absolutely unpalatable. Writing on October 18, 1960, in a report conspicuously entitled "No More Laughter," he showed just how deep his own biases were:

> This was once a land of smiling, laughing happy people. Rich or poor, it didn't matter. Wherever you went, day or night, you were welcome and there was a smile to greet you. That was the Cuba that I loved thirty-five years ago, and apparently it lasted until say a couple of years ago.
>
> Now ... there is no more laughter. There is no temptation to stroll

the streets of Old Havana even in daytime, much less at night. Laughter is replaced by suspicion, hatred and fear. You will probably not be molested if you stroll, but the gaiety is gone, and the under-currents are no longer sympathetic. We do not stroll.[49]

It comes as no surprise, therefore, that in light of such consistently negative reports on the first years of the Cuban revolutionary process, Canadian diplomats in Havana should regard Canadian-Cuban relations with such a jaundiced view. Indeed with the value of hindsight it seems that some of Ambassador Cruz's suspicions at the time concerning the lack of valid analysis on Cuba were correct. Writing in the summer of 1962, for instance, he informed his minister of a recent meeting with the deputy director of the Latin American Division: "I have expressed to the Ministry on several earlier occasions that I believe the Department of External Affairs here can not be giving positive reports on developments in Cuba. . . . The most surprising aspect about my recent conversation with Mr. West is that he was unaware of the daily provocations by North American planes and boats, and in reply informed me that 'He hadn't read anything about that in the *New York Times*.'"[50] Clearly there was a superficial, one-dimensional view of a multifaceted reality—a problem facing the diplomatic service of all countries.

Ambassador Anderson in particular was quite emotional in his vehement denunciations of what he perceived to be Cuban cynicism. Fearful of potential Cuban aggression against all countries of the Americas ("I, all of my staff, and all other Canadians of my acquaintance here are left without even the tiniest grain of doubt that this government is a communist bridgehead directed at the Americas, and that *all* American countries had better look to their fences"),[51] he was convinced of the necessarily short-term nature of Canadian-Cuban relations. Moreover, he stated on several occasions that the Cubans were deliberately exploiting claims of friendship with great insincerity to meet their own political ends:

> This naturally tends to strengthen our feeling that our conclusions are correct, that the Castro Government is not only pro-communist but communist-controlled, that the present flowery expressions of friendship for Canada are totally insincere and false, and that their sole purpose is to get, while it is still possible, whatever goods can be got from Canada to fill the various needs which cannot be supplied from the Sino-Soviet group.[52]

Three weeks earlier he had made this point even more directly: "I am still doing my best to maintain friendly relations and as you know, the Cuban officials are showing friendship, but I cannot help knowing that this is only on the surface. *There is not, and cannot be, any genuine friendship.*"[53]

The October 1962 Missile Crisis: Its Impact on Bilateral Ties

It is significant that, despite the limited commercial benefits resulting from the rupture of diplomatic relations with Washington and the generally negative tenor of reports on Cuba from External Affairs, Prime Minister Diefenbaker stayed the diplomatic course in maintaining Canadian relations with the revolutionary government. This approach was subjected to an even greater trial with the Missile Crisis. In October 1962 Cold War tension reached its zenith, with the polarized East and West camps each staking out their territory, while daring the other to do something about it. Undoubtedly the closest situation to thermonuclear war to which the entire world has ever come, it also constituted a time at which allies of both superpowers were expected to—indeed were obliged to—state their support. It was a test of loyalty, and from Washington's perspective, one that John Diefenbaker failed miserably. Once again the bilateral relationship was pulled into the vortex of U.S. foreign policy, becoming a trilateral one.

For the prime minister, John Kennedy's major address to the U.S. people in October 1962 was the beginning of the whole sad episode, which would culminate in Diefenbaker's electoral defeat at the hands of Lester Pearson. The president charged the Soviet Union with threatening world peace by seeking to install nuclear missiles in Cuba and called for a naval blockade (the more diplomatic-sounding term "quarantine" was used) around Cuba. Just two hours prior to President Kennedy's live address, the prime minister received Livingston Merchant, who had recently retired as U.S. ambassador to Canada and who came now as a special emissary of John Kennedy to give prior warning of the content of the president's speech. Unlike British Prime Minister Harold Macmillan, who had been consulted about the brewing Cuban crisis on several occasions by Kennedy, Diefenbaker was not considered particularly helpful by Kennedy's staff, and it bothered the Canadian prime minister to be presented with virtually a fait accompli. Of course he was concerned about the threat of nuclear war and agreed that Kennedy had no alternative but to seek to prevent the installation of the missiles in Cuba, yet at the same time he was annoyed at the lack of prior consultation and was concerned at possible rash actions that the U.S. president might take.

That same night, shortly after the president's address, Diefenbaker gave a statement to the House of Commons in which he condemned the idea of the missile pads in Cuba and urged an on-site inspection to be organized by the United Nations as a means of verifying the true nature of the Soviet installations. This response had been prepared by the Department of Ex-ternal Affairs *before* the Kennedy speech and was intended to seek some form of dialogue between Moscow and Washington at an early stage of the looming crisis, before both sides felt sufficiently threatened to harden their positions irrevocably. Unfortunately, this attempt at gaining time was poorly received in Washington, where it was interpreted as a lack of faith in care-fully collected evidence by U-2 spy planes and a lack of confidence in Kennedy's ability to handle the rapidly escalating situation. Writing later in his memoirs, Diefenbaker explained why in fact he did have little confi-dence in Kennedy's judgment:

> I knew that President Kennedy was still smarting over the 1961 Bay of Pigs fiasco. . . . I knew also that the President thought he had something to prove in his personal dealings with Khruschev after their unpleasant Vienna meeting, where Khruschev had treated him like a child, referring to him as 'the boy.' I considered that he was perfectly capable of taking the world to the brink of thermonuclear destruc-tion to prove himself the man for our times, a courageous champion of a Western democracy.[54]

From that point it was all downhill in terms of U.S.-Canadian coopera-tion, which led to an even greater strain in bilateral ties. The official re-quest by Washington for Canada to follow the U.S. example and place its air defense forces on an increased alert (Defcon 3) was deliberately delayed in Ottawa, leading to a bitterly angry telephone call on the afternoon of October 23 from John Kennedy, who sought a far stronger response from Diefenbaker.[55] The prime minister continued to voice official Canadian support for its ally, condemning the "direct menace" to the entire world that the Soviet missiles represented and calling for a U.N.-supervised solu-tion to the problem, although for the Kennedy administration the Cana-dian position was clearly one of "too little, too late." By Thursday, Octo-ber 25, the first Soviet vessels transporting the missiles to Cuba were ap-proaching the U.S. warships, and the world waited fearfully to see what would happen. Washington had urged Ottawa again to place its air de-fense forces on a higher alert, something that Diefenbaker—fearful of what he perceived to be Kennedy's political immaturity—was greatly reluctant to do. Meanwhile Defence Minister Douglas Harkness, frustrated with the position of Diefenbaker, took unilateral action and did so without telling his prime minister. The apparent waffling and uncertainty by the Diefenbaker government, its hesitation to support the Kennedy strategy, the delay in following the U.S. lead to place Canadian forces on a higher alert, the fact that permission was given for only eight flights by U.S. aircraft carrying nuclear weapons when requests for 640 flights were made, and the refusal to allow U.S. forces to move nuclear warheads over Canadian airspace from Bangor, Maine, to U.S. bases in Labrador and Newfoundland all led to increasing political problems for Diefenbaker.

In Washington Diefenbaker's conduct had destroyed any remaining shreds of credibility with the Kennedy White House, and the U.S. president took delight in scheming to obtain vengeance for Diefenbaker's diplomatic cold shoulder. It was no accident that, in the general election the following year, John Kennedy assisted Lester Pearson in several ways, by meeting with him for strategy sessions and photo opportunities and encouraging his pollster Lou Harris to meet with Pearson and provide invaluable assistance to the Liberal Party. In Canada, too, the prime minister's position on the Cuban Missile Crisis brought him much criticism for his dithering at a time when a poll taken by the Canadian Peace Research Institute showed that almost 80 percent of Canadians backed Kennedy's position.

The irony of the situation is that, while Diefenbaker can be criticized for delaying so long in supporting the actions of the United States, Ambassador Cruz in Ottawa was left in no doubt as to where Canadian loyalties lay. On September 4, 1962, for example, the director of the Latin American Division, Alfred Pick, in a somber mood, expressed to Cruz his "fear that the Soviets would take control of Cuba, so that in addition to losing our sovereignty we would then also constitute a threat to the Americas."[56] On October 18, the Cuban ambassador informed his minister that the Canadian government had just denied permission to the Soviet embassy in Canada for Soviet planes to refuel in Gander on their way to Cuba. Six days later he cabled Havana that, according to international treaties, no arms were to be transported to Cuba through Canadian waters and that all Cuban vessels would be searched in Canada. In the wake of the Missile Crisis, he noted a stormy meeting with Pick at which the Canadian diplomat informed him that "Cuba had lost its independence, since it was now in Soviet hands."[57] All Cuban aircraft landing in Canada would in future be thoroughly searched, he was notified. That same day he recounted his meeting with Secretary of State for External Affairs Howard Green, who "insisted yet again on the same ideas as ever—that Canada had to align itself with the United States, and that therefore it was absolutely necessary for Cuba to remove the Soviet bases."[58] A week later, in a meeting with Under-Secretary of State for External Affairs Norman Robertson, the Cuban ambassador received a similar message of Canadian support for Washington.[59] Once again, however, Diefenbaker's initiatives were seen by Kennedy as being too limited and coming too late. The very fact that Canada continued to trade with Cuba and retained diplomatic relations with Havana, despite the official view that Cuba had been the catalyst that had brought the world to the brink of nuclear destruction, was, in Washington's eyes, proof positive that Canada could not be trusted during John Diefenbaker's tenure.

Diplomatic Ambivalence

If any two expressions can be used to summarize the dynamic of bilateral relations during this crucial formative stage, they would be "mutual suspicion" and "ambivalence." The relationship began with the best of intentions, as can be seen from Howard Green's instructions to incoming Ambassador Anderson in 1959 and the frequent declarations of appreciation from Cuban leaders for Canada's maintenance of diplomatic relations. Yet soon the nature of the political reforms and the wave of economic nationalization in Cuba caused growing concern among Canadian policymakers— a process that was not made easier by increasing pressure from the Kennedy administration to support its policies. Canada wanted to maintain as normal a policy with Cuba as the circumstances would allow, but at this stage found it a difficult policy to pursue. Ambivalence soon became the dominant theme, at least from Ottawa's perspective.

To take the example of trade, it is important to note that at all times Canada had encouraged the development of bilateral trade, yet at the same time collaborated assiduously with Washington to prevent the transshipment of U.S.-made goods. In December 1961, commenting on Ottawa's role in this regard, Secretary of State Dean Rusk at confidential Senate Foreign Relations Committee hearings noted that "Canada has helped us very well in preventing the flow of American parts and American produce to Cuba."[60] Another example of how Cuban policymakers increasingly looked askance at Canada's claims of friendship can be seen in the treatment of the media: Canadian journalists flocked to Cuba to cover the rapidly changing political scene, but in Canada the government insisted on the closing of Prensa Latina, the Cuban news agency and would not even allow journalists to cover the 1963 federal election.

Finally, one can cite the manner in which Ottawa acceded to Cuban requests by allowing cargo flights to begin a somewhat erratic service, yet in November 1960 the Canadians refused to sell Beaver aircraft to Cuba, fearing that they might be used for military purposes, and in 1963 refused to allow tourist charter flights to fly to Cuba. Writing in May 1963, Ambassador Cruz, reporting on a meeting at External Affairs, informed his minister that the latter measure "had been taken because it would be politically embarassing [sic] for the government, in the midst of an electoral campaign, to have Canadians travel to Cuba—especially because those who would go would be 'communists and fellow travellers,' to use their words."[61] No wonder that Ambassador Cruz should write back to his minister, as the Canadian election campaign drew to a close, that he felt his four years of attempting to improve bilateral relations had largely been in vain: "despite our best efforts to comply with Canadian requests, Ottawa was now taking measures which are normally only taken with governments with which they do not have cordial relations."[62]

If ambivalence was the dominant note in the bilateral relationship during the Diefenbaker years, it was accompanied by an ongoing undercurrent of misunderstanding. At times this might be attributed to some degree of malevolence, but it was usually the result of an inability to bridge the cultural gap. One amusing incident will perhaps illustrate how, despite the best of intentions, a diplomatic gesture could easily go awry. On May 16, 1961, Ambassador Cruz—who apart from this incident proved an effective spokesman for his country—had been informed by the head of protocol at External Affairs that a gift he had sent to Prime Minister Diefenbaker was unacceptable because of an accompanying note and was therefore being returned. The gift in question was a box of cigars in a hand-tooled leather case on which the prime minister's name had been embossed. He therefore sought advice from the ministry, since he simply could not understand why the gift was deemed unacceptable and was concerned at the diplomatic impact that it might produce:

> If we accept the principle that there was no word or sentence in the letter that could offend anybody, I therefore have to reach the conclusion that it was sent back for some political reason which I cannot fathom. I suspect, however, that it may be because of the great friendship between Canada and the United States, which we have seen so openly expressed at the time of the failed invasion of our territory.
> . . .
> After analyzing it time and time again, I cannot think of any other explanation: the gift was sent on May 3 (that is, many days after the failure of the imperialist invasion of Cuba), and it is also surprising to note that they should wait until May 16, exactly the day when President Kennedy arrives here, before returning the box of cigars. . . .
> I should clarify by noting that the Ministry knows that such boxes of cigars have been given to innumerable people throughout the world without ever having provoked such a reaction. I should also add that approximately two months ago I made the same gift to the Minister of External Affairs, without any similar reaction resulting.[63]

Precisely what was the wording that the prime minister found unaccept-able in the letter accompanying the box of cigars and that the ambassador thought normal? The exact text stated: "Dear Prime Minister . . . I hope that as you smoke these cigars you will have 'the name of Cuba on your lips,' and that your thoughts will be on my courageous people who con-tinue to resist so firmly the imperialist aggression."

The incident is important, for it reveals the ambassador's lack of appre-ciation of Anglo-Saxon sensitivities; the florid, emotional language sounds rhetorical and bombastic to Canadian ears, all the more so because of the overdone clichés applied somewhat belligerently to Canada's greatest trad-ing partner, neighbor, and ally. It was, in short, totally inappropriate. More troubling, though, than the ambassador's lack of political sensitivity in writing such a note was the fact that he should have spent time racking his brains in an effort to discover why the note was so poorly received and, even then, could discern nothing that Ottawa might have found objection-able. To say that this particular incident revealed a gross lack of diplomatic sensitivity would appear a fair comment in the circumstances but, in light of some of his Canadian counterparts' comments, one that was hardly lim-ited to Cuban ambassadors.

Yet, diplomatic faux pas and insensitivity apart, it is important to note that another key element remained in the Canadian-Cuban dynamic that needs to be emphasized: the political will to maintain the relationship held firm. That is, while the Ottawa-Havana axis was perceived through a strong filter of ambivalence and misunderstanding, an even firmer conviction about the need to keep the relationship afloat predominated. Despite the uncer-tainty felt in Ottawa about the course of the Cuban revolution and a vari-ety of errors made in diplomatic analyses in Havana and Ottawa, there was no misrepresentation of either country's position in the diplomatic dia-logue. This mixture of cooperation and conflict in the relationship, together with Canada's close alliance with the United States, at times made for diffi-cult diplomatic moments. Yet in the final analysis neither Ottawa nor Ha-vana deliberately fooled the other—a point that needs to be recognized. In June 1961, M. N. Bow, chargé d'affaires for a four-month spell, wrote his final impressions, noting that despite the obvious difficulties in the rela-tionship, "so long as such a possibility exists, however remote it may be, Canada should pursue a policy of friendly but not fraternal relations with Cuba, and should adamantly oppose any suggestion of outside interven-tion in Cuban affairs."[64] More than thirty-five years later that same ap-proach remained in effect.

3

Coldly Correct
The Pearson Policy toward Cuba

All this will be true just as long as we get the result that everybody is hoping for, namely that the Conservative Party will again hold a majority in the House of Commons, and will retain power.

On the other hand, if the Liberals win the elections the panorama would be gloomier. First because this party has shown itself time and time again to be openly opposed to trading with our country, and has attacked it almost daily in the House. And secondly because if Paul Martin (a sworn enemy of Cuba and a leader of the Catholic community) is named Secretary of State for External Relations, as is expected, then this will mean that he will be alongside . . . that defender of the United States, Mr. Pearson as Prime Minister. [If that were to happen] relations with Cuba, and with all the socialist countries, would suffer a most radical change.

Ambassador Américo Cruz

The Cuban ambassador to Canada, Américo Cruz, in this May 4, 1962, dispatch to his minister, was expressing a profoundly held concern about the pro-U.S. leanings of Lester Pearson. Eleven months later, with the election of the Liberals, Cuban worries understandably rose again. In light of Prime Minister Pearson's excellent personal ties with President John Kennedy and his extensive connections with the Washington bureaucracy and local elite that were the result of a lifelong diplomatic career, Cruz was right to be concerned. In addition, Pearson had taken a dramatic decision (largely in the wake of the October 1962 Missile Crisis) to reverse his long-held opposition to nuclear weapons and support Canada's acquisition of nuclear arms. He had done this at the request of Washington as a deterrent to Soviet expansionism. The Cubans were indeed right to be wary of the incoming prime minister.

Yet the Cuban diplomats also needed to take into account Canada's traditional foreign policy leanings, a nascent Canadian nationalism in the wake of growing U.S. control of the economy, the basis of Canadian-Cuban relations established during the Diefenbaker years, and Prime Minister Pearson's own strongly pragmatic view of politics. What resulted was a dynamic involving Pearson's efforts to repair the damaged U.S.-Canadian "special relationship" in the wake of the tension caused by the Diefenbaker-Kennedy schism, and his own personal view that Canadian-Cuban relations should be allowed to progress slowly and correctly.

This chapter examines the nature of that unusual relationship. The first section examines Pearson's views on international politics, including his assessment of Canadian-U.S. relations and how they pertained to the government's handling of the Cuban question. The core of the chapter concerns the actual events and trends in bilateral relations. Drawing heavily on diplomatic correspondence, this section analyzes the "cut and thrust" of diplomatic problems and successes. The chapter concludes with an assessment of this five-year period within the overall scheme of Canadian-Cuban relations.

Pearson's Views of the United States

In a lecture given in 1968, Lester Pearson spoke about Canada's position in supporting U.S. demands for Soviet missiles to be withdrawn from Cuba: "Canada supported the United States in its determination to get Russian nuclear missiles out of our part of the world. In a *hostile country, such as Cuba had become,* they were a provocation and a threat to peace."[1] In emphasizing that Cuba had become a "hostile country" while noting his support for Washington, Pearson showed where his political preferences lay, a theme to which he referred unabashedly and frequently. Six years earlier, for example, in an address to the Council on World Tensions held at the University of Bahia in northern Brazil, he had shown his sweeping support for U.S. goals in Latin America and had claimed that Washington's aims for the region had been poorly understood: "So, I beg of you, my Latin American friends, be careful; but don't misjudge the Americans. They are a wonderful and generous people, the least imperialistically-minded people that ever had world power thrust on them."[2]

In staking out these positions that were so supportive of U.S. foreign policy and that could only have sent shivers of despair through Cuban diplomats, Lester Pearson was merely restating a policy to which he had long adhered, namely, that the United States was both the leader and the friend of the Free World, the natural ally of Western nations and implacable foe of communism. His response to a Soviet motion at the United Nations reveals unequivocally these strong ideological preferences:

> The truth is that the nations of the world outside the Soviet bloc know
> that the power of the United States will not be used for purposes of

aggressive war. They know that the policies of the United States though we may not always support them, or even approve them—are not designed to lead to war.

We in Canada know this country and its people well. We know them as good neighbors who respect the rights of others, who don't ask for or get automatic support from smaller countries through pressure or threats or promises. We know that they accept the fact that co-operation between large and smaller countries can only exist on a basis of mutual confidence and mutual respect.[3]

An essential supplementary component of this support for Washington's international policy was Pearson's unswerving commitment to NATO, which was clearly spearheaded by the U.S. government. On the occasion of the signing of the treaty itself in April 1949, Lester Pearson left no doubt as to who the enemy was and why NATO had been formed. He noted succinctly that NATO had been born out of two basic emotions—fear and frustration—the responsibility for which he laid at the feet of international communism. NATO was thus a necessary deterrent because of communist tactics, he noted, given the collective "fear of the aggressive and subversive policies of communism and the effect of those policies on our own peace, security and well-being; frustration over the obstinate obstruction by communist states of our efforts to make the United Nations function effectively as a universal security system."[4] A fervent booster of NATO's strategic role, and of Washington's leadership of the organization,[5] he emphasized in January 1963 that the world had just recently clawed its way back from the abyss of nuclear annihilation: "We owe our escape from catastrophe to a combination—notably in Washington—of skilful diplomacy and adequate deterrent military strength. We will continue to need both in the days ahead," he added significantly.[6]

It was only natural for a man of Pearson's upbringing, personal diplomatic connections, and many years of experience in the United States to be favorably impressed with U.S. foreign policy. His firm support of NATO was also understandable, although he disliked the overwhelming emphasis placed on military force to the detriment of broader socioeconomic considerations. What was most surprising, however, was his rapid conversion in January 1963 to a position supporting nuclear weapons. This change of heart by Pearson reversed a long-held Liberal view (re-affirmed at the party's 1961 convention) and led to major rifts within his own party.

Pearson had clearly been shocked by the October 1962 Missile Crisis and sincerely felt that the Canadian government had failed to live up to its defense commitments with its U.S. neighbors.[7] It was undoubtedly a difficult decision for him to make, flying as it did in the face of his party's long-standing policy as well as his own publicly stated position, and it led to many fellow Liberals shunning him. Future Prime Minister Trudeau condemned his leader and openly scorned him as the "unfrocked priest of peace."[8] Although it caused discomfort to many of his fellow Liberals, in many ways Pearson's position was the logical conclusion of his long-standing trust in Washington and personal belief that it was in Canada's best interests to accept the military leadership of the United States and its own role as a junior partner in this relationship. Consequently, the Cuban ambassador was wise to be wary of Pearson's pro-Washington penchants.

Yet while Pearson was unabashedly in favor of many aspects of U.S. policy, domestic and international, he was also aware of the rising current of nationalism in Canada and the fact that many people were increasingly wary of growing U.S. control and ownership of the Canadian economy. On the one hand, Pearson waxed eloquent about the sound bilateral relationship while, on the other, his government was obliged by public pressure to respond to increasing economic nationalism. The 1965 Auto Pact, which allowed duty-free trade in automotive products while leading to an increase in exports of such products to the United States, was also widely seen as a further example of the Canadian government trading political control of its economy for a fistful of American dollars. Canadian nationalists felt seriously concerned by the way in which the lucrative auto industry was thereby "dovetailed" with its much larger U.S. counterpart. Concerns of nationalists were further heightened by the powerful lobby orchestrated by *Time* and *Reader's Digest,* which, in the wake of the 1965 budget stipulating that advertising in foreign-owned publications would no longer be tax-deductible, managed to wrest an exemption from the Pearson government.

The opening of the international exhibition Expo 67, together with its nationalistic hoopla and yearlong ceremonies, accentuated the mood of national pride. The disturbing meddling of President de Gaulle in his ill-fated speech in Montreal also heightened emotions as Canada celebrated its centennial. In this context of increased national awareness, it was understandable that political figures would reflect on the growing role of U.S. interests in the Canadian economy and the political influence that would result. In his memoirs, Prime Minister Pearson himself reveals this concern in a surprisingly frank manner:

> The signing of the Auto Pact raises the question of our economic relations with the United States. There was (and is) a growing popular concern in this country over American economic penetration and

business takeovers. Almost 40 per cent of the over 2500 business takeovers and mergers in the sixties were promoted by foreign, mainly
American, interests. I regard this trend to American domination of
Canadian resources and the Canadian market as an urgent problem
that we, or any government, would have to deal with.[9]

Still, Pearson was an unwavering proponent of the "special relationship" between Canada and the United States, although that did not mean
he was blind to the problems with the U.S. system. At best a rather tepid
nationalist and by contrast a leader possessing a strong continentalist perspective, his innate respect and admiration for the United States was quite
noticeable. At the same time, he became increasingly unconvinced by U.S.
foreign policy, particularly with the evident decrease in pursuing diplomatic
solutions to world "hot spots" accompanied by an increase in militaristic
approaches to those same problems. When seeking to interpret the multifaceted nature of Canadian foreign policy, therefore, it is important to bear
this complex relationship in mind.

Disagreement of Pearson with U.S. Foreign Policy

It is easy for Canadian nationalists to criticize the continentalist policies of
Pearson and to accuse him of having sold out to U.S. corporate interests.
Yet it is clear from a study of Canadian foreign policy initiatives of this
time that it would be incredibly simplistic to interpret Lester Pearson's support for certain U.S. foreign policies as a general rubber-stamping of all of
Washington's international endeavors. There were thus significant differences of general philosophy between Washington and Ottawa, as well as
specific disagreements over concrete philosophy—seen most clearly concerning Vietnam and, to a lesser extent, Korea and China. As early as October 1949, shortly after the People's Republic leadership came to power,
Canadian envoy to China Chester Ronning had recommended that Canada
observe its time-honored tradition of recognizing the de facto government,
a position favored by Pearson.

One telling anecdote about the differences in Canadian and U.S. feelings about Communist China stems from the 1954 Geneva Conference. In
his memoirs, Pearson notes that during the first tea break he went with
Chester Ronning to meet Chou En-lai, after which he visited the Chinese
leader at the official residence, much to the consternation of U.S. delegates:
"They did not like it at all. And General Bedell-Smith, who was the American delegate, let me know that I was letting the side down badly by such
normal fraternization. He felt it was wrong to let the Chinese feel they had

any friends at all in the Western camp."[10] That said, Pearson clearly felt that a pragmatic foreign policy, based more on political realism than ideological concerns, made eminent sense.

The essence of the difference of opinion over China between Ottawa and Washington was that the Canadian government did not believe in the need of force to show opposition to the Communist government. Pearson obviously did not agree with many of its policies but, in light of traditional diplomatic practices, including the necessary recognition of a government enjoying significant popular support, believed that the U.S. emphasis on a state of permanent antagonism was self-defeating. Negotiation, not blustering, was the hallmark of the Pearsonian school of diplomacy, regardless of the ideological label of other governments.

The Canadian position on Korea also differed somewhat from that adopted by the United States. Ottawa interpreted the invasion of South Korea by the North as an act of aggression and rapidly responded to the U.N. Security Council's request for support. At the same time, Pearson harbored deep mistrust of General MacArthur's handling of the war, especially when the U.S. military leader showed that he wanted to turn a defensive policy protecting South Korea into an offensive against the North. From the outset Pearson made known his concern that China might become embroiled in the ensuing struggle and also expressed his worry that General MacArthur's punitive expeditions went far beyond the parameters laid out by the United Nations. Similarly the Canadian foreign minister spoke out forcefully against President Truman's insinuation that nuclear weapons might prove necessary to resolve the Korean crisis and intimated that such a policy might well destroy NATO. Canadian troops did participate in the U.N.-sponsored mission, but it was clear that Pearson held profound reservations about the way in which the war was pursued by the U.S. leadership. Indeed, Pearson tried valiantly to moderate or mitigate the adventurous tendencies of Washington by having the war conducted under the auspices of the U.N.

If Pearson's views on China and Korea diverged from the official U.S. position, he held a radically different position on the conflict in Vietnam. Nowhere was this clearer than in a speech he gave on April 2, 1965, at Philadelphia's Temple University. He had gone there to accept the university's World Peace Award but used the occasion to weigh in with a skillfully crafted speech during the course of which he called for a suspension or pause in the U.S. bombing of North Vietnam. The next day Prime Minister Pearson lunched with President Johnson at the presidential retreat Camp David, at which time he was seriously taken to task by Johnson for his undiplomatic language. (Usually it is a matter of diplomatic protocol that visiting political dignitaries do not criticize policies of the host government.) In the prime minister's diary he noted the strong reaction of President Johnson.[11] Veteran journalist Knowlton Nash sums up the bizarre incident with some irony: the U.S. president "exploded at the speech when they met the next day for lunch at Camp David. 'Lester, you pissed on my rug!' exclaimed Johnson in an extraordinary, non-stop, fist-waving, expletive-filled harangue."[12]

This complex, ambiguous, and occasionally contradictory position on international relations reveals in Pearson a man who in general was prepared to support U.S. leadership in world politics yet at the same time harbored some deep reservations about Washington's grasp of the subtleties of international dynamics. Clearly unafraid of standing out through his disagreement with Britain over a policy concerning the Suez crisis or with the United States as seen in this section, Pearson sought to pursue a genuinely independent Canadian foreign policy. Undoubtedly hampered by a strong bias in favor of Washington's policies, Pearson did strive honestly to overcome that innate prejudice and actually succeeded in some policy decisions.

Canadian-Cuban Relations: The View from Ottawa

The same approach can be seen in the Pearson government's position on Cuba. If one examines the diplomatic records in Ottawa and Havana on bilateral matters, a fascinating image emerges—fascinating because the main thrust of the documents available in Ottawa is remarkably different from the emphasis of those obtained in Havana. Through piecing together the issues encountered in both diplomatic archives, a picture emerges of two nations that sought to develop a commercial relationship without really coming to terms with their own limitations or their partner's true interests. The result of this diplomatic struggle to determine what they imagined, often incorrectly, to be the other's *true* goals forms the basis of this chapter.

During this period it is fair to say that there were no major diplomatic breakthroughs on the bilateral front; nor were there any significant scandals that threatened to damage or set back bilateral relations. As will be seen below, Ottawa was more concerned with containing Cuban influence—refusing to allow Cuban initiatives to take root, ensuring that no official decision indicated sympathy for the Castro government, and inhibiting the growth of relations between the two countries. At the same time as Ottawa extended the diplomatic "cold shoulder," however, it was clear that significant differences of opinion on Cuban matters existed between it and Washington. In essence, the Canadian government wanted to maintain some sort of status quo, keeping Havana at arm's length although not seeking to overthrow the revolutionary government, while also disagreeing with many fundamental aspects of U.S. policy.

This "coldly correct" policy proved extremely difficult to decipher for Cuban diplomats in Canada, as an analysis of their correspondence reveals. They constantly felt themselves to be on the defensive, in no small part because of the rise of terrorist activities against Cuban diplomatic missions in Canada, and because of suspicions concerning the origins of a series of hidden microphones that they encountered in the embassy. On the broader diplomatic front, it is obvious that they were consistently received coolly by External Affairs officials, who studiously avoided giving encouraging signs, and were pressured on a number of questions ranging from Fidel Castro's presence at Expo 67, which Ottawa discouraged strongly, to alleged broadcasting of classes in guerrilla warfare to North American Indian groups, for which no evidence was provided. The result of this pressure was to create (not unreasonably) some sort of siege mentality on the part of Cuban diplomats in Canada. This led to a cloud of diplomatic coolness that shrouded the dynamic of bilateral relations throughout this period, as Havana sought to expand ties and Ottawa struggled to find a policy with which it felt comfortable. It was a blend of uncertainty and confusion, lightly sprinkled with prejudice, that would form the basis of this uneasy relationship for more than twenty years. Put quite simply, official Ottawa did not know how best to react to revolutionary Cuba; it felt the need to maintain diplomatic relations yet was concerned at both the Castro government's international role and its domestic reforms. For its part, Havana tried desperately to improve its economic standing with Canada but, hampered by its own lack of diplomatic sophistication on the one hand and Canadian coolness on the other, soon found itself ignored by starchy bureaucrats in Ottawa.

One episode from the Canadian diplomatic files will perhaps illustrate Ottawa's reluctance to seek closer ties with the revolutionary government. It concerned a small engineering enterprise initiated by John Wies, proprietor of a repair shop in Delhi, Ontario, who had approached the Canadian government with a plan to repair Cuban agricultural machinery. He had previously dealt with tobacco machinery in Cuba and saw the great potential for dealing with unserviceable farm equipment. His plan was based on the idea of setting up a machine shop in Saint John, New Brunswick, to which broken tractors and farm equipment would be shipped. There they would be repaired and then loaded back on Cuban freighters. Since Cuba had already contracted with Canadian companies to repair its aging Britannia aircraft and to vulcanize automotive tires, Wies's plan interested George Schuther, assistant director of the Trade Services Branch, who contacted colleagues in External Affairs for their opinions.

Once again, however, the decision was taken to discourage such an action. In part, this was allegedly because many of the farm implements in question would be of U.S. origin, although Schuther had announced in his previous letter that, because of the embargo, U.S. spare parts would specifically not be used, but there were political interests at stake too. Accordingly the response from O. G. Stoner was wholly negative: "It is evident that Mr. Wies' plans would involve intricate export licensing problems and that it would be difficult to control the scheme satisfactorily. Additionally, there are political considerations which would make such an operation generally undesirable from the point of view of External Affairs. Our advice would be that you should discourage Mr. Wies from proceeding with it."[13]

In the summer of 1963, Ambassador Cruz wrote to his minister to explain yet another area in which he believed that Canada was deliberately stalling on a Cuban initiative. It concerned attempts to revive the tourist industry, which was by now almost defunct in Cuba. Cuba officially requested permission to fly tourist flights from Canada but was turned down by Ottawa. Cruz protested to Alfred Pick, reminding the head of the Latin American Division about Canada's previous refusal to allow planes bought by Havana from the Soviet Union to refuel in Canada and pointing out the irony that those same planes had been allowed to land in Montreal on diplomatic and commercial matters when they had been operated by the Soviet Union. For Ambassador Cruz it was a matter of basic discrimination, brought about by Canadian vulnerability to the United States:

> Mr. Pick had to admit that this was so, and that it was all because there was a state of extreme sensitivity about the Cuban revolution, and that it was necessary to be very careful in dealings with Cuba. . . . He indicated to me that Canada could not afford to irritate the U.S. government by granting favors to Cuba, and noted that I had to understand that relations between Canada and the United States were very close—as well as very delicate, given both the huge U.S. investments in Canada and the constant media propaganda against Cuba originating from the United States.[14]

Obviously, the official position was cooler than at any time since the Cuban revolution, and in the face of uncertainty as to precisely what was expected of Ottawa, the Department of External Affairs merely threw a diplomatic wet blanket on any initiatives designed to improve bilateral relations. Policymakers in Ottawa thus fell back on the status quo, refraining from encouraging initiatives that would make changes, waiting for time to pass, and the matter in question to be forgotten.

Keeping Up the Pressure

In the previous section examples were provided of Canadian policies that, it was suggested, were clearly designed by Ottawa to maintain a diplomatic chill in its policy toward Havana. But there were also a series of incidents that took place, some of an official nature, which had a similarly negative effect on the bilateral relationship. On October 17, 1967, for example, Social Credit leader Robert Thompson informed the House of Commons—without any evidence—that Radio Havana was broadcasting a daily program in Cree on guerrilla warfare to indigenous groups in Canada. He would later claim (again without any evidence) that Cuban security guards at the Expo site had set up a guerrilla training camp in the Laurentian mountains. The following day, Secretary of State for External Affairs Paul Martin met with the Cuban chargé d'affaires, Roberto Márquez, who vehemently denied the charges. Martin noted that Canada had no hard evidence about the alleged programs but noted that External Affairs officials "were in contact with another country which did have them. Everybody understood this to mean—as the media pointed out—that he was referring to the United States."[15] The archives of the Cuban Ministry of External Relations have a substantial report on the incident, with a minute listing of all programs broadcast during the days in question, the times that they were on the air, and the languages in which the shows were broadcast.

Radio Havana showed that it did broadcast in two of the indigenous languages of South America (Guaraní and Quechua) but none at all of North America. Its lengthy report, in which Vice-President Carlos Rafael Rodríguez himself participated, so concerned were the Cubans at the allegations, claimed that it had never editorialized about Canada's internal problems (particularly significant given the nascent separatist movement in the province of Quebec), nor had it even given any unfavorable news coverage about Canada. In the detailed summary of French programming broadcast to Quebec, the Cubans showed exceptional sensitivity to the national unity question. They had always maintained a policy of ignoring separatist desires as a deliberate strategy, claiming that their ties were with Canada as a country, and on the occasion of General de Gaulle's stormy speech from the balcony of the Montreal Town Hall had broadcast just two cautiously worded reports. For the entire year there had been only two editorial comments on Canada—one in English praising Expo 67 and another in French supporting Canada for accepting U.S. draft dodgers from the Vietnam War.

On the diplomatic front, several other incidents occurred that aggravated the bilateral relationship. A strong diplomatic note was lodged, for instance, by External Affairs at a Cuban photo exhibit at their Expo site. One photograph in particular caused problems because it showed a photograph under which Cuban officials had written the caption "The Andes will prove to be the Sierra Maestra of Ecuador." Contacted by Ecuadorean officials (albeit several months after the offending caption had been in place), Ottawa sent a "strong and imperative" diplomatic note, "practically ordering it to be withdrawn," in the words of the Cuban chargé d'affaires.[16] More serious, however, was the insistent pressure placed on Havana to prevent Fidel Castro from attending the Expo celebrations. The Cubans wanted their leader to attend the festivities but had been told in no uncertain terms by Canadian officials that this was not desirable. In a revealing letter of June 1, 1967, Ambassador Cruz informed his minister of a meeting to which he had been summoned by Secretary of State for External Affairs Paul Martin "to try and find a solution to the problems caused by the insistence of the Canadian government that Dr. Castro not come to the Expo celebrations. . . . They did not want Prime Minister Castro to come, alleging motives of security."[17]

Ambassador Cruz had noticed a distinctive cooling in Paul Martin's treatment of the matter since the previous month—a fact he not unreasonably attributed to pressure from Washington. At the same time, however, there had been continuous pressure, usually through intimidation and bomb threats, against Cuban diplomats in Canada during this time, particularly in 1967, the year of Expo. Undoubtedly this had to be a factor in the Canadian government's decision, which was probably not fully appreciated by the Cuban diplomats.

There had been several acts of political intimidation in the mid-1960s, both against the Cuban embassy in Ottawa and its consulate in Montreal. In September 1966, a rocket exploded outside the embassy, shattering all the windows of the house and sending exploding shrapnel into the building. A second rocket was defused. In November, the ambassador protested a general lack of security to External Affairs after several people had been surprised in the gardens of the embassy. Threats, both written and by telephone, were received by Cuban diplomats, a Cuban freighter was bombed in Montreal, in March 1967 a bomb exploded at a Montreal auction house that was selling Cuban goods, and the following month at the Cuban Expo site a bazooka shell (with the words written on it "Washington No, Moscow No, Cuba Yes") was found. Understandably, the number of incidents and their nature were of grave concern to Cuban authorities.

In August further incidents occurred. One diplomat found his car opened and obviously searched. The same month police asked all Cuban diplomats to leave their quarters on one occasion at 4 A.M., after a suspicious-looking individual had been observed placing a bomb in the embassy garden. The Cuban Ambassador, concerned that his house would soon be singled out for similar treatment, took the highly unusual step of "advising the Department of External Affairs that he would shoot at anyone he found in the garden."[18] In September reports also surfaced of another bomb, allegedly placed in a suitcase, found in a neighboring building. Meanwhile, the Cuban workers preparing the Expo site in Montreal received many death and bomb threats. Most of these were false alarms, but of course the Cubans and police alike could take no chances. Writing to his minister on September 11, the Cuban ambassador commented about the "suitcase bomb," noting: "All of this is highly suspicious. We think that there probably was no bomb and that the whole thing has been invented, either to terrorize us or to create an unfavorable climate for Cuba in this country."[19]

If the exile groups caused Cuban diplomats considerable anxiety and frustration during this period, it can also be said that Canadian law enforcement officers and counter-espionage specialists aggravated the situation. A brief note from Ambassador Cruz to his minister in February 1964 noted that three hidden microphones had been found in the walls and in the casing for the doorbell. Accordingly, he was requesting that the Cuban government send "an electronics expert to revise our residence, since we are living without being able to talk aloud. We also need eight telephones since we are certain that they have been bugged."[20] Cuban officials were convinced that these devices had been planted with the collusion of Canadian security officials. A year later, more hidden microphones were discovered, leading to an angry confrontation between the Cuban ambassador and First Secretary Roberto Márquez on one side and Secretary of State for External Affairs Paul Martin and Alfred Pick of the Latin American Division on the other.

The Cuban diplomats handed over the microphone and three transmitters to the Canadian officials and presented them with a most energetic letter of diplomatic protest. Martin noted that the Canadian government was totally unaware of these deeds, but the Cuban ambassador officially requested him to convey their profound anger to the prime minister and then launched into a fierce criticism of the Canadian position: "I insisted time and time again that this should never be repeated. It was indeed quite unacceptable that the Canadian government should talk to us continuously about the need for freedom, while it placed microphones in the embassies of countries which have shown their friendship to Canada." Interestingly enough, despite his outburst, the ambassador noted in his dispatch to Havana that he expected such activities to continue, "since I believe that it's not the work of the Canadian police, but rather was done by the CIA, which apparently has a lot of influence here over the RCMP."[21] The result of this mixture—bomb threats, hijackings, charges of espionage and counterespionage, rumors about guerrilla training camps—was the continuation of the black legend about Cuba. At a time when Washington continued its pressure on Havana, when Cuba had lost its ally in Diefenbaker, and when Ottawa viewed as controversial both the social reforms and foreign policy of revolutionary Cuba, this combination can only have contributed to the climate of uncertainty and distrust that would plague the bilateral relationship for many years to come.

Problems in Understanding

From a survey of the pertinent diplomatic documentation corresponding to this period, it is quite clear that the official position in Ottawa was one of concern about the direction in which—seemingly under growing Soviet tutelage—revolutionary Cuba was heading. In part the reason for this critical treatment came from the negative assessment by Canadian diplomats of events in Cuba, and in this regard they followed the example of their predecessors. Canadian ambassador Léon Mayrand was close to retirement and displeased with the direction of the revolutionary government. He personally became involved in the cases of many Cubans who wished to leave the country and complained most vociferously, as the archives of the Cuban Ministry of External Relations reveal, when people whose cases he had supported were not allowed to leave.

In August 1967, on the occasion of a visit to Ottawa by Mayrand, he and Américo Cruz met and talked about shared interests. Their conversation on the state of things in Cuba, as reported to Havana by Cruz, was quite revealing:

> To my question as to how things were going he replied that "pretty bad, and the worst thing of all was that there were many people who went to bed hungry at night—especially poor people." He also said that "meat was to be more heavily rationed because the rest of it was being exported to Europe," and the "amount of goods rationed had

not improved and that as a result people were getting increasingly upset." . . . From this account you can judge what his feelings are toward the revolution, something which quite logically will be reflected in the reports which he submits to the Secretary of State for External Affairs.[22]

This phenomenon, of course, was not a novel one, as early chapters have attested. It was expected to some degree, because of the particular nature of the Cuban revolutionary process and the lack of pertinent diplomatic experience with such a government, but the prejudices of some career diplomats (even those with many years' experience) made bilateral understanding a more difficult matter than it might otherwise have been. A year after Lester Pearson had been elected, for example, his secretary of state for external affairs in an interview with Américo Cruz informed the ambassador that "for now there would be no change in Canadian policy toward Cuba, but that they would be obliged to change that policy if Cuba gave them a pretext to do so—or if international pressure were to become too great."[23]

For his part Prime Minister Pearson, now faced with a host of problems ranging from a rising separatist threat in Quebec to a profound wave of economic nationalism as the Canadian economy suffered a series of crises, had precious little time for formulating foreign policy. This of course continued to fascinate him but was now set largely by Paul Martin, who perhaps could be criticized for not having the broader worldview of his prime minister. In any event, Pearson continued to hold ambiguous feelings about revolutionary Cuba, largely because of the points outlined earlier in this chapter. A fair summary of his position can be gleaned by the diplomatic dispatch sent by Ambassador Cruz to Havana on October 7, 1966, on the occasion of a meeting with the prime minister. The United States, commented Pearson, "had pursued a mistaken policy towards Cuba, and were full of passion concerning the Cuban problem."[24] He also emphasized what Cruz had already notified Havana about on several occasions—namely, that Canada would maintain normal diplomatic relations with Havana, but that Cuba should at all times understand the nature of the "special relationship" between Canada and the United States.

The dynamic of misunderstanding developed throughout the Pearson years, largely because of this climate of suspicion toward Havana's intentions, but also because Canadian policymakers and diplomats alike were simply unprepared for the mercurial political persona of Fidel Castro, much less the radical sociopolitical reforms on which he embarked. In those circumstances Ottawa reacted with a mixture of paternalism, ignorance, indecision, and distaste. No initiatives were taken to assist Havana during the Pearson years, although the minimum diplomatic civilities were observed. For their part, Cuban diplomats read into the ensuing tension and climate of distrust yet another example of Canada's role as a lackey of U.S. imperialism. Typical of Havana's reaction was a letter to Cruz from the director of the division for the Americas and Western Europe of the Ministry of External Relations, in which he claimed that Canada's policy toward Cuba was due "fundamentally to the influence exercised by the United States over Canada, which subordinates the commercial policy of the Canadians to Washington's designs."[25] Of course the economic dependence of Canada on the United States was a decisive factor in setting Ottawa's foreign policy, but it was nowhere near the simplistic scenario that Cuban diplomats often depicted. For this reason they, like their Canadian counterparts, failed to perceive the many nuances in internal political dynamics and as a result presented faulty analysis to their ministries.

The Validity of the Coldly Correct Policy?

International diplomacy exists for two basic reasons: to preserve a climate of dialogue, comprehension, civility, and (it is hoped) respect among nations and to protect one's own interests. An analysis of the diplomatic records of Canada and Cuba during this time reveals clearly that, in pursuing these goals, there was a noticeably different emphasis placed on their realization in Havana and Ottawa. Each country possessed a different agenda: one seeking desperately to survive economically and to diversify its trade and the other diffident and standoffish, having decided apparently that there was little to gain from developing closer ties. Combined with this uneven interest in making the relationship work was a mild distaste in Ottawa for the practices, ideology, and style of Cuban diplomacy, which acted as a filter through which the Ottawa mandarins viewed Havana's erratic revolutionary path. The increasing frustration of Washington at the revolutionary government's policies understandably added an extra dimension of influence—albeit mild—to the official Ottawa view.

For Cuba, trade with Canada was extremely important, yet in that area too there was a clear imbalance, again in Canada's favor. Canadian exports to Cuba increased dramatically during the Pearson years, proof positive of the "business is business" philosophy in international commercial matters. In 1963, for instance, Canada exported goods valued at $16.4 million, but in 1964—due largely to a dramatic rise in the price of sugar on the world market—this increased to $60.9 million. The remaining years of the Pearson government saw Canadian exports continue at a reasonably stable rate: $52.5 million in 1965, $61.4 million in 1966, $42.3 million in

1967, and $44.9 million in 1968. Canadian imports remained consistently low, usually approximately one-ninth of their exports to Cuba: $13.0 million in 1963, $3.4 million in 1964, $5.3 million in 1965, $5.6 million in 1966, $6.3 million in 1967, $5.1 million in 1968. An analysis of this trade relationship reveals the imbalance in bilateral commerce. Cuba suffered consistently from a shortage of hard currency, and this factor, together with a lack of confidence in the Cuban economy, meant that very little credit was extended to Havana. Tariff preferences given to other Commonwealth nations meant that Canada bought very little sugar (approximately 8 percent of total sugar purchases by the late 1960s), while large Soviet purchases of Canadian flour (750,000 tons) and wheat (225,000 tons) for Cuba in September 1963 further skewed the balance of payments.

A meeting on July 25, 1967, between Canadian Minister of Trade and Commerce Winters and the Cuban ministers of foreign trade and education, the vice-minister of foreign trade, and Ambassador Cruz examined the clear disparities in bilateral trade. In essence they argued that Canada should provide an act of good faith in seeking to level off the disparities to some degree. The Cuban minister of foreign trade stressed the dramatic rise in Cuban imports from Canada (not matched, he noted, by Canadian imports) and officially requested that Cuba receive the same access to the Canadian market as West Indian sugar. He was told, however, that many countries in the West Indies depended more on sugar for their economic survival than did Cuba. The Cubans then asked that Cuban rum, which had been sold in Canada before the revolution, be again stocked in Canada but was told by Winters that liquor sales were a provincial matter. The Cubans countered by raising the fact that many exports, especially synthetic fiber, were now cut out of the Canadian market by the use of U.S. prices to establish fair market value, and Winters stated that possible upcoming international trade negotiations might remedy this. Finally the Cuban minister of foreign trade noted that some Canadian banks were not willing to extend credit to Cuba, to which Winters replied that each bank was free to set its own credit policy. In each response, the Canadian minister was correct and precise—but it is also clear that he was not prepared to make a single concession to the Cuban delegation. The central thrust of his argument was that business was business, and if the status quo favored the strong trading partner in all of these matters, that was just an economic fact of life. What was not discussed, but which constituted a backdrop for this meeting, was a series of factors that militated against the meaningful development of bilateral trade: Canadian exporters were advised by External Affairs to sell only against irrevocable confirmed letters of credit, no credit was granted by the Canadian government to Cuba, controls were rigidly applied to ensure that no strategic goods or goods of U.S. origin were exported to Cuba, and strict controls on all flights to Cuba from Soviet bloc countries were applied.

This dramatic trade differential is an eloquent illustration of the imbalance in the political-diplomatic relationship. Cuba badly needed to keep channels open with as many Western countries as possible. Its exclusion from the Organization of American States in 1962 and its isolation from all countries in the Americas (apart from Canada and Mexico) had dealt the Cuban revolution a hard blow. Cognizant of José Martí's advice on the need to trade with as many countries as possible, and wary too of Soviet designs, the Cuban government was particularly careful about protecting its ties with Canada.

As this chapter has sought to show, this determination was not reciprocated by Canada, whose diplomats and officials seemed unable to decide precisely what kind of relationship they wanted with revolutionary Cuba. They were certain, however, that they felt uneasy with the status quo, and while they would not support the demise of the Castro government, they would do nothing dramatic to support or favor it. There were many elements at play here: concern with both the discourse and the actions of the revolution, recognition of the Havana government as a popular one, the determination to uphold Canadian diplomatic tradition, a profound disagreement with the approach toward Cuba taken by the U.S. government, and the possibility of an increase in Canadian exports.

The Canadian position toward Cuba can be gleaned from a few official documents of the time. Take, for instance, the view in the "Talking Points" outlined for the NATO ministerial meeting in December 1963:

> The Canadian Government, of course, holds no sympathy for the present dictatorial régime in Cuba, which has betrayed the Cuban revolution's original objectives of liberal social and political reforms and has reduced Cuba to the status of an economically backward police-state dependent upon the Soviet Bloc. . . . we remain deeply disturbed by the presence in the Western Hemisphere of a communist régime aligned with the Soviet Union and by the transformation of Cuba into an area which still retains a potential for disturbing East-West relations and the stability of the Hemisphere.[26]

Such a dour, one-dimensional interpretation, even given the fact that it was prepared for NATO, could hardly be said to inspire confidence in developing the bilateral relationship.

The most thorough summary of the nature of Canadian policy toward Cuba can be gleaned from the document prepared by External Affairs for

Prime Minister Pearson on the occasion of his 1964 meeting with President Johnson. Dated January 13, 1964, the lengthy discussion paper emphasized that, despite some economic problems,[27] a rise in dissension, and a deterioration in the standard of living, the revolutionary government remained firmly in control. Given that reality, the official position was that any attempt to isolate Cuba, diplomatically or economically, would probably be unsuccessful. Accordingly, Canada had determined to maintain diplomatic relations, since that enabled embassy personnel to protect the interests of Canadian citizens, stay informed about events in Cuba ("of particular importance because of the Cuban alignment with international communism"),[28] and develop trade in nonstrategic goods.

On a tactical level, the Canadian position had garnered for Ottawa the image of political independence since it did maintain diplomatic and commercial relations with Havana. The last section of the position paper, however, showed that Canada took into account U.S. concerns about Cuba, listing a litany of concessions made by Ottawa to comply with U.S. requests. Of these concessions, the first summed up the Canadian government's general thrust because it committed itself to fulfilling "the indication given to President Kennedy at the Hyannis Port meeting last year that *the Canadian government would do or say nothing to show support for the Castro government.*"[29] In economic matters the government promised to respect the status quo, thus maintaining a ban on the transshipment of U.S.-manufactured goods. In questions of transportation several policies were upheld by the Canadian government, the general aim of which was to inhibit international communication: "the refusal of permission for flights from Canada of passenger-carrying aircraft . . . the continuing search of Czech and Cuban aircraft passing through Gander or Halifax on route from Eastern Europe to Havana" and "the general ban on flights over Canada of Cuba-bound aircraft of the Soviet Union."[30]

Finally under the broad rubric of political monitoring and information-gathering, the paper prepared for the prime minister showed clearly that Ottawa was prepared to be a team player. A visa control system had recently been put in place to monitor the movement to Canada of all Cuban official personnel, while further measures, as yet unspecified, were being prepared in order "to control carefully the carriage of Cuban officials and other very restricted categories of passengers on the charter flights between Havana and Montreal, in either direction."[31] Finally, External Affairs officials, aware of the lack of U.S. personnel in Havana, reminded the two leaders of the strategic importance for Washington of having Canadian diplomats there since it resulted in "the collection by our Embassy in Havana of information of interest to the United States."[32]

This section began with a pointed question: "The Validity of the Coldly Correct Policy?" It was not meant to be a rhetorical query, for it can be argued that a policy of this nature was precisely what was needed at such a time. After all, the memory of the October 1962 Missile Crisis was still very fresh in the mind of the world community, the Cuban government continued along an increasingly radical sociopolitical program, and its international policy, particularly in Latin America, was seen by Ottawa as being essentially reckless and destabilizing. The influence of Washington of course had to be taken into account, given the cultural similarities, the dependence of the Canadian economy on trade with the United States, and the personal affinity between diplomats and policymakers in both countries.

A final element to be considered was the nature of domestic political and economic matters in Canada. The rise of economic nationalism, the growing economic problems faced by Prime Minister Pearson, the question of the future of Quebec (which would finally explode during the tenure of his successor, Pierre Elliot Trudeau), and the comparative unimportance of Cuba for the Canadian government all contributed to the general downgrading of the "Cuban question" as a matter about which to become concerned. The prime minister himself, as was noted earlier, disagreed with many aspects of the U.S. policy toward Cuba (and indeed more so toward Indo-China) and firmly believed in the traditional tenet of Canadian foreign policy that all governments that evidently enjoyed popular support should be recognized. Yet there was a major difference between respecting that theoretical diplomatic position and actually doing anything to support, much less strengthen, bilateral ties, and that was precisely the core thrust of the Pearson years.

For a variety of reasons, as outlined above, the Pearson government decided that this was not an issue that it should actively support. Instead it would adopt a position of waiting to see if the Castro government would remain in power or fall, refusing to do anything at all to hasten either possibility. This was not, however, as impartial a position as at first appeared. One should remember the commitment made by Pearson to John F. Kennedy to do or say nothing that might be taken as support for the revolutionary government, as well as the exchange of intelligence, and possibly illegal activities by Canadian security forces in information-gathering. It is also important to bear in mind that the Canadian government during these years sought to dissuade any initiative to foster or improve bilateral relations. It was one thing to export Canadian wheat, but quite another to look at any other attempts to redress the obvious trade imbalance.

In short, Canadian diplomats could claim success, for the "coldly correct" policies worked. Trade increased, intelligence was provided to U.S. officials, and Canada was seen by the world community to be independent of its superpower neighbor. Yet this is a superficial reading, for this essentially negative policy of "wait and see" did nothing to further Canadian long-term interests and damaged the image of Lester Pearson as a world statesman. A case can be made to show that Ottawa's treatment of Cuba during these years was a triumph of inertia. The Trudeau years would change all that, as Pearson's bland, unimaginative policy gave way to a burst of creativity in the handling of the Cuban question—a policy that was daring, controversial, productive, never dull, and quite successful.

4

The Trudeau Years
A Fresh Approach

Canada and Cuba have apparently overcome the difficulties of the 1960s. . . . Canadians and Cubans have also become less distrustful of one another, and this has somewhat reduced suspicion, though it would be unduly optimistic to expect peoples of such divergent views and backgrounds to be completely at ease with one another.

Jack Ogelsby, "A Trudean Decade"

Writing in 1979, Jack Ogelsby identified accurately the fundamental dynamic at play in the bilateral relationship during the Trudeau years (in essence 1968–84, with a short—nine-month—Conservative government under Joe Clark in 1979–80). On one level the earlier difficulties had been overcome, since trade expanded rapidly during the 1970s, Canadian development aid was granted for the first time to the revolutionary government, Canadian tourism began in earnest, and a list of high-ranking government officials from both countries visited the other's capital. The extremely successful Trudeau visit to Cuba in 1976 was, of course, the highlight of this dynamic, typical in many ways of the first eight years of his innovative foreign policy. On another level, however, there were also significant difficulties in the relationship. Trade, for instance, dropped sharply in the 1980s after rising precipitously from 1969 to 1981. There was an embarrassing spy scandal at the Cuban consulate in Montreal, after which several Cubans were asked to leave Canada, while the RCMP were implicated in counterespionage activities, which led to the death of a Cuban security guard in Montreal. In 1978, just a few years after the introduction of the government aid program to Cuba administered by the Canadian International Development Agency (CIDA), opposition pressure led to its termination. There was also a profound disagreement between Ottawa and Havana on the Cuban role in Africa. On a personal level this latter issue proved to be a major sticking point in the strong personal friendship between

Castro and Trudeau, who otherwise agreed on many aspects of international relations and development issues. Moreover, it can be argued that, from Ottawa's perspective, it was the issue of Cuba's role in Angola that led to the gradual unraveling of what had been until then a surprisingly cordial relationship. As can be seen, the bilateral dynamic was in many ways of a volatile nature, yet throughout these years it was one from which both countries benefited on domestic and international levels. More important, perhaps, was the fact that both governments recognized the value of this relationship, warts and all, and sought to maintain its viability. In this, they were notably successful.

This chapter seeks to trace the highs and lows that characterized this unique period in the bilateral relationship. Without any doubt the Trudeau years—particularly the first decade—were the most significant period in the development and historical evolution of Canadian-Cuban relations. Even the Diefenbaker government's refusal to toe the U.S. line despite significant pressure from Washington pales in comparison with the importance of the Trudeau years and his innovative policy toward Cuba, particularly during his first eight years in power. All that has happened since to the bilateral relationship has been marked in some way or another by the extraordinary nature of the Canadian government approach of 1968–78 to the Cuban case. In sum, one cannot understand the highly unusual, and occasionally contradictory, nature of this relationship without taking into account the impact of the Trudeau initiative toward Cuba.

This chapter is composed of two distinctive parts. The first assesses the unique factor of Trudeau's extraordinary influence on Canada in the early years of his government. It also outlines his political philosophy and domestic social programs (particularly important because he consistently emphasized that Canadian foreign policy was designed to support these same domestic initiatives). The 1970 crisis involving the Front de Libération du Québec (FLQ) terrorist group will also be examined briefly since, at Ottawa's request, the individuals involved were granted asylum in Cuba. The section concludes with an analysis of the various changes brought to Canadian foreign policy by Trudeau—especially during the early years of his term in office.

The second half of this chapter concentrates on the diplomatic "nuts and bolts" of relations between Canada and Cuba during this period. It begins with a detailed analysis of the development of bilateral trade matters. The essence of the relationship between Canada and Cuba since colonial days had been commerce, and this continued to be the case throughout the Trudeau years. This section analyzes the rise and fall of bilateral trade, the nature of export credits and insurance extended for the first time to revolutionary Cuba, and the commercial trends that can be traced. Two additional sections follow, dealing respectively with the positive and negative developments during this period.

This is the longest chapter of the book—a feature that is no accident in light of the major improvement in bilateral relations. It is thus no surprise that Pierre Elliott Trudeau is still so highly regarded in Cuba and has visited the island on several occasions since leaving political life. His contribution to the evolving bilateral relationship was, without doubt, the most enduring made by a Canadian prime minister.

Trudeau and the Reshaping of Canadian Foreign Policy

The basic facts of Pierre Trudeau's prime ministerial career are straightforward. He first became prime minister in 1968. In 1972 he lost his government majority (109 seats in Parliament, as opposed to 107 for the Conservatives, with the New Democratic Party, the social democrats, holding the balance of power with 31 members). A majority government in 1974, a defeat at the hands of Joe Clark's Conservatives in 1979, and political revenge on February 18, 1980 (when he again won a majority government) are mere historical details of a long political career that succeeded in placing his own political priorities as the basis for the national agenda. They disguise the many achievements of his government, the manifest problems it encountered, and tremendous personal turmoil as his storybook marriage to Margaret Sinclair rapidly went sour. Yet they give little indication of the philosophical underpinnings of Pierre Trudeau, which, with some notable variations, remained basically the same in 1984 when he retired as in 1968 when he first stepped into the political spotlight as prime minister.

The warm relationship between Prime Minister Lester Pearson and the staff in the Department of External Affairs, and the extremely high mutual regard that existed, suffered a rude awakening with the arrival of Pierre Elliott Trudeau. He was an outsider, skeptical both about the privileged treatment given to officials at "External" and about the usefulness of traditional diplomatic practices. As he explained in a January 1, 1969, television interview on CBC, it was time for a more updated approach: "I think that the whole concept of diplomacy today . . . is a little bit outmoded. I believe much of it goes back to the early days of the telegraph when you needed a dispatch to know what was happening in country A. Whereas now most of the time you can read it in a good newspaper. In that sense I believe there is a need for a basic re-examination of the function of the diplomat."[1] Between 1968 and 1970, a thorough review of both Canadian foreign policy and of the department itself took place, which understandably caused great consternation among diplomats. When the dust finally settled, and the government's white paper titled *Foreign Policy for Canadians* had emerged in 1970, significant changes were proposed for both. The Department of External Affairs, for instance, saw its budget cut by $7.5 million, with compulsory separation for sixty foreign-service officers and 110 support staff and the closure of seven missions abroad. In all, this amounted to 7 percent of the department's staff, but the impact of the review process left far greater psychological scars that took many years to heal.

Just a month after coming to power, Trudeau released a statement (on May 29, 1968) announcing the launching of a major foreign policy review, comprising defense, economic, and aid policies. Among other areas to be studied closely were Canada's role in NATO, which Trudeau wanted to decrease, and relations with Latin America and the Pacific Rim, which he favored increasing. In the same statement it was announced that Canada would finally recognize the People's Republic of China, would reduce Canada's troop commitment to NATO by 50 percent, would increase its foreign aid, and would develop significantly its relations with francophone Africa. The review proper was a significant and profound study of Canadian foreign relations, with the underlying goal of revamping them to better reflect a changing world environment and, more important, better serve current Canadian objectives and priorities.

Once again Trudeau's determination that pragmatic policies be devised and carefully applied is obvious. Six booklets resulted from this review, the underlying thesis of which was that both foreign and domestic policies were to be subordinated to the same goal, namely, to develop objectives of *national* importance. Gone were the days of Lester Pearson when External Affairs devised ways for Canada to be a "helpful fixer" around the globe; no longer would Canada, under a Trudeau government, consider an activist middle power role in international circles. In its place now was a determination to apply principles of realpolitik and to subordinate foreign policy to domestic goals and national interests.

One example of this revamped policy was the development of relations with the Soviet Union. In a press conference held in Moscow on May 20, 1971, Trudeau explained the rationale for this policy. It was not merely a case of seeking out improved trade with Moscow but was also part of the overall strategy to improve trade around the globe, thereby lessening its dependency on one principal market—the United States: "Canada has increasingly found it important to diversify its channels of communication because of the overpowering presence of the United States of America and that is reflected in a growing consciousness amongst Canadians of the danger to our national identity from a cultural, economic and perhaps even military point of view."[2] Back in Washington such concerns were, understandably, poorly received.

Canadian-Latin American Relations under Trudeau

In line with the Trudeau approach to develop alternative trading relations, his initiative toward Cuba was really not that extraordinary, notwithstanding Washington's fears to the contrary. It should be viewed as merely another comparatively small facet of a multifaceted strategy of trade diversification. Trudeau wanted to seize on fresh trading opportunities as part of his much heralded Third Option, and Latin American nations regardless of their political leanings were seen as prime targets for this commercial expansion. This approach afforded him a certain degree of independence from Canadian policies vis-à-vis Great Britain and the United States, traditionally the two major trading partners of Canada. It is precisely in this context that ties with Havana developed, in essence as just one further string in a bow of diplomatic options. Under Trudeau, Latin America thus became a target area for the expansion of Canadian trade and investment.

There were other significant developments in Canadian-Latin American relations at this time, which should be seen as the backdrop for the Trudeau initiative on Cuba. After several reviews of the question of whether or not to belong to the Organization of American States (OAS), Ottawa decided to apply for and received Permanent Observer status. The same year, following eight years of arm's length dealings, Canada also became a member of the Inter-American Development Bank. The prime minister took a strong personal interest in the ensuing revamped foreign policy, traveling to the area in 1976 (including the Cuba leg of a journey to Mexico and Venezuela) and 1979. Moreover, twenty-five official government missions also visited Latin America between 1973 and 1977, the highest percentage by government officials apart from official delegations to Western Europe between 1968 and 1980.

The basis for this flurry of activity was quite simply that Canada wanted to expand commercial activity with the region. In doing so, Ottawa was not particularly bothered who its business partners were in the region, and those policymakers in Washington concerned about Pierre Trudeau's good personal relationship with Fidel Castro should have taken some comfort from the Canadian government's determination to increase exports to Argentina, Brazil, and Chile—then in the grip of right-wing military dictatorships that had assassinated thousands of their dissenting citizens. Pragmatism was again the dominant note of this approach, one that paid off handsomely for Canadian investors: within a decade of the review of Canadian policy toward the region, exports to Latin America had quadrupled to more than $3 billion, and the book value of direct investment in the region had doubled to more than $2.5 billion, while fully 80 percent of private, direct Canadian investment in the developing world was in the region.[3] It was true by the 1980s that Canadian trade with Latin America represented only 5 percent of Canada's total trade (given the enormous bilateral relationship with the United States), but it was also true that Latin America was Canada's leading trade partner in the developing world, with some 42.8 percent of total 1980 trade.[4]

Trade relations with Latin America thus increased dramatically, in no small measure because it was the sine qua non of the new Canadian policy. Imports from Central America, in thousands of Canadian dollars, the same measurement for all subsequent figures in this section, increased steadily over the decade despite civil war and domestic turmoil in the region: $213,786 (1970), $401,098 (1975), $603,057 (1978), $689,038 (1979), and $1,028,068 (1980). Increases in imports from South America were even more impressive: $476,891 (1970), $1,393,363 (1975), $1,930,195 (1978), $2,226,031 (1979), and $2,978,547 (1980). Canadian exports to these two regions also increased significantly during the same time. In the case of Central America, again in thousands of Canadian dollars, they increased almost fourfold, from $378,742 in 1970 to $1,528,360 in 1980. Exports to South America posted even bigger gains, from $365,496 in 1970, which was almost double the $191,939 of goods exported just five years earlier, to $2,249,847 in 1980.[5]

A study of bilateral trade figures shows that throughout the Trudeau years there were four target countries for enhanced Canadian trade in the region: Brazil, Venezuela, Mexico, and Cuba. Canadian exports to these countries rose steadily during the Trudeau years, regardless of the official government ideology. Exports to Brazil increased, in thousands of Canadian dollars, from $17,508 (1965) to $87,386 (1970), $194,466 (1975), $415,784 (1978), $418,560 (1979), and $893,225 (1980). In second place, exports to Venezuela showed a similar increase over the first Trudeau decade: $111,390 in 1970 to $652,924 in 1980. The same was true of exports to Mexico: from $91,697 in 1970 to $482,903 in 1980.

Canadian imports from these target countries show a remarkably consistent pattern of development. The case of Brazil, for instance, saw an increase of Canadian imports from $87,386 in 1970 to $893,225 in 1980. Venezuela (at that time a key supplier of fuel to eastern Canada) saw the value of its exports to Canada increase from $111,390 (1970) to $652,924 (1980). Mexico posted a similar rate of growth: from $91,697 in 1970 to $482,903 in 1980. When seen in this light, Canadian exports to Cuba (from $58,899 in 1970 to $415,298 in 1980)[6] were merely the continuation of the same Trudeau policy to *all* countries of the region interested in increasing their trade.

Venezuela or Mexico, or even Brazil (run by a right-wing military regime with an appalling human rights record throughout Trudeau's governments), did not, of course, have the negative cachet of Castro's Cuba. As a result, the very fact of increasing trade with Havana was a bold step undertaken by the prime minister. The Cubans certainly knew that, and with their economy becoming increasingly linked to that of the Soviet Union and its satellites, they were extremely pleased to see trade relations begin to flourish. The visit of Trudeau to Cuba, his fluency in Spanish, the extremely positive personal rapport between him and Fidel Castro, the beginning of Canadian development aid soon afterward, and the increase in bilateral commerce were all positive developments for Havana, particularly when the Cuban government was being drawn into a costly war in Southern Africa.

While they were under no illusions about the reasons behind this enhanced bilateral trade, the Cubans appreciated Trudeau's lack of ideological blinkers and were determined to develop the relationship as much as they could. From the Canadian perspective, meanwhile, the risks of bothering Washington were easily outweighed by the advantages of improving Canadian external trade, developing the Third Option, showing political independence to the domestic electorate, and following the prime minister's own freewheeling approach. The main rationale for the policy, however, was in many ways the same that sparked a fivefold increase in trade with Pinochet's Chile, or a fourfold increase with Stroessner's Paraguay during the same years, and in the final analysis it came down to increasing bilateral trade with the whole region.

Breaking the Logjam in Canadian-Cuban Relations

Undoubtedly there was a logjam concerning Cuba in the Department of External Affairs. For a variety of reasons, including ongoing pressure from Washington, an official rejection of communism resulting from the constant dynamic of the Cold War, the unusual nature of the relationship during Diefenbaker's tenure, and concern at Cuba's international role, considered by Canadian bureaucrats schooled in more traditional approaches as the antithesis of sound diplomatic practices, Ottawa continued to maintain its coldly correct dealings with the revolutionary government in Havana. Although there were major difficulties and differences of opinion, the logjam did, however, slowly begin to disintegrate. This can be seen, among other things, in the number of official ministerial visits between both countries in the mid-1970s, the significant growth of bilateral trade, and the personal rapport between Trudeau and Castro. The remainder of this chapter seeks to document how this process slowly, and with several major stumbling blocks, evolved.

We begin this section with an acknowledgment of the contribution made to improving bilateral relations by the Cuban ambassador at the time, José Fernández de Cossío, who remained as ambassador until 1976. As the diplomatic dispatches from the archives of both Canada and Cuba show, he lobbied constantly for increased trade between both countries, showing the inconsistencies in Canadian policy, emphasizing the value to Canadian business from such enhanced trade, and underlining the political value that would accrue to Ottawa from such initiatives. Typical of the Cuban ambassador's position was his request for Canadian export credits in a meeting with the prime minister and P. A. Bridle of the Latin American Division of the Department of External Affairs held on December 23, 1968, shortly after he had arrived in Canada. The memo prepared by Bridle on the meeting reveals the leading role taken by Fernández de Cossío in the interview:

> The Ambassador referred in positive terms to Canada's increased interest in Latin America and, in this context, made the case for Canadian credit arrangements to foster Cuban purchases of Canadian goods. . . . To attain a sufficient rate of growth, Cuba must import large quantities of equipment and specialized products such as fertilizer. Many western countries such as France, Britain and Switzerland extended credits to Cuba, and Cuba would like to buy a great deal more in Canada—fertilizer, for example, which Canada makes very well. Would it not, the Ambassador asked, be appropriate if Canada's move toward closer relations with Latin American countries were to include credit financing of Canadian exports to Cuba, especially of products needed for development purposes?[7]

Significantly, at the end of the meeting Trudeau asked Bridle to have a brief prepared for him on whether the Canadian government "might not extend export credits to Cuba in the same way that it does to other countries." He was clearly open to new concepts and to investigating whether a mutually beneficial commercial approach could be pursued—a strategy that was a major change from his predecessor.

The background to this meeting at which Cossío presented his credentials as Cuba's new ambassador is worth noting. He and Trudeau had first met at Expo 67 in Montreal, during the Cuban's tenure as director of the Cuban pavilion. The following year, when Cossío arrived to present his official credentials, Trudeau greeted the Cuban ambassador in Spanish and talked fondly about their earlier meeting. The entire discussion took place in Spanish, much to the chagrin of the head of the Latin American Division of External Affairs, who did not speak the language. At the end of the meeting, when he asked what to report about the meeting, Cossío offered to send over to External Affairs the notes that he would be preparing to send to his ministry in Havana. The highly unconventional nature of the Canadian-Cuban dynamic during these six years was colored by the receptivity of Trudeau and his confidant in international politics, Ivan Head, as well as Cossío, to new initiatives, as they sought to inject new vitality into the relationship. In an assessment of Ambassador Cossío's contribution to the dramatic resuscitation of the bilateral relationship, the Department of External Affairs' assessment of early 1974 is instructive:

> In recent years our relationship with Cuba has changed from one of mere cordiality to a much more positive and substantial one which we believe is mutually beneficial. . . . In no small measure Mr. de Cossío deserves a good deal of credit for the way in which Canada-Cuba relations have blossomed lately. He is perhaps the most astute and hardest working head of post in Ottawa.[8]

In an interview with Fernández de Cossío in May 1993, the Cuban diplomat (then Cuban ambassador to Mexico and now director of the Horizontes hotel chain in Havana) talked about those heady days of the bilateral relationship. Cuba was partially to blame for the lack of progress in developing the relationship at that time, he admitted, since prior to his arrival the post of Cuban ambassador had remained vacant for eight months. From his arrival he lobbied the Canadian government steadfastly, showing how the relations between Ottawa and Havana had become frozen, producing little benefit for either of the two countries, and instead urging the pursuit of mutual benefits. This was to prove a drawn-out and tedious process, particularly in the early years of the ambassador's tenure. Ultimately, however, this new approach did provide significant benefits for both countries. In essence Trudeau was open to considering this strategy of Cossío, while the Cubans were keen to increase their trade with the capitalist world. For virtually a decade, then, a wholly new approach to Canadian-Cuban relations ensued, the climax of which came in early 1976 with Trudeau's visit to Havana. Fittingly, when the Trudeau entourage arrived at José Martí international airport, one of the first people to greet the prime minister was Fernández de Cossío, who had been promoted to the position of deputy-minister of external relations.

In 1969 Fernández de Cossío again extended a challenge to Ottawa, inviting the Canadian government to support Havana's efforts to develop the tourist trade by allowing Cuban charter flights to land on a regular basis in Canada and by encouraging various trade missions to investigate how best to develop the tourist industry. The Department of External Affairs forwarded the Cubans' initiative to the Canadian embassy in Havana for assessment, which turned out to be totally negative. The Canadian embassy in Havana rejected Fernández de Cossío's project for two basic reasons: the poor state of Cuban hotels and a lack of Cuban government support.[9] Undaunted by the cold diplomatic shoulder extended by External Affairs, Cossío continued his personal lobbying efforts. In November 1969, the Cuban ambassador sought to pursue a different tack in his promotion of Canadian-Cuban trade, calling for the exchange of trade ministers in 1970. In particular, he lobbied the commercial sector, his greatest success being the decision by the large mining company Sherritt Gordon to begin trading with Cuba. This process started in 1972, when Cossío first made contact with Sherritt officials, and twenty-five years later that company is the single largest foreign investor in Cuba. Cossío also pursued the question of Canadian technical assistance for Cuba and was rewarded by support in a highly regarded series of programs organized by CUSO, Canadian University Services Overseas, from 1969 to 1981. This was the first foreign nongovernmental organization (NGO) to assist revolutionary Cuba. Moreover Ambassador Cossío also proposed biweekly mail and cargo service, a suggestion that was eventually approved by External Affairs.

In the initial years of the first Trudeau government, the relentless efforts of the Cuban ambassador met with limited success, although his imaginative suggestions were politely ignored on many occasions. Officials in the Department of External Affairs were perplexed at the apparently untiring energy of the ambassador and probably wished that he would leave them alone; yet at the same time they did seriously consider some of his suggestions. Canadian ambassador to Cuba Léon Mayrand, for example, responded unequivocally and with some sympathy to the barrage of suggestions made by his Cuban counterpart in Ottawa in a January 15, 1969, letter to External Affairs:

> If we have been less than forthcoming here in response to the frequent mention by Cuban officials of their credit needs, this has been simply as a result of Canada's general trade policy towards Cuba during the past decade. The Canadian approach was accurately described in the Trade and Commerce memorandum attached to your letter No. XL-837 of November 6, 1968 as "very passive" and this has, of course, characterized our attitude during conversations with officials here on topics such as credit.

Contrary to the Cuban Ambassador's remark, we have in fact been extremely conscious of the great importance of credit facilities to the Cubans. We have raised the matter several times with the Department in recent years. . . . We think that the present would be a suitable point at which to review our Cuban trade policy. However, we would reiterate the view contained therein (which is supported by Ambassador Cossío's remarks), that if any substantial increase in sales to Cuba is to be realized, then some acceptable credit arrangements will have to be worked out.[10]

Fully ten years after the Cuban revolution, then, the official Ottawa position on Cuba remained in essence a "passive" one. Cuba might praise Canadian "solidarity" (which was clearly nothing of the sort) in official media, and talk of Canadian courage in maintaining diplomatic and commercial relations with Havana despite constant pressure from Washington, yet the real story was remarkably different. Despite the occasional prodding from Canadian diplomats in Havana and the energetic lobbying of their Cuban counterparts in Ottawa, the Department of External Affairs wanted to do as little as it could about the Cuban question. Lethargy had settled in comfortably, and it was easier to discount Cossío's initiatives and the occasional suggestion from the Canadian embassy than to pursue them actively. Unsettled too by the ongoing strength of the Cuban revolution despite economic hardships and the growing ties between Havana and Moscow on the one hand, and influenced by Washington's frustration at the Castro leadership on the other, Canadian policymakers in 1969 simply did not know what to do about Cuba. As a result, they talked in generalities about Cuban issues but at all times remained indecisive, preferring not to alienate Washington while adopting a "wait-and-see" approach.

The concern about appeasing Washington was deeply rooted in the Department of External Affairs, notwithstanding Havana's claims of Canadian solidarity. The deference shown to the U.S. position on Cuba was clearly visible in a large number of official documents dealing with Cuba. Take, for instance, a memorandum prepared for Prime Minister Trudeau by the Department of External Affairs on April 17, 1969, concerning whether Canada should extend export credit insurance to companies trading with Cuba. The memo stated that the Canadian government neither extended credit to Cuba nor insured sales to that country. What were the reasons for this policy? "Initially this decision was taken by the ECIC Board because Cuba was not considered to be credit-worthy. Although this is no longer the case, the Board has maintained its policy primarily for political reasons: we do not wish to give offense to the U.S., or to other OAS countries

such as Venezuela or Bolivia which have strong views about Cuban interference in their affairs."[11] The memo concluded by stating that "there is
considerable scope for expansion of trade with Cuba if we are prepared to
co-operate with regard to export credit" (2), but it was also clear that nobody in External Affairs was prepared to rise to this particular challenge.

The sale of 5,000 cattle to Cuba (again the result of a Cossío initiative)
at a cost of $10 million is another excellent illustration of Ottawa's tre-
mendous fear of upsetting Washington. Export insurance credit was provided after much lobbying by the Cubans and by the Holstein-Fresian Association of Canada (assiduously courted by Ambassador Cossío), which
pressured the Canadian government. Advisors in the Ministry of Industry,
Trade and Commerce were clearly less ideologically hampered than their
colleagues in External Affairs and swiftly supported the large cattle deal,
particularly at the ministerial and deputy-ministerial levels. When the negotiations were completed, External Affairs accepted it as a fait accompli
yet were still extremely worried as to how the sale of Canadian cows would
be received in Washington. In a confidential memo of April 29, 1969, to
the under-secretary of state for external affairs, J. C. Langley sought to
justify the extension of export insurance credits to Cuba, noting that the
sale of cattle was a modest change by Canada in a market where Japanese
and Western European countries were now extending more generous terms.
He hastened to add his concern as to how the news of the cattle sale would
be received in Washington, and therefore he advised that "it will be necessary to have available a fairly convincing rationale to use in explaining this
move," preferably tying it into the results of the ongoing review of Canadian foreign policy.[12]

Both of these points—consistent deference to Washington and the potential trade advantage—were outlined succinctly in the confidential brief-
ing papers prepared for Trudeau on the occasion of his March 1969 meetings with Richard Nixon. In the section dealing with Canadian policy
toward Cuba, for example, the diplomats who prepared the document noted:

> The principal reason we have withheld credits from Cuba is that the
> U.S. and some other OAS countries have from time to time made
> clear that they deplore this sort of economic assistance to a country
> which promotes violent revolution in the hemisphere. Any trade with
> Cuba of course runs counter to their policy of economic blockade of
> Cuba.
>
> If we should nevertheless wish to make Canadian trade with Cuba
> less passive and more on par with other Latin American countries
> there are several ways—including provision of export financing—in

which this could be done. . . . It remains to be seen if the time has arrived for modification of our present policy on trade with Cuba.[13]

Two years later, despite the solid lobbying efforts of Ambassador Fernández de Cossío, little had changed at the political level. A meeting held in Ottawa on November 10, 1971, with the objective of analyzing the current state of bilateral relations (attended by twenty-five high-ranking bureaucrats) was told by Canadian ambassador Brown that "our relations with Cuba had not improved in the past year because of a lack of initiative and desire on the part of the Canadian authorities, caused by a 'Washington syndrome' (rather than treating Canada-Cuba relations on a purely bilateral basis)." His superior, head of the Western Hemisphere section Klaus Goldschlag, corrected the ambassador, noting that "Canada-Cuba relations would never be treated on a simply bilateral basis because of the attitude in Washington, but as far as possible the goal was for 'normal' relations."[14] All developments in Canadian-Cuban relations, based on this approach, had to pass through the filter of U.S.-Canadian relations and, implicitly, if they were seen as offensive to Washington, would presumably be quashed.

The official position of External Affairs toward Cuba was thus an essentially conservative and guarded one. Trade with Cuba could indeed prove profitable for Canadian exporters, a fact readily accepted by policymakers in Ottawa, yet U.S. criticism remained a major obstacle. As a result, it "remained to be seen" whether it was a propitious moment for such an initiative to be pursued. It was precisely the passive sort of approach that Pierre Elliott Trudeau found reprehensible. When alerted to the potential for enhanced bilateral trade both by Fernández de Cossío and his own officials, he went out of his way to emphasize the need for a more proactive approach toward Cuba.

The Trade Question

In a press conference held in Washington on March 25, 1969, Prime Minister Trudeau was questioned about Canada's ongoing trade with Cuba, and whether such commerce constituted a subsidy for Cuban subversive activities in Latin America. Trudeau responded that trade represented one of the best approaches to understanding other countries and to exercising influence on them. The Canadian philosophy, he maintained, was that trade and political concerns should not be confused: "Short of being at the state of war with another nation, we do not believe that curtailment of trade is in any sense conducive to a lessening of tensions between countries. On the contrary. We trade with Communist China. We trade with Cuba."[15] This determination of the prime minister to assist the development of Canadian exports regardless of the political ideology of the trading partner would be sorely put to the test in the ensuing years.

Attractive and mutually beneficial trade deals were worked out over a variety of items in the following years. Cattle, fertilizer, steel, locomotives, and ships were all exported to Cuba, but all the sales were brought about only after overcoming both substantial pressure from Washington and grave reservations held by External Affairs mandarins. Most of this activity took place in the 1970s, and was based on the steady growth of Canadian exports (up from $40 million to $58 million between 1969 and 1972, with major increases to $81 million in 1973, $144 million in 1974, and $260 million in 1976. Meanwhile Cuban exports to Canada had also grown steadily: from $7 million (1969) to $16 million (1973) and $76 million (1974). To accommodate the flood of Canadian business representatives heading to Cuba, two trade officers were appointed to the embassy in Havana, replacing the trade representative, who had been listed as a second secretary, with no reference to his commercial activities, so as not to flag Canadian business interests to Washington and potentially engender its diplomatic wrath.[16] Again it is significant to point out that the initiative for this development came from outside External Affairs (from the Department of Industry, Trade and Commerce), who pursued it because of "the excellent market prospects existing in Cuba."

In the mid-1970s a number of Canadian subsidiaries of U.S.-based multinationals experienced difficulties in attempting to sell equipment to Cuba, a development that forced Ottawa to revisit its Cuban policy. One of the first cases involved the profitable sale in 1974 of twenty-five locomotives by a Montreal firm, MLW-Worthington, at a cost of $15 million. The parent company, Studebaker-Worthington, had applied for a permit as required by the Trading with the Enemy Act, but this had been denied in Washington. The Trudeau government was incensed by this decision, arguing that U.S. law should not be allowed to hinder an export sale by a Canadian company. Official protests were made by the Canadian embassy in Washington, and a number of government ministers decried this heavy-handed U.S. interference in a Canadian matter.

A similar controversy erupted later in 1974 over the sale of $500,000 worth of office equipment by the Cole Division of Litton Business equipment. The company, based in Scarborough, Ontario, was a wholly owned subsidiary of Litton Industries Inc. of Beverly Hills, and again U.S. officials rejected applications by the parent company. Alastair Gillespie, the minister of industry, trade and commerce, protested Washington's decision, noting in a press conference that he deplored the U.S. actions, which he found appalling, and concluded: "This . . . return to a type of commercial colonialism we find intolerable."[17] Canadian corporations, he noted, should be allowed to trade with any country, and U.S. interference was totally unacceptable. In January 1975, the *Ottawa Citizen* broke the story of a similar problem involving the sale of $2 million worth of typewriter equipment by IBM Canada Ltd., which again had been stalled by U.S. legislation.

The reaction of the Canadian government to Washington's continuous pressure on U.S.-based companies to limit trade between their subsidiaries and Cuba was firm and clear. It was not unlike the current Liberal government's opposition to the Helms-Burton law. Individual ministers, as well as Prime Minister Trudeau, expressed their frustration. In February 1975 Washington backed down, allowing Litton to sell its equipment to Cuba, with a State Department official noting that "our relations with Canada were obviously of importance in a decision on this case."[18] The deal with MLW-Worthington Ltd. was also resolved successfully but again not without major pressure from Ottawa. The next month Alastair Gillespie, minister of industry, trade and commerce, visited Cuba along with twenty-seven journalists and representatives of business, industry, and the academic community. This was the first official visit to Cuba by a Canadian cabinet minister, and it revealed the growing interest in expanding bilateral commercial ties. In August 1975, speaking about a further U.S. ruling that allowed Canadian subsidiaries of U.S.-based corporations to trade with Cuba, he noted that this was "a useful step but it doesn't go far enough."[19] For his part, External Affairs Minister Allan MacEachen, commenting on the sale of office furniture by Litton (after considerable lobbying by the Canadian government), noted that what was really needed so that these problems would not recur was a change in U.S. law.

In many ways it was the joint position of Industry, Trade and Commerce, a strong business lobby eagerly pointing out growing sales opportunities in Cuba, and Prime Minister Trudeau that succeeded in implementing this novel Canadian policy toward Cuba, despite the reservations still felt by policymakers in External Affairs. Loan agreements providing Cuba with a $100 million line of credit were drawn up and used by Cuba to purchase locomotives, railway cars, steel, and grain and to arrange several extensive servicing contracts. On his Cuba trip, Trade Minister Gillespie himself signed contracts worth $25 million in the steel, machinery, and foodstuffs sectors, with additional accords for trade totaling $440 million over a five-year period.[20]

A study of newspaper accounts and government bulletins of the first half of the 1970s reveals a long list of commercial initiatives undertaken by both sides. Typical of these was the December 1974 announcement by Industry, Trade and Commerce that the Export Development Corporation had agreed to lend $24 million to the Cuban government, which wanted to purchase three 10,160-ton tankers, to be built in Quebec. The Canadian loan equaled approximately 80 percent of the purchase price of the tankers. To assist Cuban development projects while expanding exports, in February 1975 it was announced that CIDA would extend a $10 million line of credit for three years at a low interest rate and provide a $2.67 million grant to Cuba for the purchase of Canadian goods and services. External Affairs Minister MacEachen noted that this development assistance was "one expression of Canada's close relations with Cuba. These relations have been expanding considerably in the past few years and Cuba has become an increasingly important market for Canadian business."[21] This can be seen by the substantial growth in Canadian exports to Cuba between the early 1970s and early 1980s.

Smaller delegations than the large entourage of Industry, Trade and Commerce Minister Gillespie arrived in Cuba, ranging from a trade mission of the Maritime Lumber Bureau in May 1976, which announced that trial quantities of a variety of lumber would be shipped to Cuba, to the December 1977 trade delegation to Cuba headed by Nova Scotia Premier Gerald Regan, who came to encourage the sale of steel and coal. In February 1979 it was Ontario's turn, as provincial officials and representatives of local business came on a market-identification mission.

While many of these agreements expired once the funds had been expended or, as in the case of CIDA grants, were not renewed, one of the most successful commercial ventures—a fishing agreement—has withstood the test of time and continues today to be mutually beneficial. This agreement was signed in Havana in May 1977, at a ceremony attended by Canadian Fisheries Minister Roméo Le Blanc (now Canada's governor-general) and his Cuban counterpart. The agreement provides Cuba with the right to fish within Canadian waters and establishes a plan for fisheries development between both countries. Significantly, it was the first agreement undertaken by Canada with any other country since it had extended its fishing limits from 12 to 200 miles. It was drawn up for an initial five-year period, with annual negotiations on fishing quotas and fees to be established, and has continued to the present. For 1977 Cuba was allowed to fish some 60,000 metric tons, approximately 6 percent of the catch allowed in Canadian waters.

In September 1975, in an attempt to formalize these many initiatives and provide a basic framework at the government level for their development, the first meeting of a Cuba-Canada Joint Committee on Economic and Trade Relations was held in Ottawa. The committee had been proposed in March, at the time of Alastair Gillespie's trade mission to Cuba. At the end of the meetings, loan agreements worth $20 million to be expended on the purchase of Canadian equipment and services were drawn up. The existence of this body at this time, despite the reservations of many in External Affairs, symbolized the optimism of both governments in expanding commercial ties. It was a relationship that provided significant tangible and symbolic benefits to both, and one that flourished until the end of the 1970s.

The Cuban Position on Quebec

While steadily increasing trade figures showed the mutual advantages from this rapprochement, the Cuban government also showed its good faith in developing this relationship by helping Ottawa to resolve a particularly thorny political problem—the matter of the FLQ terrorists. In an interview with former Cuban ambassador to Canada José Fernández de Cossío in May 1993, the theme of Canada's appreciation of Cuban support at the time of the 1970 FLQ crisis was emphasized. Anybody who has studied Canadian history in the twentieth century must be aware of the enormous significance that this particular episode held, and continues to hold, for the all-encompassing question of the relationship between the federal government and nationalist aspirations in Quebec. The murder of an elected parliamentarian—a minister of the government of Quebec—and the kidnapping of the British trade commissioner in Montreal, together with the presence of thousands of federal troops on the streets of Quebec and the rounding up of hundreds of suspected Québécois sympathizers, were all events that had not been seen before. The Trudeau government was facing a major political crisis, and an area of great sensitivity.

The Cuban role should be understood against this background. Both prior to the events of 1970 and since, Cuban diplomats have occupied an extremely difficult position in Quebec. There are clear cultural affinities between the Québécois and the Cubans, which might explain why roughly one-half of all Canadian vacationers are from Quebec. As one small illustration, the 1993 Varadero carnival featured advertisements for the winter carnival in Quebec City, and the principal organizers from the Quebec event participated in the Varadero parade, while the Cuban colors were highlighted during the Quebec carnival. In addition, the goals of the social democrat Québécois politician René Lévesque, and many of his aspirations for Quebec, were probably appreciated by Cuban diplomats, particularly those based in Montreal, where the Cubans have a large consulate, as well as tourist and trade offices.

At the same time, Cuba's relations are with the federal government of Canada, with whom they have established a solid diplomatic tradition and excellent commercial relations. Consequently, despite the blandishments of pro-independence Québécois politicians, Havana has always emphasized to its diplomats based in Canada the need to respect above all else the federal relationship. It was of course both permissible and indeed necessary to have firm relationships with provincial government representatives, whether members of the Parti Québécois or the Liberals, but it was also important not to give the appearance—given the constant surveillance of Cuban officials by Canadian security agents—of favoring the Quebec government and therefore risk alienating Ottawa. In sum, the Cubans were sensitive to the dynamic between the federal and provincial governments, and sought to be respectful of both.

One example from the archives of the Department of External Affairs will perhaps illustrate the delicate line that the Cubans had to tread. In December 1980 the Cuban Ministry of Foreign Relations sent a telegram to the Canadian embassy, advising them of an invitation that the government of Quebec had extended to the Cuban minister of external trade, Ricardo Cabrisas, to lead a trade delegation to Quebec. This was seen as offensive to the federal government, which insisted that the proper procedure would have been for the provincial government to approach Ottawa and have External Affairs extend the invitation on behalf of the Quebec government. Otherwise a direct link would be extended between Havana and Quebec City, which could lead to a diminution of the status of the federal government in Quebec. The Cubans were therefore requested to respect the appropriate chain of command and politely decline the invitation from the provincial government until Ottawa had granted its approval. It is important to note that the Cubans had drawn the matter of the invitation to Ottawa's intention in the first place, since they were aware of the confusing complexity of relations between the federal government and Quebec.

Despite this tradition of sensitivity to the problem of Quebec-federal government relations, critics in Canada have also been prepared to manipulate the black legend of Cuba and emphasize Havana's attempts to take advantage of this political and cultural difference. In 1967, for example, Robert Thompson, M.P., accused Radio Habana Cuba, without any evidence, of broadcasting classes in guerrilla warfare in Cree and French to the province of Quebec. There was no foundation to the charges made, but in many ways the damage was already done, adding to the "subversive mystique" of Cuba—a rich legacy indeed. The extremely detailed analysis of "Canadian content" in Radio Habana Cuba reporting ordered in the wake of these allegations revealed Havana's sensitivity to the case of Quebec. The report noted, for instance, that, "due to the special circumstances of the separatist movement in Québec, we have always taken care to avoid any commentary in our programs. As a result, the stormy visit of President De Gaulle to that Canadian province was reported only twice, with bulletins from Canada and France."[22]

The same report also highlighted two other pieces of misinformation that had been circulated recently in Canada. One concerned the matter of "harangues" by Cuban radio, inciting the French-Canadian population to rise in arms. Finally in this report it was claimed that on Cuba's national holiday, July 26, Montreal police had been obliged to move in swiftly to break up a mob of Cubans who had been heading toward the U.S. pavilion at the Expo site. In fact the Cubans had formed a conga and were dancing and weaving their way through the grounds of Expo. In the fall of 1969 two other allegations, again without foundation, surfaced. The first resulted from a press conference given on October 6 by the recently appointed commissioner of the RCMP, Higgitt, who claimed that some of Quebec's subversives had been in Cuba, while the second was an insinuation by the premier of Quebec that a bomb that had exploded at the official residence of the mayor of Montreal the week before had been placed by terrorists trained in Cuba. Once again the black legend had made its presence felt.

Against this backdrop of tension between Ottawa and Quebec City, with rumors swirling that revolutionary Cuba was assisting actively subversive separatist groups in Quebec, events came to a head in 1970. On his arrival in Canada in 1968, and in a move designed to dispel any concerns that Pierre Trudeau might have harbored, Ambassador Fernández de Cossío presented a personal commitment from Fidel Castro to the Canadian prime minister. He noted the false rumors that had circulated at Expo, where he had been director of the Cuban pavilion, "making Cuba appear as if it were undermining the national integrity of Canada. As a result the President of Cuba had instructed him to guarantee expressly that our country had never supported these goals."[23]

It was of course ironic, given the rumors about Cuban guerrilla training of Québécois separatists, that when the October 1970 crisis occurred, Ottawa should turn to Cuba for assistance in defusing the political crisis of the time. Following the discovery of the body of Quebec Labour Minister Pierre Laporte and the location of the FLQ cell by security forces, a protracted series of delicate negotiations took place. The kidnappers promised to assassinate British trade commissioner James Cross unless their demands were met, including safe transportation from Canada. Ottawa approached two other countries to ask if they would accept the kidnappers, only to be turned down, before approaching Cuba. The negotiations between Cuban and Canadian officials took two months to complete, with constant contacts between officials from both countries. In December 1970, in a minutely planned operation, the kidnappers and their hostage were driven to the Cuban pavilion at the former Expo site and from there to the airport, where they left for exile in Cuba.

Then-ambassador Fernández de Cossío credits the experience resulting from this episode as having been of great importance in improving bilateral relations at that time. Until Cuba's acceptance of the FLQ terrorists, the Canadian government had been in a quandary about resolving the crisis—particularly after its first two choices of countries to accept the FLQ terrorists had refused to do so. Cuba's agreement to aid Canada in this delicate situation was therefore highly appreciated by Ottawa since it allowed the situation to be resolved at a time when this looked increasingly unlikely. The Trudeau government expressed its gratitude most clearly, and this undoubtedly prepared the way for a more favorable evaluation of Cuba's interests and requests.[24]

A footnote to this dramatic episode is perhaps in order. In a dispatch to Ottawa in early 1977, Serge April of the Canadian embassy in Havana noted his recent conversations with Roberto Regalado, a specialist in Canadian matters with the Department of the Americas in the Central Committee of the Communist Party. The FLQ terrorists had recently left Cuba for France, upset because the Cubans, among other things, had refused to provide them with guerrilla training, a conscious decision by Havana since in Regalado's reported words, "Cuba does not want to do anything that could harm Canada." April also referred to a meeting in which he had participated with Regalado and Canadian and Québécois Communist Party leaders in November, and which confirmed these views: "one of the things which Regalado said to them was that they would continue to enjoy the solidarity of the Communist Party of Cuba, but only if they did not participate in any activities that could harm the Canadian government."[25] It was extremely clear, then, that Cuba had gone out of its way to accommodate Canada in a most difficult situation for Ottawa. It is also true that Cuban diplomats had sought diligently to avoid contact with separatist groups and to be extremely careful—and sensitive to national aspirations of Canada—in dealing with officials of the government of Quebec. Just as important, when the Trudeau government had asked Havana for support in defusing the most explosive political crisis it had faced, the Cubans had complied with that request and lived up to the agreement for several years, when the FLQ members left for France and ultimately returned to Canada.

Enhanced Bilateral Ties: Beyond the Commercial

It is easy to point to the dramatic increase in commercial ties and wax eloquent about the value of improved relations. The figures are stark in their simplicity. Canadian exports to Cuba rose more than tenfold, from $40 million in 1969 to $450 million in 1981, while Cuban exports during the same period also rose dramatically, from a mere $7 million in 1969 to $196 million in 1981. But there was more to this improving relationship than commercial benefits, as both countries endeavored to shore up and strengthen the developing bilateral ties. In this they were reasonably successful, despite ongoing problems and despite a profound disagreement concerning the nature of Cuba's role in Angola.

To a large extent this flurry of activity, following many years of what could be considered diplomatic stagnation, or at least studied disinterest on the part of Ottawa, was due to the combination of Cossío's persistence, the openness of Trudeau, the clear economic benefits to be obtained for both countries, support from officials in Industry, Trade and Commerce, and the political advantages for both countries of greater independence in their international agenda. It was therefore no accident that by 1981 Canada had become Cuba's principal non-Communist trading partner, outstripping Japan, France, and Spain.

It is important to note, however, that these enhanced relations, passing from diplomatic cordiality to an economically and politically advantageous arrangement, were shored up by a number of activities not related directly to commercial matters. Mention was made earlier of the bilateral fishing agreement, which has proved beneficial to both countries. Cuba received (and continues to receive) cheap protein for domestic consumption from under-utilized species (largely silver hake, redfish, and squid) not traditionally harvested by the Canadian fishing industry. Canada in turn receives payment for the fishing rights (approximately $450,000 in 1993), as well as salaries for the mandatory fishing observers aboard and employment in Atlantic Canada for fish-plant workers who process the excess fish landed in Canada by the Cuban fishing fleet. Perhaps just as significant given the importance of the fishing industry in Canada is the support traditionally given the Canadian position by Cuba in the workings of the North Atlantic Fisheries Organization (NAFO) and, in particular, in matters pertaining to conservation measures and criticism of overfishing, including those nations with which Cuba has cordial diplomatic relations.

Table 4.1. Canada-Cuba merchandise trade: exports and imports, 1960–84 (in thousands of $Canadian)

Year	Exports to Canada	Imports from Canada	Total two-way trade
1960	7.2	13.0	20.2
1961	5.2	31.1	36.3
1962	2.8	10.8	13.6
1963	13.0	16.4	29.4
1964	3.5	60.9	64.4
1965	5.3	60.9	64.4
1966	5.6	61.4	67.0
1967	6.3	42.4	48.7
1968	5.1	45.0	50.1
1969	7.8	40.7	48.5
1970	9.5	58.9	68.4
1971	10.4	56.0	66.4
1972	11.1	58.7	69.8
1973	16.6	81.8	98.4
1974	76.3	144.6	220.9
1975*	—	—	—
1976	60.6	260.7	321.3
1977	45.4	184.0	229.4
1978	60.4	217.8	278.2
1979	106.8	257.4	364.1
1980	163.5	416.5	580.0
1981	196.5	452.4	648.9
1982	94.8	324.4	419.2
1983	56.3	360.6	416.9
1984	62.7	335.8	398.5

Source: Ministry of Foreign Relations, Government of Cuba.

*data unavailable

Another important bilateral agreement signed during this time was the 1973 agreement on hijacking, which has been renewed regularly since. Signed by External Affairs Minister Mitchell Sharp and Vice-Foreign Minister René Castillo in February 1973, this agreement required each country either to prosecute hijackers in its courts or to send them back to the country where the crime had been committed. Given the number of air-hijackings to Cuba in the early 1970s, this was an extremely useful accord—one that stood in marked contrast to the difficulties encountered in attempts to secure a similar agreement between Washington and Havana.

Enhanced bilateral diplomatic relations also meant that outstanding problems now became easier to solve, as both sides sought to employ their good offices and the new-found will to resolve such difficulties. A good example was the case of Ronald Patrick Lippert, arrested in 1963 and sentenced to thirty years in prison for smuggling arms to counterrevolutionaries. On the tenth anniversary of his imprisonment, Tom Cossitt, M.P., moved successfully that the Canadian Parliament request that Havana release Lippert on humanitarian grounds. The following month the Cuban government acceded to this request and emphasized that it was doing so because of the desire to cooperate with the wishes of the Canadian government. Many prior requests for Lippert's release had been rejected by Havana, but it was clear that the Cuban government badly wanted to maintain the momentum in improving bilateral relations. Since penalties for counterrevolutionary activities are rarely commuted, this was an unusual step by Havana.

By the same token, the few remaining claims against the revolutionary government by Canadian citizens, largely the result of nationalization of property, were also resolved, with the exception of claims by the insurance companies, during 1980 and 1981. On June 18, 1981, the agreement was ratified, with the Foreign Claims Commission given responsibility to assure that the $850,000 agreed to was equitably distributed. Ottawa recognized that this amount fell short of full compensation, but in view of Cuba's limited resources, recognized that this was the best arrangement that could be made. All approved claims would be paid up to the first $10,000, with the remaining funds shared on a prorated basis.

The warming of this relationship was illustrated during the early and mid-1970s by the significant number of visits by high-ranking political leaders of both countries, indicating the increased importance accorded the cultivation of bilateral relations by both countries. Coming after the neglect of the 1960s (and from 1984 to the present), it constituted an important development. The visit of Paul Gérin-Lajoie, president of CIDA, in February 1974 was particularly important at that time. The agreement signed in Havana provided Cuba with invaluable foreign support and represented the first major development assistance agreement signed by revolutionary Cuba and a capitalist country. The importance of the agreement for Canada can be deduced from the full-page photograph of Gérin-Lajoie cutting sugarcane in Cuba that graced page 4 of the annual review of CIDA's activities.

An incomplete list of such high-level visits would include details of parliamentarians, provincial trade delegations, and a number of cabinet ministers from the federal government. In January 1974, a seven-member delegation of members of Parliament participated in a week-long visit to Cuba at the invitation of the Cuban government. In March of that year a delegation led by the deputy-minister of industry, trade and commerce (including also representatives from the Departments of External Affairs, Finance, and Agriculture) visited Cuba with the express purpose of discussing trade expansion. The large entourage accompanying Alastair Gillespie, minister of industry, trade and commerce, in March 1975 was important because it was the first official visit by a federal Canadian cabinet minister. The following month Marc Lalonde, minister of health and welfare, visited Cuba to discuss the implementation of a program that would exchange health professionals between both countries for further training. In May 1977 Roméo Le Blanc, minister of fisheries, visited Cuba to sign the bilateral fishing agreement that is still in effect today. In December of that year, the premier of Nova Scotia, Gerald Regan, headed an official trade delegation to Cuba and met with Fidel Castro, his brother Ramón (who is still a personal friend), and high-ranking government officials. In September 1979 a trade mission from Ontario, consisting of provincial government officials and eleven representatives of Canadian businesses, visited Cuba to explore possible areas of investment.

For its part Cuba also sent a number of high-ranking officials. In February 1975, Raúl León, president of the National Bank of Cuba, visited Ottawa for negotiations on loans being provided to Cuba by the Canadian government. In September 1975, Cuban vice-president Carlos Rafael Rodríguez came to Ottawa for three days of talks with Prime Minister Trudeau and a variety of cabinet members. In 1979, a year in which bilateral trade increased by 30 percent, the president of the National Bank of Cuba again visited Canadian financial leaders, while the minister of electricity visited the Hydro-Québec plant at James Bay. In addition, in preparation for the 1976 Olympic Games in Montreal, a number of Cuban teams had trained and played exhibition games in Canada, with Canadian athletes also traveling to Havana.

The Trudeau Visit of 1976 and Its Aftermath

The pinnacle of Canadian-Cuban relations during the Trudeau years undoubtedly came during the visit of the prime minister to Cuba in early 1976 (a visit that had been in the planning stage for at least two years), the importance of which can be gauged by the fact that a large photograph of the two leaders was plastered on the front cover of the February 9, 1976, issue of *Time* (Canada). The personal relationship that developed between Fidel Castro and Pierre Trudeau has been well described by *Time* correspondent William Mader: "Whatever their ideological and political differences, there is no question about the affinity between Trudeau and Castro. Both are essentially shy men, yet utterly determined. Trudeau is an intellectual, Castro a bright pragmatist. But there was a special chemistry between them that amounts to a personal friendship."[26] This "special chemistry" and the friendship have continued over the years, and Trudeau has returned to Cuba on several occasions since.

The highlight of the 1976 state visit to Cuba came during his speech to some 25,000 people in Cienfuegos. During his speech, which he gave in more than acceptable Spanish, Trudeau paid tribute to Castro's "undoubted dedication to bettering the lives of Cubans." Referring in all probability to Cuba's recent incursions into Angola, with which he disagreed profoundly, the Canadian prime minister noted: "we have found that we are not able to agree on every issue. We have found instead something more important . . . that we can disagree honorably and without disrespect."[27] He ended his speech with a dramatic flourish: "Viva Cuba y el pueblo cubano. . . . Viva el Primer Ministro Fidel Castro. Viva la amistad cubano-canadiense."[28]

While both leaders agreed on a number of themes—the need for nuclear disarmament, support for the United Nations and its agencies, the importance of aiding the aspirations of developing countries, and advancement of the Law of the Sea—they disagreed fundamentally on the question of Angola. They discussed the situation of Southern Africa in general and Angola in particular, and while they failed to agree, Trudeau was impressed by Castro's broad knowledge of the area. At a press conference held on January 29, he noted that the Cuban prime minister had made his decision to intervene militarily in Angola after a great deal of thought, and that while he did not agree with the decision, he did understand the basis for Cuban intervention.

He was questioned, inevitably, about whether his visit to revolutionary Cuba and the developing bilateral relations with Havana would cause problems for Canadian relations with Washington. Trudeau replied that there were important lessons to be learned about Cuba, particularly in areas of food, health care, education, and housing, and that it was "in many senses a model which will be followed by developing countries." Moreover, he added, the United States should accept the obvious fact that the Cuban revolution was still strong despite the ongoing U.S. blockade, and the issue of normalization of relations needed to be dealt with. In his own case, as leader of a NATO country visiting communist Cuba, he noted dryly that "a very short time after I had been to Peking, President Nixon went to Peking; a very short time after I had been to Moscow, President Nixon went to Moscow."[29]

Back in Canada a barrage of criticism was leveled at the prime minister for traveling to Cuba at a time when Cuban troops were so heavily involved in Angola, since it appeared that by doing so Canada was approving Havana's actions. Leading the attack against Trudeau was John Diefenbaker, who predicted that Canada would receive an international "black eye" for allowing the prime minister to visit Cuba at that moment. Trudeau responded on several levels to the impassioned criticisms of his Cuba policy. First, he noted, Canada had made abundantly clear its opposition to Cuba's role in Angola, and for almost three hours he and the Cuban prime minister had argued over the topic. "I felt that Cuba, and I said so, was making a very serious mistake from the point of view of its own involvement in that Angolan situation. Regardless of the harm that they might be doing in Africa, I thought they were doing a fair amount of harm to themselves, and I made that quite clear," he noted in the House of Commons.[30] Second, he argued, Canada wanted to continue the tradition of improving bilateral relations that had originated during Diefenbaker's own tenure. Finally, he stated that the visit had been planned far before Cuban incursions into Angola, and as a result cancellation would have been received in Havana "as not only a condemnation of its action, which it knows we have made, but also as a definite slight and a cooling, if not a breaking, in our relations."[31]

Notwithstanding the prime minister's spirited defense of his actions, it was clear that Trudeau's perceived audacity was an issue that opposition politicians could exploit, as much for domestic political advantage as anything else. The criticism increased and remained constant for many months afterward, and in part it was criticism that the prime minister himself could appreciate, given his own profound disagreement with Cuban policy in Angola. A cloud of unease and uncertainty began to settle over the whole question of Cuban involvement in Africa. In late January 1976 two non-scheduled flights of Cubana de Aviación passed through Gander airport in Newfoundland, one en route to Guinea-Bissau and one returning from Brazzaville, and were the occasion for the secretary of state for external affairs to note that Cuba had been warned not to use Canadian airports for refueling if they were in any way involved with the war effort. In March Conservative M.P. Sinclair Stevens berated Trudeau, calling on Ottawa to take a responsible approach to its principal trading partner (the United States). At a time when President Gerald Ford was denouncing Fidel Castro as "an international outlaw," the Canadian prime minister had been in Cuba lavishing praise on him—an unacceptable practice.

The ambitious aid program to Cuba was soon to become the sacrificial victim of this growing frustration. The juxtaposition of the expulsion of

four Cubans from Canada in January 1977[32] and the ongoing concern about
Cuba's role in Africa led to an impassioned debate about the utility of Canadian aid. Conservative M.P. Doug Roche demanded that all CIDA assistance be cut off immediately, noting that "whatever good CIDA's agricultural projects are doing in Cuba, it is not possible to support them when
Cuba finds the resources to send troops to Angola and also to train guerril-
las for war against Rhodesia's white minority. The expulsion of Cuban
diplomats from Canada for conducting an intelligence operation in Montreal
raises further questions about CIDA being duped."[33] Sensing that Canada's
development assistance program in Cuba was an area in which the Trudeau
government was vulnerable, opposition M.P.'s redoubled their attacks, embarrassing the government.

In the spring of 1978, the Conservative party mounted a major assault on
Canada's policy toward Cuba, with aid again the focus of their attack, but
this time focusing on export development credits. Parliamentarian Lloyd
Crouse questioned the utility of a mandatory arms embargo against South
Africa while Canadian aid continued to be sent to Cuba, whose troops were
being sent to Angola in increasing numbers. On May 23 John Diefenbaker
again entered the fray, calling for the cessation of all technical assistance to
Cuba in view of Cuba's "disruptive role" in Africa. And on June 6 Douglas
Roche expanded the question, asking when the government would go further and terminate all export credits to Havana. The secretary of state for
external affairs, Donald Jamieson, wearily noted the government's position:
both officially and unofficially Ottawa had expressed its grave concern to
Havana about Cuban incursions into Angola on many occasions, and at that
time Canada was concluding various development assistance projects that
pre-dated Cuba's role in Africa. In May the prime minister finally entered
the fray, noting that all CIDA programs were now being terminated, and
that there were no further projects being considered. Canada's venture into
aiding development projects in Cuba was thus brusquely curtailed and, despite Cuba's subsequent withdrawal from Africa, have yet to be renewed at
the bilateral (government-to-government) level. At the same time, the few—
essentially medical and scientific—programs administered through the International Development Research Centre (IDRC) have remained functioning,
and have been remarkably successful.

A study of the annual reports of the Canadian International Development Agency speaks volumes about how the rising star of aid for Cuba
came crashing down so abruptly. CIDA's director, Paul Gérin-Lajoie, might
have figured in a full-scale photograph cutting sugar cane in Cuba for the
1974 report, but it was an image that the Trudeau government was soon
keen to dispel, particularly in light of the increasing attacks in Parliament

of the issue of Canadian aid to Cuba. The annual review for 1972–73 made absolutely no mention of aid to Cuba, while in comparison the 1976–77 report showed the dramatic increase in disbursements to Cuba: nothing in 1971–72, $.05 million (1972–73), $0.43 million (1974–75), $3.68 million (1975–76), and $4.26 million (1976–77). In 1978, $4.52 million were given to Cuba, but the annual review for 1977–78 noted that greater emphasis was now being placed on the poorer countries, and as a result Cuba was being phased out—the official face-saving rationale. As a result, aid disbursements fell to $1.06 million for 1978–79, nothing in 1979–80, and –$0.2 million for 1980–81.[34]

These were never significant amounts, particularly when seen in the light of the continuing trade increases on which both countries understandably focused. Nevertheless, they do reveal initial Canadian support for development projects, followed by a noticeable disaffection in Ottawa with Cuban matters. The bloom started to come off the rose as the Trudeau government turned its attention away from Cuba to broader multilateral concerns of international development and nuclear disarmament, thereby defusing domestic criticism of the prime minister's interest in Cuba. It may well be that this would have happened in any event, regardless of Cuban involvement in Angola, since some key figures in External Affairs clearly felt uncomfortable with the increasingly friendly ties with Havana (and, it could be argued, Trudeau's early personal interest had already moved to other areas). The sending of Cuban troops to Africa acted as a catalyst in bringing about this process, especially when it led to significant domestic criticism of the advisability of giving development assistance to Cuba at a time when Havana could apparently afford to send large numbers of soldiers to fight in Angola. In sum, after Angola nothing was ever the same in Canadian-Cuban relations.[35]

Other Irritants in the Bilateral Relationship

While the furor over Angola was undoubtedly the single most important negative element to influence the official Canadian position over Cuba, there were several other matters for Ottawa and Havana alike which of necessity colored the way in which each government considered the other. These were many and varied, and in fairness both sides felt that they possessed genuine and valid complaints. A study of these problem areas reveals that there were many minor concerns and incidents, but that by far the most severe problem area fell, once again, in the field of foreign relations, and in particular with security concerns.

During the 1970s there was great suspicion of Cuban espionage activities in Canada by the intelligence-gathering community. Visitors to Cuban ships in Canadian ports were followed by RCMP officers, sympathizers of the Cuban revolution were visited regularly by Canadian intelligence officials, and potential visitors to Cuba were invited by RCMP officers to see an extremely simplistic bipolar "documentary" on totalitarian communist systems. In a rather one-dimensional fashion, Canada was presented by Canadian counterespionage officers to potential sympathizers with the Cuban revolution as the "soft underbelly" to the United States and hence an attractive target for Cuban intelligence officials. In 1995, Svend Robinson, a member of Parliament for Burnaby, near Vancouver, noted that some of his constituents, keen to open a business in Cuba, had been approached by officials from the main Canadian counterintelligence agency, CSIS, and advised firmly not to do so. Robinson maintained that this was a policy of harassment. It is clear that old attitudes die hard, as is shown by the fact that, even in the post-Cold War era, Cuba remains a "scheduled" country for Canadian security officials, with a reservoir of suspicion intact.

For their part, too, the Cubans had security problems, although these were of a different kind. Throughout the 1960s their embassy and consulates had been harassed by Cuban exile groups, while formal complaints had been made to the Department of External Affairs on several occasions after hidden microphones had been found in the embassy building and the ambassador's house. Fidel Castro was keen to attend the Expo 67 festivities, but was dissuaded from doing so by Canadian officials, nervous about security concerns. It has been claimed that the RCMP Security Service's Cuba Desk was tipped off by the CIA that Cuban exiles had smuggled in a 4.5 inch rocket launcher and were planning to destroy the Cuban pavilion. Apparently they were arrested and the armaments seized.[36] In April 1967 a note was sent by a group called the "Exiled Cubans Association" of New York to all the tenants of the building where the Montreal consulate was housed, advising them to pressure the landlord to break the lease with the Cubans: "Inasmuch as you are neighbours we wish to advise you in advance that it is the aim of our organization to harass and cause possible damage as a result of such harassment to all property maintained and paid for by the Cuban government. The fact that this office is located in your building places you in danger."[37] In 1967 a bomb was located in the Montreal consulate, and again in 1971 an incendiary bomb was located and dismantled by Montreal police.

As bilateral relations warmed up during the Trudeau years, Cuban exile groups became more daring. On December 5, 1970, the day after the FLQ kidnappers of James Cross flew to Cuba, the Cuban consulate in Toronto was firebombed. In late March 1972 explosive devices had been found near the ambassador's residence and less than a week later at the embassy itself. The most serious incident, however, took place at the building that housed both the trade commission and the Cuban consulate on April 4, 1972, when a powerful bomb exploded, killing Cuban security guard Sergio Pérez. It has been alleged that RCMP Security Service personnel were involved in the bombing, which, it is claimed, was meant as a ruse so that Canadian security officials could gain access to sensitive material. In the wake of the explosion Canadian security officials had allegedly carted away armfuls of sensitive documents, including a codebook allegedly used in espionage activities: "Within hours the entire cache, code books and all, landed on a desk in CIA headquarters in Langley, Virginia. In this case the RCMP Cuban Desk served mainly as a messenger service."[38]

Yet while such concerns were understandably troubling matters for both governments, they were usually dealt with by security services and officials who had little influence on the lofty matters of bilateral political relations. In this realm the impact of charges and countercharges undoubtedly created a filter through which the larger picture of international relations was perceived, but there was little direct effect on how the two nations conducted business with each other. Steadily, however, as the interest of the Trudeau government in Cuba began to wane, the previously ignored ideological concerns again entered the equation and became a significant factor in the evaluation of bilateral relations.

Despite his barely concealed scorn for Ronald Reagan and for what could be termed his tenuous grasp of international affairs, Prime Minister Trudeau did little to contradict the U.S. president in his views on Cuba. Partly because of his own disillusionment with Cuban activities in Angola, but more likely because he was now pursuing broader development and nuclear disarmament goals and had therefore simply lost interest in Cuba, Trudeau began paying less attention to Cuban matters. As a result, an increasingly pre-Trudeau, ideologically based, conservative interpretation of Cuba again made the rounds through the corridors of the Department of External Affairs.

This attitude can be seen in a March 25, 1981, memo, prepared for a meeting with Joaquín Más Martínez, who was to come to Ottawa as a special envoy of President Castro. The memo noted with some concern the significant international role of Havana, not only because of its role in Africa, but also because of its leadership until 1982 of the Non-Aligned Movement. Cuba's role in the Caribbean was an important one, the memo noted, but, without any documentation, was "generally negative to Canadian and Western interests." Closer to home, it advised the minister that "intelligence activities by Cubans in Canada are of concern to this country and have led to expulsions of Cubans, as well as numerous visa denials."

What, therefore, should the minister do about the impending visit of Más Martínez? And what views should he hold about Havana's emissaries? The authors of the memo advised him in solid Cold War terminology to remember that, in essence, Cuba was part of the enemy camp: "Cuba's orthodox Communist government, its close economic and political dependence on the Soviet Union, its activities in Africa, and its interference in Central America and the Caribbean, the mutually hostile relationship between the United States and Cuba place severe restraints on the development of closer relations."[39] In no way critical of the Reagan policy in the region, instead it stated that Havana's "orthodox" Communist government, which in fact was nothing of the sort, and its "interference" in Central America (presumably the U.S. activities were acceptable to Ottawa) constituted a challenge for the West as a whole.

An indication of this new hard-line approach to Cuba came in 1980, again over the turmoil in Central America. By now the special relationship that had characterized the first decade of the Trudeau government had long disappeared and, in the words of one Ottawa mandarin, "a number of events have occurred over the past two or three years which have brought Canadian-Cuban relations more in line with our relations with the Soviet Union and Eastern European countries." As a result, CIDA assistance had been phased out, and 1979 was the first year that a ministerial-level visit had not taken place. Dividing the world in solid Manichean fashion, it was noted that since 1978 Cuba "had increased its political activity in the Commonwealth Caribbean and Central America *in a way that is in opposition to our interests* and those of the Western world generally" (emphasis added).[40]

The increase in tension over Central America and Cuba's support both for the Sandinista government in Nicaragua and, until the early 1980s, for the Farabundo Martí Front for National Liberation (FMLN) in El Salvador, rapidly inserted themselves in an inextricable manner into Canadian foreign policy. Canadian-Cuban relations, already flagging in the wake of Havana's intervention in Angola, steadily declined as a combination of Trudeau's growing disinterest, competition for attention resulting from his growing interest in nuclear disarmament, the return of External Affairs hawkishness, a solid working relationship between U.S. Secretary of State George Schultz and his Canadian counterpart (and former MIT colleague) Allan MacEachen, and of course the omnipresent Canadian economic dependence on the United States.

This fresh element in the returning chill in bilateral relations can be seen in a variety of External Affairs communications throughout the early 1980s. A telegram from Ottawa to Ambassador Bartleman in May 1982, for instance, noted that policymakers were concerned at Cuban activities in Central America, that Washington had "legitimate security interests" to defend, and that Havana was "playing a dangerous game" in underestimating the "public tolerance of perceived Cuban provocation." The telegram assured Ambassador Bartleman that Ottawa was aware of the "long and tortured history" of Cuban-U.S. relations, but noted that "Cuban acquiescence in bringing world to brink of nuclear war during Missile Crisis affords disturbing precedent of Cuban willingness to bait USA beyond limits of endurance."[41] The searching of planes for arms at Gander en route from the Soviet Union and Eastern Europe via Havana to Nicaragua by the RCMP occurred on several occasions. Canada had apparently decided, largely over Central America, that it was time to send strong signals of displeasure to Havana.

The degree to which Trudeau and Castro had drifted apart in their analysis of North-South issues can be seen in microcosm in letters dealing with El Salvador that they exchanged between April and June 1981. Trudeau expressed his hope that Cuba would use its influence "to help diminish the tensions in our hemisphere." Specifically he asked the Cuban president to refrain from influencing events in El Salvador: "The Government of El Salvador should be given the opportunity to institute its promised reform measures and to allow the development of a broad consensus between men of good will on both sides which will lead to democratic elections."[42] On June 17 Castro responded civilly, but one can detect the icy frustration behind his reply: "I feel, however, that, if we are to assume a realistic and fair approach, it is first necessary to put an end to the interference, the pressure, the military aid and advising, as well as the participation of those who in the past armed the repressive forces of El Salvador, and to this day are still arming, training and supplying them."[43] The Trudeau-Castro honeymoon was over, with each possessing an extremely different interpretation of the basis of North-South development, and each disagreeing radically with the other on world "hot spots" such as Southern Africa and Central America.

Toward an Understanding of the Canadian-Cuban Dynamic, 1968–84

As this chapter has attempted to show, the difficulties involved in attempting to grasp as fluid and as complex a matter as the evolution of this particular bilateral relationship are many. Combined with the backcloth of superpower politics and the dependency of both Canada and Cuba on different trading blocs and "patrons," there were several other factors that need to be considered when assessing the demands of policy formulation:

the particular micro-and macro-concerns of Canadian and Cuban leaders, the political agenda on the world stage, interests of their own political or corporate elites, the demands of domestic political life, media coverage, the evolution of the leaders themselves, and finally information supplied by their diplomatic and intelligence corps. It is important also to remember that the period under study, apart from the brief Clark government of 1980, covers almost a decade and a half, a time when the danger of world destruction through thermonuclear war became a definite possibility, and when North-South concerns finally became an important topic of global concern, even if it soon passed from popular consciousness. Trudeau's obsession with seeking a solution to Cold War tensions made him somewhat contemptuous of Ronald Reagan's grasp on international affairs. In his memoirs he noted dryly that "President Reagan was not a man for thoughtful policy discussions, but he was pleasant and congenial and my children found him entertaining,"[44] yet it was also clear that he had to engage Washington in this quest, which was far easier said than done.

If Cuban officials were unsure of the confusing signals given by Ottawa, no less uncertain were their Canadian colleagues. Shortly before returning to Canada, Ambassador Léon Mayrand, about whose views the Cubans had protested energetically on several occasions, noted with evident bitterness that "this Cuban approach of always smiling [will] be re-invigorated with the arrival of my successor. Just like they have done with me until the point where they realized that I knew them too well to be totally favorable to them in everything. This is a post in which one should not spend too much time if you don't want any bother or complications."[45] If we compare this with his colleague Mac Bow just four years later, it is immediately clear that a totally different approach was advocated:

> In our opinion, Canadian interests cannot be protected from a passive and responsive position. If we wish to control the pace of Canadian-Cuban relations, the initiative cannot be left to Cuban impulses to which Canada responds negatively or timidly. Instead, we should develop proposals designed to enhance Canadian political, commercial and other interests in Cuba, Latin America and in the ongoing process of changing international power relationships and detente. Such a controlled and modulated development of relations should be based on sincerity and on well-defined Canadian objectives.[46]

Following a study of diplomatic correspondence from both countries for much of this period it is clear that there are two basic schools of thought, found in both countries. On the one hand is the traditional conservative approach, which in general has sought to quash Cuban initiatives and occasionally react to them. Inherently suspicious of Cuban overtures, this model is characterized by an overt fear of angering Washington, a fear that permeates Canadian diplomatic correspondence concerning Cuba. Dozens of examples can be cited from official correspondence, but one will perhaps suffice. In 1983 a major debate took place surrounding an invitation issued to Ramón Castro to visit Canada.

He had been invited to give an address to the Canadian Holstein-Fresian Breeders' Association. Ramón Castro, a life-long farmer, had made a number of trips to Canada, buying several thousand Canadian Holstein, and was a renowned cattle-breeder. The memo on the possible invitation, prepared by the Cuba Desk officer, H. R. Rousseau, described Ramón both as "apolitical" and as a "friend of Canada," who on several occasions had invited Canadian delegations to the state farm he directed. He would be pleased to accept an invitation to Canada, "a country for which he has much respect and admiration." On the other hand, Rousseau noted, an invitation might indicate support "for the régime," while there were also American members of the Association who "might see this invitation as a sort of provocation." As a result of these divergent factors, while a private invitation ("if kept low key with no public exposure, and it could be justified on trade purposes") was feasible, "in view of these negative factors it would be best if Ramón Castro *not* be invited."[47]

In addition to being exceptionally careful not to upset Washington, this school of thought was also concerned that Canada not take any leadership in improving its relations with Cuba. This view was opposed to that of the prime minister, but it was one that had held sway since the revolution and would once again become the predominant current. The basis for this approach was that Canada had little to gain by developing bilateral relations with Cuba unless other countries were to do so. It was well summed up in a September 1974 intradepartmental memo:

> The pace of our initiatives towards Havana has to be continually measured against the speed with which other countries of the Hemisphere attempt to reach an accommodation with Havana. Our relations with the United States and with several leading nations of Latin America, and in particular Mexico, Brazil and Venezuela are more important than those with Cuba. . . . Canada has more significant bilateral aid programmes in several other Latin American countries and is participating actively in a number of Inter-American organizations, including the Inter-American Development Bank, of which Cuba is not part. Various Latin American countries are also becoming an

important source of immigrants and immigration officers will soon have been established in four of them. Cuba has no potential in this regard.[48]

While this conservative approach has undoubtedly been the predominant school of thought for most of the revolutionary period, there have been times when it fell into disfavor. As this chapter has sought to show, when Prime Minister Trudeau took an active interest in the development of bilateral relations, an amazing array of initiatives suddenly materialized. The years 1968–76, then, can be seen as the "golden age" of Canadian-Cuban relations. At that time it seemed that Fidel Castro's oft-cited sentiment that the "Canadian-Cuban relationship could become the example of cooperation between socialist and capitalist countries that could show the way to other Latin American nations and other regions of the world"[49] could actually be realized. An exception during several decades of Canadian-Cuban relations, what distinguishes it from prior and subsequent periods was the fact that, for the first time, it was a proactive policy that was not afraid to pursue overtly Canadian goals without first deferring to Washington. Had Trudeau's interest not waned following Cuba's role in Angola and his assuming broader multilateral interests, it is interesting to speculate on precisely what would have happened in the evolution of the relationship.

A final element needs to be introduced, though, if we are to appreciate the dynamic of this bilateral evolution, namely, the issue of misreading cultural signals, of not understanding the political culture of the other country. Two rather bizarre examples might help us understand this phenomenon. The first is related to the awkward-sounding title of "Municipal Regulations concerning Fires and the Cuban Embassy." It concerns a complaint raised by the first secretary of the Ottawa embassy in the wake of an incident that had occurred on May 26, 1969. On that day Cuban officials had decided to burn confidential documents in the backyard of the embassy. Unfortunately a neighbor, after spotting the smoke, had alerted the fire brigade, and there had ensued a Chaplinesque sequence with "a massive descent of fire-fighters armed with axes" on the embassy, Cuban officials protesting about an invasion of Cuban territory, and the firefighters informing the diplomats that burning paper in the open constituted an infraction against municipal air pollution regulations. The Cuban ambassador wanted to inform External Affairs about the incident, and to inform them that in the future confidential documents would be burned in the furnace. ("The idea of a paper-shredder had still not occurred to them," the author of the memo noted dryly.)[50]

The second concerns an incident involving the renowned Canadian photographer Youssef Karsh in 1971 after he had returned from a trip to Havana, where he had photographed Fidel Castro. During his trip he had praised a particular Cuban palm tree (the "palma macana"), whereupon Fidel Castro had promised to send him one. True to his word, the Cuban leader did so, which caused grave concern in Ottawa because of the regulations involved. As an enterprising bureaucrat in the Department of Agriculture informed the Canadian embassy in Havana, a significant amount of red tape was involved: "1) Plant must come completely free of soil as import of soil is prohibited from all countries except continental US. 2) Plant must be accompanied by phytosanitary certificate (i.e. plant health certificate) issued by plant quarantine authorities of Dirección Nacional de Sanidad Vegetal."[51]

Why dwell on these two cases? The answer is that both reveal a glaring lack of awareness of one culture for another. In both cases parties from the Canadian and Cuban sides acted with the best of intentions, and in both cases a form of cultural communication breakdown occurred. In both cases, then, we encounter a microcosm of the difficulties of cross-cultural communication, all the more severe, of course, when there are ideological differences and resultant prejudices, as well as powerful patrons whose priorities are to be kept in mind at all times.

The value of the Trudeau years, and especially the first nine years of his government, was that Ottawa (perhaps despite itself) managed to shrug off, for a time at least, the restraints that had hindered it in the past and since then have largely been rebuilt. Earnestly pursuing the idea of a "Third Option," Trudeau was probably less hindered by ideological baggage than any of his predecessors and certainly possessed a greater appreciation of world politics than most leaders of his day. Moreover, his policy was beneficial on an economic plane, since he undoubtedly created employment for Canadians as exports to Cuba soared dramatically. It is to his credit, then, that for several years he managed to pursue an independent path for Canada and to develop a level of communication with Cuba that was beneficial to both. In sum, with the exception of John Diefenbaker, who maintained diplomatic relations with Cuba for largely visceral reasons, the first eight years of the Trudeau policy for Cuba (before he appeared to lose interest) bore a "made-in-Canada" stamp for Ottawa's foreign policy. It was a phenomenon that has not been seen since.

5

The Mulroney Tenure
Studied Neglect

The socioeconomic situation in revolutionary Cuba reached its nadir by the early summer of 1993. The demise of the Soviet Union two years earlier had devastated the island's economy, destroying in one fell swoop its major export market, principal supplier of a vast array of products from food to industrial plant, and traditional alliance in the ongoing struggle against Washington. The lack of fuel was a particularly harsh blow, and anybody traveling to Cuba in the early 1990s can vouch for the horrendous lineups for transportation, the closed factories, and the many cars stored on concrete blocks. Tens of thousands of Chinese bicycles helped to transport Cubans, but clearly the country was in crisis.

Then came the "storm of the century" between March 12 and 14, 1993. Its effect was limited in North America, but in Cuba it left a trail of destruction in its wake. Some 150,000 people were left homeless, many crops were devastated (six million banana trees were uprooted), hundreds of industrial facilities were destroyed, planes were flipped over at the Havana airport, and waves roared over the Malecón sea wall in Havana, reaching almost half a mile inland and filling the tunnels in the city. In all, more than a billion dollars of damage resulted.

This already grave situation was made worse by an unprecedented medical epidemic that affected more than 40,000 Cubans. Officially termed polyneuropathy, it hospitalized more than 20,000 people, many of whom temporarily lost their sight. Linked to vitamin deficiency, and particularly to a lack of vitamin B complex, the result of a lack of milk and cereals in the diet, it caused a great psychological shock among Cubans and showed the stark reality of the crisis they were experiencing. The final blow came with torrential storms in late spring, which devastated the sugar crop, producing the second lowest harvest in the entire 34-year revolutionary process, forcing Cuba to break many of its international contracts for the export of sugar and reducing sharply its supply of badly needed hard currency.

Appeals by Cuba for international humanitarian assistance for the first time during the entire revolutionary process brought a mixed response.

Just ten days after the March storm, Peru sent sixteen tons of medicine and equipment. The Ukraine, itself facing dire economic circumstances, sent 300 tons of food products. Most European countries, as well as the European Community itself, sent food or medical assistance, as did many from Latin America and the Caribbean. Yet while impoverished Honduras, tiny Belize, and Nicaragua (the latter, of course, no ideological fellow-traveler of Cuba), John Major's Britain, India, Chile, Japan, and a host of other countries all provided humanitarian assistance, a glaring omission could be found in Canada's position.

Canada gave no official aid to Cuba, and apart from some technical assistance through the International Development Research Centre, had not for nearly a decade and a half. The Cuban government used its official newspaper *Granma* to list the countries that had shown humanitarian solidarity with Cuba at this moment of great need.[1] It was claimed that Ottawa had sent 5,000 tons of potatoes as a symbol of solidarity, yet Cuban officials knew better: the potatoes, which were the result of a glut in Canada, were about to be ploughed under, and the donation was the result of the generosity of the provincial government of New Brunswick and the sharp thinking of Cuban ambassador to Canada Carlos Castillo.[2] They had actually been obtained before the storm hit Cuba in mid-March.

Embarrassed by the lack of official response from the federal government, a number of NGOs and churches sought to prod Ottawa into action. The lead role was taken by OXFAM-Canada, with active support from the United Church of Canada, which had maintained an active 30-year program in Cuba, the Anglican Church of Canada, the Jesuit Centre for Social Faith and Justice and CUSO (Canadian Universities Service Overseas), which had organized some very successful projects in Cuba in the mid-1970s until Ottawa cut funding for all CIDA-funded projects in Cuba. In Cuba their counterpart was the Ecumenical Council of Cuba, which brought together all mainstream Protestant Churches on the island. They put together an ambitious proposal for $250,000 in medicines and hospital supplies, which was approved by CIDA and sent for final approval to the office of then secretary of state for external affairs, Barbara McDougall.

McDougall simply refused to sign the request from CIDA, an unusual development in itself, and sent it back for further consideration at CIDA. According to Monique Vézina, an aide to the minister responsible for CIDA, "the delay in approving Canadian relief was due to the policy implications of saying Yes to Cuba."[3] So, while many European, Latin American, and Caribbean countries, regardless of ideology, responded to Cuba's appeals for immediate humanitarian assistance, and while one branch of the Canadian government (together with the leading churches and NGOs) was lobbying for medical aid, the federal government of Canada deliberately refrained from responding.

It is important to bear in mind these two elements—the context of Cuba's crisis situation and the decision not to respond to Havana's appeal for humanitarian relief—to appreciate the neglect of Cuba shown by Ottawa during this nine-year period, particularly after 1991. The Mulroney government had nothing to lose by supporting an initiative in which Japan, Germany, Mexico, and a couple of dozen other countries were participating. Yet it refused to respond to the need, despite the fact that Canadians constituted the largest number of foreign tourists to Cuba and had the largest single foreign investment there. So much for the historic relationship, and the fact that, apart from Mexico, Canada was the only country of the Americas not to break with Cuba thirty years earlier. The Mulroney period brought an entirely new element to bear in the relationship: studied neglect. This chapter seeks to show that there was no serious attempt to destroy the bilateral relationship, despite fundamental ideological differences between Ottawa and Havana and the Mulroney government's deliberate courting of Washington. Rather, it emphasizes that the Conservative government merely put the relationship with Havana into a veritable diplomatic deep freeze. There was nothing that Ottawa could gain from cultivating closer ties with the revolutionary government, and the Reagan and Bush administrations would undoubtedly have been displeased by any attempt to pursue such an initiative. As a result, much like Lester Pearson had done in the early 1960s, the Mulroney government deliberately ignored Havana and waited for the Cubans to get the message.

This chapter seeks to analyze two basic questions: why the Mulroney government pursued this path and how it went about achieving such a goal. In addition, however, it assesses the overall development of the bilateral relationship, which, despite the official diplomatic cold shoulder extended by Ottawa, nevertheless did produce some interesting and unexpected developments. The premise again is that the role of the prime minister is of paramount importance in setting the parameters for the relationship. The chapter will therefore begin with an examination of the ideology and goals of Brian Mulroney. A further factor concerns Canada's reinvigorated policy toward Latin America in general (for example, the decision to join the OAS and the government's warm embrace of NAFTA), against which the Cuba policy should be examined.

The chapter is divided into three main parts. The first examines the views of Prime Minister Mulroney (and to a lesser extent of his secretary of state for external affairs, Joe Clark). It is based on an understanding that the two men had a different approach to the question of Cuba, and that it is important to draw out those differences. The second section assesses the nature and extent of the "discovery" of a Latin American strategy by Ottawa during the Mulroney years. The third, and most substantial, section analyzes the development of the bilateral relationship, and how it waxed and waned during this nine-year period. It seeks to determine to what extent, despite profound reservations about Cuba by Canada and an extremely pro-Washington position by the prime minister, the dynamic of ties between Ottawa and Havana continued relatively stable, in no small part because of the traditions already established.

The Mulroney View of International Relations

"Good relations, superb relations with the United States of America will be the cornerstone of our foreign policy."

   Brian Mulroney, 1983

In many ways the election of Brian Mulroney in 1984 marked a totally new direction for Canada. The incoming prime minister was the first industrial working-class leader of the country (his father was an electrician from Quebec), and he understood life on the other side of the political tracks. It can be argued that Mulroney was also the first prime minister in decades to understand clearly the aspirations of the body politic in Quebec, as opposed to Pierre Trudeau whose somewhat cerebral and elitist appreciation failed to grasp fully the nationalist sentiments that played and continue to play a major role in provincial politics. A self-made man, Mulroney was an old-style conservative who firmly believed in his role to guide Canada along a diametrically opposed path to that blazed by his Liberal predecessor. This was true as much for domestic concerns as it was for the Mulroney program for foreign policy.

From 1984 to 1993, when he resigned as prime minister, Brian Mulroney provided strong, decisive, and toward the end, unpopular leadership. (Shortly before the end of his mandate, the government's popular support fell to an all-time low of 16 percent.) In domestic policy he introduced sweeping change, as he himself explained: "Free trade, NAFTA, tax reform, the GST, privatizations and deficit reduction, fighting inflation and lowering interest rates. . . . None will accuse us, I think, of having chosen to evade our responsibilities by sidestepping the most controversial questions of our time."[4] But there was also a negative side to the policy: there were record bankruptcy rates, the national debt doubled to $450 billion from $206.3 billion during this time, and unemployment increased to 11.3 percent.

Mulroney was also, without doubt, the prime minister most supportive of Washington's policies, both domestic and international, in the entire history of Canada. He recognized that, with 80 percent of Canadian exports going to the United States, strong bilateral relations were the major foreign policy consideration for any prime minister. A strong ideological advocate of privatization, he dismantled a host of national, government-supported programs that had been enshrined by previous governments, including Conservative ones, and largely supported the international policies of the Reagan and Bush administrations. Brian Mulroney went out of his way to encourage and develop his personal relationship with the rich and the powerful in Washington, not just because he saw it as the best form of aiding Canada, but also because he apparently believed that this ideological approach was the necessary path to follow if Canada were to shed the consequences of Trudeauism and to prosper. Mirroring in many ways the beliefs of his U.S. mentors Reagan and Bush, with both of whom he struck up a particularly warm personal friendship, Brian Mulroney steadily changed the fabric of Canadian society and increasingly adopted Washington's goals as his own. In sum, he was as different from Pierre Trudeau as could be.

In a closely argued text, Lawrence Martin has demonstrated, to cite the subtitle of his book *Pledge of Allegiance,* the "Americanization of Canada in the Mulroney years." The evidence he marshals is convincing: the Free Trade accords bound the Canadian and U.S. economies closer than they had ever been; legislation introduced in the Trudeau years that was unpopular in Washington because of its perceived nationalistic nature (in particular, the Foreign Investment Review Agency and the National Energy Program) was rescinded; tax reform was revamped and based on the U.S. model; crown corporations were privatized and sold off in record numbers; a variety of advisory councils (many critical of government performance) were closed; support for cultural programs, the Canadian Broadcasting Corporation, and the railway system (all three extremely important in maintaining a cultural identity in a country as vast as Canada) was sharply reduced; concessions were made by the government to a host of U.S.-based economic interests, dealing with everything from film rights to drug patent legislation; social spending was reduced and the universality of social programs, in many ways a sacred trust for Canada, was ended; and trade with the United States increased dramatically during the Mulroney years to the detriment of trade elsewhere. For Martin, then, the 80 percent economic dependency on the United States, the status of an economic branch plant, and the embrace of continentalism have had a devastating effect on Canada. These dramatic changes, "from 1984 to 1992, closed down the Canadian dream of building something unique and better. They were the years when, instead of attempting to contain the American influence, Canada avidly sought out that influence. They were the years when national policy was abandoned, when the goal of the Just Society was forsaken in favour of that of the American Society."[5]

But if Ottawa hurried to harmonize its domestic policies with its U.S. counterparts, it also sought to develop a stand on international relations that was very much in keeping with that of Washington. The Reagan administration was clearly relieved at Mulroney's support, particularly after Pierre Trudeau's barely concealed scorn for U.S. policy in Latin America, its Cold War belligerence best typified by the "Star Wars" plan, and what Trudeau interpreted as a widespread ignorance about North-South issues in general. At one point Lawrence Eagleburger, the under-secretary of state for political affairs, referred to Trudeau's conduct as being "akin to pot-induced behaviour by an erratic leftie."[6] It was a charge that nobody in the State Department would ever consider making about Mulroney. Indeed, secret memos between Washington and the U.S. Embassy in Ottawa waxed eloquent about the fact that Canadian support for U.S. initiatives had never been stronger and that Mulroney was a solid defender of North American values.

"Mulroney's instincts were Cleveland and Palm Springs," noted Mulroney's policy advisor for four years, Charlie McMillan. "He had a huge comfort zone on Canada-U.S. relations. What he didn't understand were Canada-Latin America, Canada-Europe, Canada-Japan relations."[7] McMillan, a friend of Mulroney and an academic specializing in Japan, was exactly right with his insightful comment. Mulroney trusted absolutely in Washington's goals, respected Presidents Reagan and Bush, and was quite prepared to show Ottawa's support for U.S. policies. "Good relations, super relations with the United States" did, then, become the cornerstone of Ottawa's foreign policy during the Mulroney years.

The Mulroney government also supported Reagan and Bush initiatives in the international arena. The only exception was on U.S. policy toward Nicaragua, where Ottawa provided limited development assistance to the Sandinista government. This was largely due to the high profile Canadian NGO presence in the country and a strong lobby against U.S. support for the contras organized by Canadian churches and NGOs. Apart from that minor aid package, however, Ottawa steadfastly refused to criticize Washington's activities in the region. In addition, the prime minister strongly supported the 1989 invasion of Panama following a late-night phone call from the U.S. president. In the 1990–91 Persian Gulf War, despite strong reservations of the Canadian public about the goals of the mission and the commitment of Kuwait to democracy, the Mulroney government responded unquestioningly and sent three Canadian warships. The U.S.-led mission to Somalia, officially under the auspices of the United Nations (as had been

Operation Desert Storm in the Gulf) but very much spearheaded by Washington, was another example of unswerving Canadian support granted swiftly by Mulroney.

In sum, Canadian international policy toward the world at large in many ways was harnessed to support the "new international order," of which the United States, as the last remaining superpower, was the leader. A junior partner in these ventures, Canada quickly earned the reputation as Washington's most dependable ally. A symbol of just how close this relationship had become was George Bush's last weekend at the presidential retreat of Camp David. He chose to invite as his guests not relatives or friends, not faithful colleagues or advisers, but instead the Mulroney family. Additionally, Caroline Mulroney (eldest daughter of the prime minister) chose to make her own way from Harvard, where she was taking an undergraduate degree, while one of his sons traveled directly from the exclusive private prep school in Massachusetts where he was studying. Jeffrey Simpson, a *Globe and Mail* columnist, accurately summarized the relationship between the Mulroney government and the White House in a recent article. There had been trade disputes and minor disagreements between the two governments: "But generally, Canadian foreign policy in the Mulroney era was characterized by a ready-ay-ready attitude towards U.S. initiatives and exceptional harmony in Canadian-US affairs. His departure will represent the high-water mark of Canadian-US harmony for the simple reason that the water cannot go higher."[8]

Canadian Policy toward Latin America

Writing in 1992, Edgar J. Dosman waxed eloquent about "the new look" of Canadian-Latin American relations:

> Canada's relations with Latin America seem to have entered a strikingly new phase since 1989. Not merely through the North American Free Trade Agreement (NAFTA) negotiations but, more broadly, as an activist in the Organization of American States (OAS), a peacekeeper in Central America, and a protagonist in the Haiti débacle. Canada has become an active participant in inter-American affairs.[9]

While this is all true, it is also fair to note the many inconsistencies in the new approach, the determination by Mulroney to harmonize Canadian and U.S. foreign policy objectives, and the tentative, rather uncertain steps taken, as Dosman himself recognizes: "But there is not yet a coherent policy — more a set of partial policies or building blocks. Despite all the positive signs since 1989, Canada's relations with Latin America retain a certain fragility, as if the historic lack of a long-term political commitment still impedes an irreversible reorientation of Canada's relations with the Americas."[10] In his well-argued analysis of the evolution of Canadian foreign policy toward Latin America published in 1994, James Rochlin pointed out that the first major foreign policy review since the one undertaken by Pierre Trudeau seventeen years earlier had been published in 1985 by the Mulroney government: yet whereas a fairly hefty pamphlet on Canadian-Latin American relations had been produced by Trudeau, and despite a noticeable strengthening of commercial and NGO connections in the 1980s, the new Conservative government spent only one page on the topic.[11] Clearly the area was of little interest to Mulroney.

In essence Ottawa's Latin American policy had been in a shambles since the end of the first decade of the Trudeau government. There were several reasons for this disinterest on the part of Ottawa, mainly revolving around more pressing domestic political matters. Moreover, in Trudeau's remaining years his own interest in Latin America decreased noticeably as he devoted himself to the crusade of bringing the two superpowers to reduce in a rational fashion their potential for world destruction. As became obvious following the election of Brian Mulroney, there were also increasingly limited funds to be given for developing countries, and once again domestic concerns played a significant role as to where they were assigned. For example, the strategic value of courting *la Francophonie,* thereby reducing nationalist tendencies in Quebec, a constant concern of the federal government, continued to be one of Mulroney's central goals.

A more profound understanding of the region was held by Secretary of State for External Affairs Joe Clark, particularly after his 1987 visit to Central America. He later developed good channels of communication with some of the foreign ministers of the Río Group, and in particular with Dante Caputo, his Argentine counterpart. Clark's attempts to forge a coherent policy were largely undercut, however, both by world developments and by the prime minister's tendency to ignore Clark and instead fashion his own policies, occasionally at Washington's request. This point should not be underestimated, since the Prime Minister's Office holds sway over virtually all aspects of government departments, which have to tailor their views according to parameters laid out by the prime minister. The prime minister's lack of awareness concerning international affairs noted above by Mulroney's advisor, together with a determination to support Washington's position abroad, acted as a filter through which Canadian policies in Latin America were consistently viewed during this nine-year period. Given the traditional lack of interest in Latin America shown by Ottawa and Brian Mulroney's support of U.S. foreign policy, it was therefore understandable that Canadian policy would differ little from that devised in Washington.

That said, it is also clear that under the tenure of Joe Clark as secretary of state for external affairs in the Mulroney government (1984–91), a sincere attempt was made to pursue a vigorous policy toward Latin America. It can be argued that much of this policy produced more acts of symbolism than of substance, yet it is undoubtedly true that even symbolic gestures were new developments following a virtual neglect of Latin American matters in Ottawa. It can also be argued that, in large part, this renewed interest resulted from increasing debts owed to Canadian banks, the vigorous lobbying by Canadian NGOs and church groups, which had sizable active representation in Central America, and from significant media interest in the region. It is also important to recognize that, given the dramatic economic and political changes taking place in the region, an attempt was made to reinvigorate Canadian policy toward Latin America.

The steps taken included ministerial visits to the region (Clark personally traveled to Central America, while the prime minister visited Mexico), an increased role in the Inter-American Development Bank, greater consultation with external specialists, an active role in supporting the Central American peace process, an increase in bilateral aid to the region, and an enhanced interest in a variety of concerns (narcotics, the environment, human rights, trade, and debt). Some equipment and training by RCMP officers was provided to Colombian officials; short-term bridge loans were extended to Argentina, Mexico, and Brazil; over a hundred officers were assigned to the UN observer force for Central America (ONUCA); Mulroney took a personal interest in restoring the government of Jean-Bertrand Aristide to power in Haiti; and the government provided the funding for the Canada-Latin America Forum (FOCAL), based in Ottawa. Canada's diplomatic representation increased slightly in the region, with a consulate opening in Santo Domingo, the establishment of a satellite office in Quito, and the upgrading of the chargé d'affaires in Guatemala City to ambassadorial level. In short, it was an attempt to develop the basis for a long-term, consistent political strategy for Canada as it sought, in Joe Clark's words, to convert its "house" in the region into a "home."[12] Moreover, following an initially vacillating approach to the OAS, Ottawa finally did see some effective Canadian input in that organization, particularly in leadership of the Unit for the Promotion of Democracy and in attempts to restore the democratically elected Aristide government in Haiti. In general, though, the impetus resulting from the tenure of Joe Clark waned when he left the portfolio. With the notable exception of bilateral policy with Mexico, the Mulroney government shelved the Clark initiatives.

In sum, it is fair to say that during this period Canada did seek to develop a coherent policy toward Latin America, particularly during the years when Joe Clark was at the helm of foreign policy. Yet it is important to note that Latin America has always been a low priority for Canadian governments, regardless of the political party in power. An important ideological note was, however, injected into the equation from the mid-1980s, with a determination by the Mulroney government not to complicate matters with the United States, at that time engaged in flexing its military might in Central America. It was this fear of endangering the "special relationship" with Washington that had acted, and clearly continues to act, as a filter through which Canada views Latin America. It is against this traditional background of neglect, deference to Washington, occasional insights and interest, potential for commercial profit, and a lack of a solid, clearly developed policy, that one can appreciate the evolution of Canada-Cuba relations.

The Evolution of Canadian-Cuban Relations, 1984–93

"We're helping Castro hang on," thundered *Toronto Sun* columnist, Eric Margolis. Decrying the acts of Canadian tourists who dared to travel to Cuba ("Every dollar spent in Cuba by Canadian tourists helps keep Fidel Castro and his communists in power"), he condemned the hypocrisy of the Canadian government for maintaining trade sanctions against South Africa while not working actively to bring down the totalitarian dictatorship of Cuba. He then asked rhetorically why Ottawa continued to back "Castro's ever more repressive police state," and answered his own question: "Because it means business for a few Canadian exporters. Because aiding Senor Castro pleases the NDP, left-wing labor unions and church groups. And, perhaps, it's a feeble way of showing some independence from the often overbearing Americans."[13]

While the tabloid journalist fumed at what he saw as Ottawa's hypocrisy and weak-kneed response to a "brutal, squalid, crumbling police state," his colleague at the *Toronto Star,* Slinger, encouraged even closer ties between Cuba and Canada. In a tongue-in-cheek article, he even urged Ottawa to consider adopting Cuba as a province of Canada. The timing was perfect, he noted: "It is a large island in the Caribbean that has come unstuck from its moorings and is bobbing around with no place to turn. 'Cuba,' we should say, 'turn to us.'" Lamenting the recent passing of the eccentric former premier of Newfoundland Joey Smallwood, he noted how political life would improve if Cuba were to become a Canadian province: "There isn't a serving premier today who has ever been accused of livening things up. Joey was charismatic, unpredictable, eccentric, a rebel, a folk hero. The same goes for Fidel." Slinger then went on to make two compelling arguments for this union: Canadian vacationers would be paying money back into the national economy and would no longer be supporting that of Mexico, Florida, Barbados, and the Dominican Republic, and "besides, Canada's about the only place left that is comfortable with socialists. But it's not simply an ideological soul-mate we're after. We're after a place where the slush doesn't stay on the ground until August. Someplace warm, growing hotter by noon, where the palm trees wave."[14]

More seriously, what was the official view that Ottawa cultivated of Havana during the Mulroney years? There have been a variety of developments and trends (in essence of a minor nature), but in general the essence of the relationship during this period was defined by Canada's roving ambassador for Latin America, Richard Gorham, in November 1989:

> Briefly stated, Canada's relations with Cuba over the past three decades have been, and continue to be, correct, cordial and as close as can be expected between two nations which have important differences on foreign policy issues, security questions, political and economic structure, and political philosophy. . . . These differences between us are a fact of life well known to all and I do not need to labor the point. Much more important, I believe, is to focus on the fact that in spite of these differences, our bilateral relations with Cuba have always been correct and cordial—indeed, friendly and close up to the point where our differences impede further proximity.[15]

Gorham, probably one of Canada's most experienced diplomats at the time, outlined with great clarity the dynamic at play. "Cordial and correct," but with firm limitations preventing greater proximity. That translated into acceptance of the Canadian diplomatic norm of respecting the established government of the day, civilized diplomatic intercourse, a polite exchange of information, and encouragement for the development of enhanced exports.

The other side of the coin was that, given Canada's close relationship with the United States, Ottawa would also look out for its ally's interests, while at the same time it would not go beyond carefully outlined parameters to assist Cuba. Hence the lack of export credits, criticism of Cuban foreign and domestic policy, support for Washington's human rights stand on Cuba, the lack of development aid, the decision not to prosecute American companies that pressured their Canadian subsidiaries to refrain from trading with Cuba (despite the Foreign Extraterritorial Measures Act, which was introduced precisely to protect the right of Canadian businesses to do so), and finally the lack of international humanitarian assistance following the March 1993 "storm of the century."

The Clark Initiatives of 1989–91

A rare exception to this trend did occur, however, during the last two years of Joe Clark's tenure as secretary of state for external affairs (1989–91), when some significant diplomatic initiatives were undertaken to explore the possibility of closer bilateral ties. From 1984 until that time, relations had maintained their traditional rhythm, with commercial questions constituting the center of bilateral attention. Then there was a flurry of activity, much of it sparked by a personal interest of Clark himself. In a major address at the University of Calgary on February 1, 1990, on Canadian policy toward Latin America, he outlined the goals of an invigorated interest in the region. Among the issues mentioned were the following references to Cuba:

> There is one further area which warrants the attention of all states in the Americas. That is the place of Cuba. Cuba has isolated itself from this hemisphere. Many states in this hemisphere have isolated themselves from Cuba. No one would deny that Cuba has had a role in the current troubles in Central America. And few can look at the economic facts and not conclude that Cuba has suffered by exclusion from the hemisphere. I will not ascribe blame here. I simply state that some of the current problems of Latin America could become more manageable if Cuba were brought back into the family of hemispheric nations. Clearly the problems here are not easy to overcome. There is a lot of history, remembered personally and bitterly by influential people throughout the Americas. Perceptions and prejudices have taken firm roots. But I refuse to believe these are insurmountable.[16]

This position was echoed by Clark's successor, Barbara McDougall, in an address to the OAS General Assembly in 1991: "We look forward to the time when the vision of the founders of the OAS for a universal hemispheric forum can be realized and Cuba will retake its place in the Organization as a full member of the hemispheric family."[17]

Two months after Clark's address, Assistant Deputy Minister for External Affairs (and subsequently Canadian ambassador to the United Nations) Louise Fréchette made the first visit to Cuba by a senior government official in many years. In an interview shortly before she left for Cuba, Joe Clark shed some light on how he regarded Cuban-U.S. relations at that time, what he considered to be troubling irritants, and what he thought

Canada's role might be in seeking to establish a climate for dialogue between Washington and Havana. He expressed concern, for instance, at U.S. government-funded TV Martí's broadcasts to Cuba ("I don't think those broadcasts are very helpful," he added), while also noting with regret Fidel Castro's condemnations of political reform in Eastern Europe: "There's not a lot of evidence that Fidel Castro is prepared to abandon his approach."

The most interesting section of the interview, however, dealt with what Clark saw as a potential role for Canada in the ongoing tension between Washington and Havana. Speaking about the possibility of helping to resolve the decades-long conflict, Clark played down the importance of possible Canadian mediation: "We are deliberately not getting involved in condemnations of either side. We are trying to go in and see what we can do." Clark added that he had brought up the issue of encouraging greater dialogue between Cuba and the United States with both Soviet Foreign Minister Eduard Shevardnadze and U.S. Secretary of State James Baker, concluding: "Canada can't solve the contest between Cuba and the United States, but we may well be able to create some conditions . . . to create some room where the principal actors might move."[18]

The visit of Louise Fréchette (April 25–28, 1990) was quite successful. In addition to meeting with Vice-President Carlos Rafael Rodríguez, the president of the National Bank and two deputy-foreign ministers, she and David Morrison (Ottawa's knowledgeable Cuba Desk officer) also had a long meeting with President Fidel Castro. Finally she gave a talk on Canadian-Cuban relations to local students at the Higher Institute of International Relations. The official communiqués released after the meetings stressed the upbeat nature of the meetings: Canada was seeking to develop a dialogue with Cuba on regional and bilateral issues. "We've always had good relations with Cuba and we propose to improve them even more," noted Fréchette.[19]

Cuban coverage of the visit stressed two main themes, the OAS and the viability of Canada mediating U.S.-Cuban tensions. Fréchette was cited as claiming that Ottawa was in favor of Havana rejoining the Organization of American States. She also commented that the inter-American community had the responsibility to create the appropriate conditions of consensus for that to happen. It was therefore necessary to reduce tensions and encourage a better understanding of the central issues. It was made clear, as Joe Clark had outlined, that Ottawa was "prepared, and willing, to contribute in an independent fashion, and according to its abilities, to a relaxation of tensions between Cuba and the United States."[20] This was not exactly the same as mediating, it was pointed out, since for that to occur both sides needed to be prepared to negotiate, which was not the case at that time. Nevertheless Canada would continue to push for a dialogue, which it deemed to be most important, and would be willing to help when called on. Ottawa was signaling its availability and interest in promoting channels of dialogue: a significant development because it had not occurred for several decades.

It can be argued that there were two divergent directions concerning a Cuban policy for Canada being pursued by diplomats and policy advisors at this time. On the one hand was the position held by Clark and others, who thought that the inter-American community would be more complete and more balanced with Cuba's inclusion, and that three decades of the same U.S. policy toward Havana had been fruitless and needed to change. It was time for a different approach, and Clark thought that Cuba would respond to a reasonable strategy. What that meant for Canada, therefore, was the pursuit of greater channels of dialogue, and an offer to Havana that, if Cuba desired, Ottawa would be prepared to use its good offices to encourage Washington to sit at the negotiating table.

On the other hand were the hawks of the department, usually resolute supporters of Washington, who were convinced that Fidel Castro's days were numbered and that, with the demise of the Soviet Union, it was only necessary to stay the course and maintain pressure on Havana for the revolutionary government to fall. In March and November 1991, for example, this viewpoint was clearly expressed by Jean-Paul Hubert, former diplomat in Havana and at the time Canada's ambassador to the OAS. When asked about the differences between Canadian and U.S. policies toward Cuba, he answered that Cuba was seen by both countries as a rotten apple tree that was in danger of imminent collapse: the only difference between the perspectives of Washington and Ottawa was that the former wanted to shake the tree and speed up the process, while the latter was prepared for it to fall with its own weight.[21] The startling contrast between his views and those of Joe Clark speak volumes about the lack of a cohesive political strategy toward Cuba, a fact that was often painfully obvious.

The Human Rights Issue

One of the major concerns of critics of the revolutionary government was its stand on human rights. It was an omnipresent concern of Ottawa and was the official reason given in 1993 for not granting development assistance to Cuba. In fact, when NGO and church leaders were lobbying for immediate humanitarian assistance in the wake of the March storm and the outbreak of optic neuritis, it was a refrain that Department of External Affairs representatives continued to cite while denying their requests. A study of Canada's voting record at the UN Human Rights Commission in

Geneva shows that it has supported all U.S. resolutions on Cuba. But during 1990 and 1991, when resolutions condemning Cuba were presented, an unusual development occurred. Considerable pressure was put by Washington on other Western countries to cosponsor these resolutions, which were supported by West Germany, the United Kingdom, the Netherlands, and Belgium. Canada refused to do so. Following the forty-sixth session of the General Assembly (October–December 1991), however, a brusque change of position can be noted, as Ottawa's moderate stand was replaced by a hawkish tone. Indeed in the February–March 1992 session, Canada not only supported the U.S. proposal to have a special rapporteur on the human rights situation appointed, but also cosponsored the proposal. The demand is now a standard feature of Canadian policy on Cuba.

On December 17, 1992, Ottawa took the unusal step of calling in the Cuban chargé d'affaires to express its official displeasure at the way in which Cuban dissident and leader of the Cuban Commission for Human Rights and National Reconciliation Elizardo Sánchez had been beaten by Rapid Response Brigades. At the same time, Canadian ambassador Julie Loranger was requested to present officially Ottawa's concern to the Ministry of External Relations. A communiqué was also published by the Department of External Affairs in which Secretary of State for External Affairs Barbara McDougall noted: "Canadians are deeply troubled by the attack last week on Mr. Elizardo Sánchez. . . . I call upon the Cuban authorities to stop the harassment of dissidents."[22]

It can be argued then that, with the exception of the period of peak interest of Joe Clark when Ottawa was seriously interested in pursuing closer ties with Cuba, the rest of the Mulroney years showed a definite neglect of Cuban matters. At the same time, serious consular problems, which Ottawa or Havana could have exploited easily, have been dealt with swiftly and correctly. The relationship may be somewhat cool, at times even strained, but it has always been important to both countries to resolve differences as constructively as possible.

The Business Connection

There was one basic thread of Canadian corporate activity during the latter years of the Mulroney government, as the Canadian business sector gradually recognized the business potential in Cuba, particularly after the disappearance of the Soviet bloc, and of course with U.S. companies still legally unable to compete for the lucrative Cuban market and investment possibilities. This low-key Canadian commercial campaign was carried out steadily, and despite a lack of initiative on the part of the Canadian government, which did very little to promote bilateral trade, and in some cases commercial counselors in Havana who discouraged initiatives, business continued to follow a fairly stable pattern.

The headlines dealing with Canadian investments from a variety of sources are worth noting: "Cuba-Canadá: Considerable aumento comercial y buenas perspectivas," *Granma Resumen Semanal* (November 18, 1990, 8), "Trade with Canada buoyant," *Cuba Business* (December 1991, 7), "Cuba glitters in investors' eyes," *Globe and Mail* (August 2, 1993, B4), "U.S. embargo aids Canadian ventures," *Toronto Star* (May 3, 1994, C1), and "Going capitalist on the Canbuck," *Maclean's* (February 13, 1995, 45) to cite only a few. What is common to them is the upbeat tone as the rapidly growing number of investments and exports was noted:

> You can see more and more of them every month in Cuba—Canadians and their investments. From French Canadian sunbathers at Playa Girón in southern Matanzas province to onshore oil derricks just outside Varadero, Canadians are becoming more visible throughout this Caribbean nation.
>
> It's not only the "Made in Canada" logo—on the automatic hand-drying machines in the bathroom of the Hotel Habana Libre or on the cheese-and-cookie packages on Cubana flights—that is an increasingly familiar sight.
>
> Half a dozen Canadian firms have signed joint-venture exploration or mining agreements with the Cuban Ministry of Basic Industry.[23]

During the latter years of the Mulroney government Canadian investors and exporters discovered the potential in Cuba, as well as the fact that their government was doing remarkably little to foster trade with this rapidly developing market. By the time that Brian Mulroney left office, Canada held an enviable position among nations trading with Cuba: Canadians constituted the largest number of tourists to Cuban beaches (approximately one-quarter), Canadian corporations had established the second-largest number of joint ventures (after the Spanish), and the largest single company working in Cuba was Canadian—Sherritt International. From the new air terminal at Varadero to much of the food sold in hard currency stores, from oil exploration in Matanzas to hotel management in Oriente, from airport landing equipment to hotel reservation systems, from Labatt's beer to Nova Scotian fish, the Canadian presence had become unmistakable. And almost all of it had been undertaken by individual businesspeople, with remarkably little support from Ottawa.

Despite some initial difficulties, Canadian investment has increased apace. Significantly, this fast-moving development was carried out in the climate of a diplomatic chill in Ottawa, with a tradition of U.S. legislative hostility to hamper efforts, and with limited support in Havana. At the same time, the weekly flights from Montreal and Havana bore witness to the dogged pursuit of commercial opportunities by entrepreneurs, laden with samples and glossy flyers. Canadian businesses that have done well in Cuba have thus done so through their own initiative.

At first glance Canadian exports did not appear that promising. They fell from $330 million (including reexports) in 1985 to $133 million in 1993. Conversely, Cuban exports to Canada rose dramatically, from $44 million to $171 million during the same time. It is important to bear in mind two factors: the extremely limited spending power of the Cubans following the collapse of the socialist bloc, since in essence they were reduced to approximately one-quarter of their purchasing capacity of 1989; and the precise nature of Canadian exports and imports. Much of the decline between 1991 and 1992 was due to the end of the purchase of wheat by the Soviet Union for Cuba. By contrast, the sale of machinery and spare parts continued to increase.

The U.S. legislative hostility is perhaps a traditionally underestimated factor that needs to be examined, since it clearly was a factor in hindering an expanded Canadian role. As was noted in other chapters, Washington had sought with some frequency to pressure allies to follow the official U.S. line on Cuba. During the Mulroney years two attempts were made to limit Canadian commercial ties with Cuba. The first, in 1990, was the Mack amendment (named after Florida Senator Connie Mack), which sought to make it illegal for subsidiaries of U.S. companies to do business in Cuba. Ottawa was opposed for several reasons: first because it represented an estimated U.S.$22 million in lost sales by the companies in question, but also because the extraterritorial nature of the legislation was viewed as an intrusion into Canadian sovereignty. It also provided the Mulroney government with the opportunity to divert domestic criticism of U.S. policy in the Persian Gulf crisis by showing that Ottawa was in full control of its foreign policy, and not blindly following Washington's dictates. Canada thus responded quickly, with Secretary of State for External Affairs Joe Clark introducing the Foreign Extraterritorial Measures Act (actually passed six years earlier), which called on Canadian-based companies, including subsidiaries of U.S. companies, to ignore the proposed Mack amendment. They were also ordered to report to Canadian authorities instructions received from their U.S. head offices that might contravene Ottawa's legislation. Eventually President George Bush vetoed the proposed bill, making the Canadian position a moot point, but not before a scathing attack from Senator Mack, for whom Canada's action "does not befit a great and free nation and should be reversed. . . . Now, as the wave of freedom sweeping the globe leaves [Cuban leader Fidel] Castro's tyranny high and dry, is not the time for free nations to help rescue Castro's economy. Now is not the time for business-as-usual masquerading as high principle. . . . How ironic that when Castro's friends around the globe have abandoned him one by one, that Canada, of all nations, would defiantly proclaim her right and intention to trade with Cuba."[24]

Not so successful, however, were Canadian objections to a subsequent piece of legislation, known as the Cuban Democracy Act or, more commonly, as the Torricelli Bill after its sponsor, Robert Torricelli of New Jersey, and passed in October 1992. The domestic political circumstances had changed, since it was now an election year, and the Democratic contender for the presidency (Bill Clinton) had assiduously courted the Cuban American vote in an unsuccessful campaign to win Florida. Once again Ottawa condemned the bill, brandishing Canadian blocking legislation and threatening Canadian companies that did not respect it with fines (up to $8,500) and even jail sentences (5 years). On October 13, 1992, Secretary of State for External Affairs Barbara McDougall and Minister of Justice Kim Campbell announced a fresh blocking order, which, in the words of Campbell, was intended "to protect the primacy of Canadian trade law and policy. If left unchallenged, the measure passed by Congress on October 5, 1992 would be an unacceptable intrusion of U.S. law into Canada and could adversely affect significant Canadian interests in relation to international trade or commerce. Canadian companies will carry out business under the laws and regulations of Canada, not those of a foreign country."[25] Denis Boulet, a spokesperson for External Affairs, expanded on this position. For Canada the legislation was a violation of the "primacy of Canadian law and trade policy," and he noted: "We cannot accept this. . . . What is at stake is the extraterritorial application of a U.S. law that would usurp a company's right to do business according to Canadian trade laws."[26]

In the end, however, of the many U.S.-based companies in Canada that ignored Canadian legislation and instead listened to their head office, not one was prosecuted by Ottawa. Estimates vary between 12 and 20 companies, with names such as Pepsi Cola, Heinz, Eli Lilly, and American Express figuring prominently. A process of self-censorship ensued in these companies, leaving both Cubans and External Affairs officials frustrated. An editorial in the *Globe and Mail* two years earlier when the Mack amendment had been introduced was prophetic in its musings: "One unattractive possibility is that U.S. subsidiaries may simply avoid trading with Cuba. While the Canadian law can attempt to coerce companies in Canada to carry out planned sales to Cuba, it is powerless to stop a wry U.S. subsidiary from ignoring Cuban markets altogether."[27] The Department of External Affairs then passed along the cases to the Department of Justice, where they appear to have been lost in a legal labyrinth. Despite much nationalistic chest-thumping, it is significant that there was not the political will to pursue the government's clearly stated policy; in addition, exports to Cuba from U.S. subsidiaries based in Canada steadily dried up.

The Changing Times

The predominant note in bilateral relations set during the Mulroney era was one of disinterest and neglect, not malevolent or mean-spirited, yet deliberate neglect nevertheless. There was also a sense of a distinct lack of direction, with the result that Canada's secretary of state for external affairs was contradicted in at least two public presentations by the country's ambassador to the OAS, who clearly rejected his minister's Cuba policy. This rudderless policy could also be seen in Canada's voting policy at the United Nations, first supporting Cuba's condemnation of the U.S. embargo in 1992 and then abstaining in 1993. A weak defense was offered by Ambassador Fréchette,[28] and it was apparent that despite overwhelming international rejection of the embargo, the Mulroney government was not prepared to criticize the Bush administration.

The common denominator of the Canadian government's approach to Cuba during this time was, then, one of fundamental disinterest, combined with a good measure of deference to Washington. Brian Mulroney, driven by his own distinctive continentalist vision for Canada's future, was not prepared to undertake any initiative toward the Cuban file, particularly when pressure from Washington resulted. True, the Conservative government had introduced the Foreign Extraterritorial Measures Act in 1990 and again in October 1992, designed to encourage Canadian subsidiaries of U.S.-based multinationals to resist legislation passed in Washington that outlawed such trade. And it was also worth noting that in December of 1992, in a speech given at Harvard University, Mulroney stated his disagreement with the Bush administration over the issue of trading with Cuba, while noting that Canadian companies, whether branch plants of U.S. companies or not, were obliged to respect Canadian law.

Yet between 1992 and the time of writing, the number of companies sued by the Canadian government for not respecting Canadian legislation was zero. Ottawa argued that these companies were Canadian, employing thousands of Canadian workers and paying taxes in Canada, and therefore were obliged to respect Canadian legislation. In all, twenty cases of subsidiaries allegedly breaking this Canadian law were passed from the Department of External Affairs to the Justice Department. Yet the silence from the government was deafening, leading columnist Jeff Sallot to write a provocative column in the *Globe and Mail,* "Don't let Washington call the shots."[29] While a case can be made to show that a process of self-censorship resulted, since the companies in question quickly learned not to inform External Affairs that their head office in the United States had obliged them to stop exporting to Cuba, in cases where the Cuban embassy produced evidence to show the Canadian government that the subsidiary in question was instead respecting U.S. legislation, there was little interest in pursuing the case. This is hardly surprising, however, for despite the hard-hitting nature of the legislation, it is difficult to imagine the CEO of HJ Heinz languishing in a Canadian prison. All bark and little bite was the nature of the government's legislation.

A fitting illustration of Canada's deferential position to U.S. interests can be seen in an incident that appears to be totally unrelated to the world of international politics. In early 1993 the Toronto Blue Jays sought to recruit a renowned third baseman from Cuba. Omar Linares was interested in moving to Canada, and the Blue Jays were equally keen to engage his services. Unfortunately major league baseball clubs were expected to respect the U.S. embargo, whether their home was in Canada or the United States, as the Toronto management was told in no uncertain terms. It would be seen as taking advantage of troubled relations between Havana and Washington if a Canadian baseball team were to seek to abuse this dynamic by importing a Cuban player. A proposal was considered that would have permitted Linares to play only at the Sky Dome in Toronto, but that too was deemed too radical by baseball's leaders. As a result, Linares remained in Cuba, with the Canadian government refusing to give any sign of discomfort at the U.S. pressure and the Blue Jays management refusing to pursue the matter—a situation that led to an outspoken editorial in the Ottawa *Citizen:* "A real *Canadian* baseball team, of course, would be more interested in getting the best players than in toadying to America's Cold War paranoia."[30]

At the same time that the official line of the government remained intransigent, however, it is interesting to note that pressure for a rapprochement with Cuba continued to build, both from the NGOs, which saw in Cuba a country with a most successful social network that was slipping badly, and from the business community, which increasingly saw in Cuba tremendous business potential. Ultimately these groups managed to advance the government agenda, regardless of Prime Minister Mulroney's neglect.

Another background factor that needs to be mentioned was the overall objective image of Cuba presented in the Canadian media. In general Canadian media coverage (notwithstanding the very conservative tabloid *Toronto Sun*) was fairly balanced, expressing concern at the human rights situation, yet praising social gains made by the revolution. When compared with mainstream U.S. coverage, for example, its Canadian counterpart seemed downright radical, despite its offering criticism of the Cuban system. The fact was that ideological concerns about Cuba were less important in Canada, in no small measure because several hundred thousand Canadians had vacationed there (largely because it is the cheapest place for vacationers to fly to escape from the long harsh winter and is safer than Florida) and felt less threatened by Cuba's existence than did the U.S. body politic.

Another factor to note is the development of solidarity activity with Cuba. Canadian solidarity groups supporting Cuba had risen from three in 1990 to nearly three dozen five years later. An important symbolic act in fusing their interests was a 1993 campaign organized in 10 Canadian cities to buy 15 tons of milk powder, which was then exported to Cuba. In 1993 Canadian solidarity groups also participated with the U.S.-based Pastors for Peace group, sending a caravan of trucks carrying medical and school supplies to join up with their U.S. counterparts—activities that continue. One final background factor should be noted: the continuing tourism boom, which was a key element in allaying fears about Cuba. The number of Canadian tourists had continued to increase steadily during this period, from 24,000 in 1984 to 85,000 by 1992 and 150,000 by 1995.

A variety of other initiatives at the grassroots level also took root: Canadian youth work brigades traveled to Cuba, protocols between several Canadian and Cuban universities were signed, and cultural activities were expanded. The film *Hello Hemingway* was the joint winner in the best film category at the 1992 Atlantic Film Festival in Halifax, while in 1993 *Spirits of Havana,* a CD recorded in Havana's EGREM studios and featuring Canadian and Cuban musicians, won a Juno award (the Canadian equivalent of the Grammy awards in the United States). A useful development was an academic conference, held in Halifax in November 1989, which analyzed three decades of the Cuban revolutionary process. Attended by more than 600 Cuba-watchers, including a 30-person Cuban delegation headed by Ricardo Alarcón, and Cuba specialists from Australia to Zimbabwe, the conference was important because it provided a forum for a balanced analysis of Cuba, warts and all.

Church groups continued to request the government to revise its policy toward Cuba. The Anglican Church had traditionally enjoyed a solid working relationship with the Episcopal Church in Cuba, since after the revolution the diocese of Cuba had been under the metropolitan authority of three archbishops, one of whom was the primate of Canada. The sixty-eighth annual meeting of the Maritime Conference of the United Church (the leading Protestant denomination, combining the Methodists, Congregationalists, and the majority of Presbyterians) in May 1992, for example, called on the Canadian government to work toward the lifting of the U.S. blockade, and to promote increased trade. Later that year the church's General Council went further, calling for humanitarian assistance to Cuba. The general secretary of the United Church, in a letter to the secretary of state for external affairs, addressed the two traditional justifications given by Ottawa for not granting aid (Cuba's involvement in Angola and Cuba's developed social network), noting: "Neither Cuban military involvement abroad or lack of need can be cited as current justification for not granting Canadian aid to Cuba. The situation of need in the areas of food and medicine is acute and Canada has the capacity and, in our view, the moral obligation to respond."[31] Not content to wait for a government response, which produced very little assistance and significantly after most other developed nations had done so, between December 1991 and July 1992, the Canadian churches (mainly the Anglican and United Churches) provided $250,000 worth of medical and hospital supplies, shipped from Montreal.

Among the NGO community, OXFAM-Canada and Canadian University Services Overseas (CUSO) were the most prominent in calling for a revamped policy. CUSO had sent its first field staff officer to Cuba in 1970, and during most of that decade it was the only foreign voluntary agency working there. Among its projects was one at the Ciudad Universitaria José Antonio Echeverría (CUJAE) in Havana to develop the engineering faculty. CIDA provided $1.1 million, and Canadian university professors taught 120 graduate-level courses. Short-term professional visits also occurred in other development projects, increasing swine production, the quality of poultry production, and cattle research. Of these the most important was the development of a breed of cattle called the F-1, which was a cross between the Cuban Zebu and the Canadian Holstein-Fresian. Finally, other projects involving tropical medicine, plant pharmacology, and public health were funded. In sum, CUSO's involvement was widely seen as being positive; Cuban research capacity improved substantially and food stocks on the island increased, while these activities also stimulated Canadian exports to Cuba: "Canada's trade surplus soared from $45 million in 1971 to a 1980 level of more than $225 million; much of the increase represented sales of Canadian cattle feed—a reflection of CUSO's involvement in Cuba."[32]

OXFAM-Canada had been involved in development assistance projects throughout Latin America and was widely recognized as an effective, progressive NGO that spent remarkably little on administration and delivered quality development assistance projects. By 1993 these two NGOs, together with the United Church, the Anglican Church, and Toronto's Jesuit Centre for Social Faith and Justice, had joined forces to lobby for the Conservative government to provide humanitarian assistance to Cuba. Finally on August 20, 1993, their efforts paid off, and a grant of $250,000 to purchase vitamins and medical supplies was approved by CIDA. Encouraged by CIDA's decision, John Foster, the national secretary of OXFAM-Canada, wrote to Perrin Beatty, then secretary of state for external affairs on September 20, 1993, stating that his organization was "most concerned that Canada's continuing refusal to restore Cuba to the list of countries eligible for Canadian humanitarian aid is causing completely unnecessary hardship for the Cuban people." He condemned the U.S. embargo of Cuba, noting that "Causing hardship and starvation is not an acceptable way to achieve political goals. It is equally unacceptable, in our view, for Canada to restrict humanitarian aid for the Cuban people because of their government's human rights record. Especially when that human rights record is substantially better than some countries which are receiving Canadian aid."[33] With the donation of vitamins and medical supplies and despite significant reservations among many Canadian policymakers, a significant breach in the wall of official opposition had been made.

Even parliamentarians began to take initiatives independently of the government. By the summer of 1993, twenty members of Parliament and senators from all major political parties had formed the Canada-Cuba Friendship Group on Parliament Hill. The Havana-Ontario Friendship Group, between the two provincial governments, was also organized in January 1993. At a special ceremony in Havana, mayor Pedro Chávez awarded the speaker of Ontario's legislature, David Warner, with the keys to the city of Havana, and member of the Ontario legislature Jim Henderson, who had led several business and academic delegations to Cuba, the July 26th Order. Material aid had also been provided by the provincial government, which donated funding for the 1991 Pan American Games, held in Havana, and various Ontario cities, which donated more than 100 used buses. Several trips to Cuba by Canadian politicians, representing all major political parties, yet without the support of the federal government, also took place during this time.

Finally, perhaps the key development during this period in bringing about the much-awaited policy change toward Cuba was the burgeoning business interest. Despite a general disinterest in Cuba shown by Ottawa and regardless of the extremely limited trade credits and lack of CIDA support,

Canadian businesspeople saw great commercial possibilities there and started to invest in and sell to Cuba. In April 1991 a telex from the Canadian embassy to Ottawa explained the potential for business in Cuba: "Despite present economic difficulties current reorientation of trade from Eastern Europe to West still makes Cuba a promising market that provides rewards for ongoing and patient marketing efforts. . . . Present is appropriate time to capitalize on this market given growing absence of trade relations with former COMECON countries and Cuba's desire to trade with Canada."[34] Investment was soon flowing into Cuba.

The groundwork had thus been prepared for the rapprochement that started after the Mulroney government had passed the torch to his successor, Kim Campbell, only to see her unceremoniously dumped by the Canadian electorate several months later. During the new government of Jean Chrétien, hardly a Cuba-supporter or political radical, the bilateral relationship would enter a new and very different phase.

6

Back in Business
The Chrétien Approach

Canadians are proud of the relationship they have enjoyed for so long with the people of Cuba. The 50 years of uninterrupted official relations we have enjoyed are proof, I believe, of our openness to the world, and of our desire to keep an open dialogue, whatever the differences of view that we may have. Canada has chosen to maintain its relations with Cuba, while other nations have chosen the path of isolation. We believe, however, that talking with people of a different mind makes us think, and helps us grow.

Speaking on April 24, 1995, at an official state dinner given in honor of Roberto Robaina, the minister of foreign relations of Cuba, Gilbert Parent, speaker of the House of Commons, explained the official Canadian position on Cuba under the Chrétien government. As can be seen from the sentiments expressed above, a noticeable difference had occurred since the fall of 1993, when Jean Chrétien was elected to lead the Canadian government. Boasting that he was an industrious "Chevrolet" prime minister in comparison to Mulroney's luxurious, self-indulgent "Cadillac" administration, and emphasizing that expanding foreign trade was to be his central goal in foreign policy, the wily veteran politician skillfully employed the Cuban situation as a means of emphasizing fundamental differences with his predecessor.

This chapter seeks to examine the rapid development of bilateral relations since late 1993 and to assess the nature of that growth. So much has happened during that time that it is difficult to know which initiatives deserve most credit. Individually, they emphasize the fact that the diplomatic relationship is indeed perceived as being mutually beneficial, while collectively they provide solid evidence of the less ideological, strongly pragmatic style of Jean Chrétien.

Cuba for him was never the issue that it had been for his mentor, Pierre Trudeau. And in ordinary circumstances the fiftieth anniversary of the establishment of official bilateral relations (March 1995) would have been merely a diplomatic footnote. Yet the growth in commercial relations, evolving ties between Canadian NGOs and their Cuban counterparts, a steady flow of high-ranking politicians between both countries, continued tourism trends, and renewed Canadian foreign policy interests in Latin America all made for a comparatively high level of interest in Ottawa. By 1997, more than 180,000 Canadian tourists were wintering in Cuba (the second largest single nationality of tourists), Canada was Cuba's leading trading partner, and bilateral relations had been strengthened as a result of the Helms-Burton law. A sea change had obviously taken place. While not a burning issue in Canadian foreign policy, nevertheless the Cuban question allowed the new government to adopt a less ideologically rigid stance, and to pursue, cautiously and in a carefully incremental fashion, increased bilateral ties. It is significant that, whereas hardly a minister of substance from either country made a courtesy call to the other's capital during the nine-year Mulroney period, Fisheries Minister Brian Tobin and the minister responsible for Latin America and Africa, Christine Stewart, would do so within a year of the new government's taking power (as did two of Canada's ten premiers); on the Cuban side, Minister of Foreign Relations Roberto Robaina, President of the National Assembly Ricardo Alarcón, and Deputy Minister of Foreign Investment Raúl Taladrid had also visited to pay their respects.

Creating Distance from Washington

When the Chrétien government was elected on October 25, 1993, it assumed a foreign policy that was in a shambles and widely perceived as revolving excessively around appeasing U.S. interests. One of the first things to be dismantled, therefore, was the rather sycophantic relationship that Prime Minister Mulroney had studiously pursued with Presidents Reagan and Bush—and one of the reasons he had been rejected by the electorate. When he was campaigning in the fall of 1993, Liberal party leader Chrétien often joked that Prime Minister Mulroney used to say "yes" to Washington even before the phone rang. By contrast, Jean Chrétien, a smart tactician and old-style populist, campaigned for office "loudly proclaiming that he was not going to try to be Bill Clinton's best buddy and he didn't care whether he is ever invited to schmooze at Camp David."[1] Opinion polls for several years had shown that Canadians felt uneasy at Mulroney's deference to Presidents Reagan and Bush. Chrétien, whose finely honed political instincts urged him to lose no opportunity to distance himself from his predecessor, and to be seen to be doing so, quickly set himself the goal of appearing more independent in developing relations with Washington. For his part, President Clinton, who made his first state visit to Ottawa in February 1995 and attended the G–7 meetings in Halifax in June of that year, assisted Chrétien in distancing himself from the "camp-follower" image of Mulroney. Gone were the extravaganzas and large state dinners of before, and the meetings held often apparently just for the sake of meeting. In their place a workmanlike attitude, complete with clearly defined goals, was established.

The February visit came fully two years after Brian Mulroney had flown to Washington to greet President Clinton for the first time since the U.S. president had taken office. In recent times it had become normal practice for the prime minister and the president, protectors of the "world's largest undefended border," to meet shortly after a change of government in either country. Mulroney had visited Ronald Reagan within two weeks of becoming prime minister in 1984. By contrast, Chrétien waited three and a half years before an official state visit. He and Clinton had already met and spoke regularly by telephone, but both observed the prime minister's desire to maintain the new image—discreet and businesslike. At their first meeting, in Washington in April 1997, in their bilateral discussions and in the context of Helms-Burton, they agreed to disagree over Castro's Cuba.

The New Foreign Policy of Ottawa: Trade above All

The Chrétien government has changed Canadian foreign policy, and the prime minister has fostered this development in his traditional, undemonstrative but quietly competent fashion. One key change can be seen in what at first glance might not appear that important: the name of the government sector that oversees the policy. When Canada was a dominion of Great Britain, most foreign policy decisions were taken in London. Then in 1909 Prime Minister Wilfrid Laurier created the Department of External Affairs. Under Chrétien, however, two significant changes took place: the new name for the organization became the Department of Foreign Affairs and International Trade and two new subcabinet posts were created, namely secretary of state for Asia-Pacific affairs, and secretary of state for Latin American and African affairs, the latter position being filled by Christine Stewart, a Spanish-speaking Member of Parliament with many years of NGO experience in Central America. Both new positions indicated the importance of these two geographical areas for the new government, especially because of the potential for enhanced trade that they represented.

These changes within the new ministry were far more than mere cosmetic tinkering. Instead they emphasized the new direction for the government as it pursued fresh foreign policy and international trade opportunities, particularly in Asia and Latin America, as possible counterweights to the U.S. market. While nowhere nearly as dramatic as the Trudeau concept of a Third Option (an attempt to minimize dependence on the traditional markets in the British Commonwealth and the United States), the Chrétien foreign policy has sought to develop other markets as counterweights, particularly in the Asia Pacific area and, to a lesser extent, Latin America. Human rights, at least rhetorically, remained important as an issue in foreign policy but were now to be subordinated to the broader issue of enhanced trade. Moreover, the key word for the foreign policy approach in the Liberal government was pragmatism, as then Foreign Affairs Minister André Ouellet noted: "Canadian values must be represented in Canadian foreign policy, but it is in Canada's interest not to be taken for a more important or bigger nation than we are."[2] So, while Washington continued to emphasize human rights abuses in Cuba while blatantly ignoring those in China and granting Beijing preferential trading treatment, Ottawa sought to be more consistent in its use of economic sanctions. Moreover, the new government expressed clear skepticism at the value of the sanctions, unless they were to have a lasting effect.

The new Canadian government did not support the concept of economic sanctions unless the international community as a whole was prepared to support the common position, the domestic population also wanted that community to impose them, and there was a reasonable chance that they would be successful. In the Cuban context, Ottawa had traditionally been opposed to the U.S. embargo, claiming that none of these conditions was pertinent. Political gestures were not taken that seriously, and the key concept for the Liberal government was enhanced trade and a ruthlessly pragmatic approach to international politics, tempered with a pinch of traditional Canadian compromise.

This policy was articulated by Ouellet in May 1995, following meetings with his counterparts from the ASEAN nations. For the new Canadian government, the most effective way of promoting human rights was through trade with the target countries, provided that they enjoyed popular support, through a process of engaging them, regardless of whether they were military dictatorships or democracies. Isolation, by contrast, was seen as not being conducive to fostering human rights. As a result, he noted, "foreign trade, which creates progress in the economy, is the best way of spreading [democracy] to the population. Therefore, Canada has expressed, through this new [Liberal] government, our desire to vigorously pursue a series of [trading] initiatives in a number of countries irrespective of their human-rights record."[3] This classic position was taken from the Trudeau days, and it has been implemented with some vigor under Chrétien.

This approach to foreign affairs was typified by the large business delegation that Prime Minister Chrétien led to China in November 1994. The irony of the situation was that in the aftermath of the Tiananmen Square massacre in June 1989, Liberal Members of Parliament had called on Prime Minister Mulroney to impose economic sanctions on Beijing. Five years later, and now in government, the Liberals had adopted a very different approach. Noting that "a lot of time has passed since then," André Ouellet sounded a cautionary note: "Human rights is one element—a very important element—but only one element in the relationship."[4] Sounding a sour note, one anonymous senior official in his ministry noted about the new approach to China of M. Ouellet: "We used to go in with lists of political prisoners we wanted released. Now we go in with lists of companies that want contracts."[5]

The November 1994 trade mission led by Jean Chrétien was in fact the largest trade mission in Canadian history, traveling to China with an impressive number of Canadian political and business leaders. In all there were 500 members, including nine of the country's ten premiers, both territorial leaders, several mayors of Canadian cities, and hundreds of business-people. It was also the most successful, bringing in $8 billion in commercial agreements and letters of understanding for Canadian companies. At a news conference given on the Great Wall of China, Prime Minister Chrétien, espousing an exceptionally aggressive business line, noted that in China "human rights are not what we would like them to be. . . . But to me, the best way to alleviate this problem is not to isolate China, but to help in the opening up of China."[6]

Just two months later Prime Minister Chrétien was on the road again, heading a trade mission of some 250 businesspeople to Latin America and the Caribbean. Again the principal concept for foreign policy was as a support for developing Canadian trade prospects. Chrétien had already visited Mexico the previous March to open Canada's largest-ever trade fair abroad. It can be argued that he deliberately chose Mexico as the location for his first trip abroad instead of the time-honored visit to the United States to distance himself from close ties cultivated with great deliberation by the Mulroney government. By going first to Mexico City and not to Washington, he was deliberately showing that his government was to follow a radically different foreign policy agenda, at least symbolically. It is significant that he played on the fear in Mexico of pressure tactics that Washington could employ on its NAFTA partners: "There is always the problem that the very friendly Americans are so big," he commented dryly.[7] The prime minister also skillfully played the French-Canadian card, emphasizing that this common "Latin blood" bound Mexico and Canada, distinguishing them from their large mutual neighbor.

Having cut his international political teeth in Mexico and in the wake of the China trip, Chrétien led a similarly impressive Canadian delegation to Latin America and the Caribbean and to the lucrative South American markets. Accompanied by International Trade Minister Roy MacLaren, he headed to Trinidad and Tobago, Uruguay, Argentina (where Canadian investment had increased from $40 million to $1 billion in the previous five years), Chile, Brazil, and Costa Rica. It was the first trip to South America by a Canadian prime minister since 1981 (again the parallel with Trudeau), and the first ever to Chile and Argentina. And once again the trip was a resounding business success, with some thirty-nine agreements in principle and contracts worth $2.8 billion signed, including $400 million in deals signed in Argentina and $1.7 billion in Chile.

The essence of Chrétien's down-to-earth approach to foreign policy can be seen in an interview he gave to the Canadian Press in November 1994. During his first year in power he had argued for the inclusion of Chile in NAFTA, and later to open up the accord to other nations in the region, noting "the more countries that will be there, the more counterweight there will be to the United States."[8] By this time he had made official visits to Beijing, Hanoi, and Mexico City but, significantly, not to Washington. And despite several meetings with President Bill Clinton in multilateral fora, there had been just one official bilateral meeting between the two leaders. One should view the reinvigorated Cuban policy of Ottawa against this backdrop of economic pragmatism and in Chrétien's deliberate attempt to distance himself from his predecessor.

Differences in Canadian and U.S. Policy toward Cuba

Nowhere can this change in official policy be seen more clearly than in observations made by leading Canadian politicians on the U.S. approach to the Cuban question. Pierre Trudeau had been known to voice scorn publicly at Reagan's foreign policy in general, a position that understandably was poorly received in Washington. Within the first year of the new Chrétien government, several key government figures had emphasized their profound disagreements with U.S. policy on Cuba and firmly but respectfully stated the Canadian government position on the Cuban question. Among the Canadian politicians to engage in this criticism of U.S. policy were Jean Chrétien, André Ouellet, and the secretary of state for Latin America, Christine Stewart. Later Foreign Trade Minister Arthur Eggleton and Lloyd Axworthy (Ouellet's successor) were just as outspoken, particularly after the Helms-Burton legislation surfaced. This new development in Canadian foreign policy was the result of what Ottawa saw as deliberate intransigence on the part of some sectors in Washington and as plain bad policy.

In June 1994, at the annual meeting of the Organization of American States held in Brazil, Stewart had pointedly remarked that "the isolation of Cuba is unhealthy," and called on the OAS to consider lifting the 1962 suspension on Cuba imposed by the OAS. A few weeks later, shortly before she announced in Havana the resumption of Canadian development assistance to Cuba to be channeled through Canadian nongovernmental organizations, her minister, André Ouellet, stated categorically that "the people of Cuba are suffering from food shortages brought on by the economic crisis, and Canadians want to help them." Turning to the U.S. obsession with Cuba, he noted: "It is time to turn the page on Cuba. The Cold War is over."[9] In the same report, Canadian consul in Miami Douglas Campbell expanded on these two ideas: "What's behind the new aid program is that we have a policy of engagement—it's the same policy we have in respect to China, El Salvador and Guatemala—to avoid isolation and encourage democratic development. . . . Canada believes it's time that the OAS and other organizations should begin to rethink Cuba's status with the end of eventual reintegration into the international community."

The reference to the OAS meeting in Belem, Brazil, was particularly important, since it allowed Canada, as a relatively new member of the inter-American community to show that it too favored the position quietly espoused by many Latin American nations. Canada had not been part of the OAS when Cuba's membership had been suspended in 1962, but thirty-two years later it appeared clear that Cuba was no longer a threat to countries in the hemisphere. Once again pragmatism was the watchword of Canadian policy. Christine Stewart noted with some precision that "it's within all of our interests to support change in Cuba that is positive and healthy," leading José Miguel Vivanco, acting executive director of the U.S. human rights group Americas Watch to comment that "Mrs. Stewart has clearly put Canada in a leadership role in regard to changing hemispheric policy toward Cuba."[10] This was a new role for Canada, and one with which it is still grappling and coming to terms. That said, the official Canadian government position has remained consistent since the election of the Chrétien government, and in a low-key but firm tone it has both distanced itself steadily from the official U.S. position and called on Washington to adopt a new policy toward the Castro government.

The frustration of Prime Minister Chrétien in late 1994 is particularly noteworthy. Just a month before the Summit of the Americas, President-Elect Ernesto Zedillo of Mexico was in Ottawa to discuss bilateral relations with Chrétien. They joked about their shared interests in the face of the United States, and, referring to Pierre Trudeau's depiction of Canada as a mouse sleeping next to an elephant (the United States), Chrétien noted what an advantage it was to have the Mexicans helping to keep an eye on the elephant too: "We will have a better chance to survive, both of us." But their barbs were also directed again at Washington when they discussed the U.S. policy toward Cuba, which the Canadian and Mexican leaders both criticized as not being helpful in the hemisphere. A normalization of relations between Havana and Washington was badly needed in the region and was surely only a matter of time, noted Chrétien. When asked how long he thought it would take for this to happen, he snapped, "the sooner the better in my book."[11]

A month later the Summit of the Americas took place, with thirty-four leaders of Latin American and Caribbean nations meeting. There was one significant omission amongst the participants (Cuba) and the location of the summit (Miami) was hardly an encouraging sign for a balanced discussion of Cuban matters. President Clinton went out of his way to emphasize Cuba's omission from the invited guests: "Only one nation in our hemisphere is not represented here. It's the only one where democracy is still denied. We support the Cuban people's desire for peaceful, democratic change, and we hope that the next time we have one of these summits . . . a leader of a democratic Cuba will take its place at the table of nations."[12] It is worth noting that Canadian Prime Minister Chrétien sounded a discordant note, speaking out publicly at the summit about the U.S. approach to Cuba in general and the deliberate exclusion of Cuba in particular: "We have a right to disagree with that position. For us, it is the normalization [of relations] that will lead to more democracy."[13] Even more outspoken in Miami was Christine Stewart, who commented that Canada "would hope that when other summits are held in the hemisphere that Cuba be present at the table. We as a nation will work to see that happens, and we will work with others in the hemisphere to see that happens."[14]

It was precisely this idea of working with others that has been pursued by the Canadian government, particularly with Mexico. This approach is not a major departure but shows that Ottawa is indeed keen to foster a normalization of relations. In 1994, in a letter to Edgar Dosman, the executive director of the Canadian Foundation for the Americas, Ouellet noted that "Cuba's isolation in the hemisphere is unhealthy. I have noted myself that this needs to change, and I certainly intend to discuss Cuba further with countries of Latin America and the Caribbean to see how we may move ahead. I do wish to assure you that Cuba remains very much an active file with me and with the Government."[15] The same year, in meetings with his counterpart Manuel Tello in Mexico City, André Ouellet spoke about the desire of both countries to see the United States "turn the page" in its relations with Cuba. Both men agreed to continue to prod Washington to change its policy, since "a new era" in international relations had arrived, whether Washington saw it or not. In an interview with Radio Canada in Mexico, the Canadian minister commended Clinton for his courageous decision to turn the page on the Vietnamese debacle after the United States normalized relations with that country, and asked the United States to show the same maturity in its relations with Cuba.

In April 1995, after the Helms-Burton Bill (designed to increase pressure on the Castro government by choking foreign investment in Cuba) surfaced, Mexican and Canadian ministers again met in Ottawa. It was the annual meeting between Canadian and Mexican ministers, but among matters of foreign policy they discussed joint strategy on Cuban policy. Indeed Ouellet and José Angel Gurria, his Mexican counterpart (the successor to Tello), planned a joint lobbying effort to convince U.S. legislators of the widespread international condemnation of the proposed legislation and the committed opposition of the two NAFTA partners to the United States. Their common position was based on an appreciation of what both regarded as a mistaken and unhelpful interpretation of the Cuban question by Washington. After a daylong meeting in April 1995, both ministers emerged to condemn the proposed Helms-Burton legislation. "We have indicated how displeased we are with the Helms' legislation," Ouellet commented. "We will work together with others to make sure that such legislation does not have consequences on third countries."[16]

That same month, after Senator Helms had called Canada a "pain in the neck" at a rally in Miami for refusing to show deference to Washington's goals in Cuba, and had compared Canada with nations that had appeased Adolf Hitler before World War II, Ouellet responded in statesmanlike language: "I think this excessive language is unnecessary. . . . Canada has maintained diplomatic relations with Cuba . . . over the years. We feel the embargo is not conducive to helping the populations who are suffering. We think we have to look forward."[17] The official Canadian policy has remained constant since Fidel Castro took over in January 1959; a policy of engagement is seen as the only effective manner of dealing with the Cuban government, and policymakers continue to look askance at what they perceive to be a myopic U.S. policy, which has been unsuccessful during all these years. Ouellet articulated these concerns well after a speech at the United Nations: "If the United States of America has been able to make peace and turn the page in regard to Vietnam, they should do the same with [Cuba], a country that . . . is no longer a threat in any way, shape or form to them."[18]

The Role of Nongovernmental Organizations

One of the reasons that Cuba has remained fairly high on the political agenda has been the resolute interest of Canadian nongovernmental organizations (NGOs) in lobbying for development assistance from Ottawa and in seeking to establish long-term projects in Cuba. It has not been an easy struggle, and the organizations have had to argue their cases with both Canadian and Cuban bureaucrats to prove the seriousness of their intentions.

The previous chapter mentioned the difficulties in breaking the bureaucratic logjam and freeing up humanitarian assistance for Cuba during the Mulroney years. Eventually in the summer of 1993, following extensive lobbying by Canadian NGOs, $250,000 was awarded by CIDA toward a shipment of vitamins and medicines, and a further $250,000 in wheat flour was provided through the UN World Food Program. That summer, too, OXFAM-Canada coordinated a successful nationwide fundraising appeal to send food and medicine to Cuba. At the same time, as the secretary of state noted sternly in September 1993 on the recent food and medicine donated by Ottawa: "Such humanitarian assistance to the Cuban people does not signify a change in Canada's aid policy. Cuba remains ineligible for bilateral assistance from Canada because of concerns about human rights in that country, and we do not have bilateral aid relations with the Cuban government."[19]

In the summer of 1994, Christine Stewart, at a conference in Havana organized by *The Economist*, indicated a major change in Canadian policy in observing that Cuba was once again eligible for Canadian development assistance. This was significant because Havana had been ineligible for any form of aid since Cuba became involved in the Angolan war. Stewart, speaking in Havana, noted that "this decision responds to concerns raised by Canadian humanitarian and religious groups that the restriction on Canadian aid interfered with their efforts to assist the people of Cuba."[20] In March 1994 Canada provided $300,000 of emergency food aid to women and children at risk of malnutrition in Cuba and a further $500,000 in food aid through the UN World Food program, again directed toward women and children and in all cases furnished through various NGOs. In late 1994 a larger grant was provided to help rebuild housing in three areas of Havana, while in 1995 some $50,000 was given to help rebuild housing in Guantánamo in the wake of tropical storm Gordon.

Funding was also provided by CIDA to the Cuba-Canada Interagency Project (CCIP) to assist this group in coordinating Canadian NGO activities in Cuba and in strengthening ties with Cuban counterparts. The steering committee consisted of organizational representatives from the Anglican Church of Canada, the Centro Félix Varela (Havana), CUSO, the Martin Luther King Jr. Memorial Centre (Havana), OXFAM-Canada, the Saskatchewan Council for International Cooperation, and the United Church of Canada. The official lead agency of this steering committee was OXFAM-Canada. The original goal was to encourage the Canadian government to support NGO activities in Cuba because it was argued that these "should begin to play a positive and constructive role in facilitating Cuba's re-entry into the international economic system and strengthening their democratic participation at all levels of Cuban society."[21] The CCIP encouraged the Canadian government to update its approach to Cuba, seeking a full normalization of official policy. At the same time it encouraged Cuban and Canadian NGOs to respond to immediate humanitarian needs and to develop long-term sustainable development projects in Cuba.

The church connection is particularly well developed, especially from the Catholic and Protestant perspective. The Canadian Jewish community has also delivered some assistance to its counterpart in Cuba, providing the services of a visiting rabbi and kosher food to the small Cuban Jewish community. The Anglican Church of Canada has held a supervisory role over the Cuban Episcopal Church for over thirty years, while it and the United Church of Canada have been active in raising funds for humanitarian aid for Cuba. The ecumenical Canadian Foodgrains Bank based in Winnipeg, Manitoba, has also helped to coordinate numerous shipments of grain to Cuba.

The Cuban Catholic Church has been assisted by the active role of Canadian missionaries, largely francophone, from the Société des Missions Etrangères, les Soeurs de Notre-Dame du Bon Conseil, and les Soeurs Servantes du Saint-Coeur de Marie. Cardinal Jaime Ortega of Havana was trained in Quebec and has maintained a solid working relationship with the Canadian Church. In 1987 a delegation of Cuban bishops visited Canada, and in April 1995 the president, vice-president, and general secretary of the Canadian Conference of Catholic Bishops traveled to Cuba, where they met with Cuban bishops, laity, Canadian missionaries, the papal nuncio, the Canadian ambassador, and Cuban government officials. While not as influential as the NGOs in influencing Ottawa's approach to Cuba, the views of the church sector are nevertheless important and are symptomatic of the wide variety of Canadian interests in Cuba.

It is important to bear in mind that, following a tradition of deliberately ignoring Cuba, it has not been easy for Ottawa mandarins to appreciate the new direction being taken by the Chrétien government. The Canadian International Development Agency (CIDA) has suddenly found itself in the midst of a variety of requests from NGOs, universities, churches, businesses, and individuals, all seeking development assistance for their respective projects and intended programs in Cuba. Prior to June 1994 there had been no official development assistance (ODA), but since Christine Stewart's announcement in June 1994, a variety of avenues have opened, and in particular the NGO division, which cofinances projects with Canadian NGOs, and the Industrial Cooperation division, which provides seed money for businesses seeking to open joint ventures in Cuba, have been swamped with requests for funding.[22] In addition, the Canadian government has provided bilateral support, particularly in restructuring the banking and tax systems in Cuba.

While the Canadian bureaucracy can be as slow and cumbersome as its Cuban counterpart, it is worth noting that things are changing rapidly in Ottawa. In CIDA, there have been several missions to Cuba undertaken by specialists in Latin American affairs to evaluate potential programs and Cuban needs. In October 1994 a consultation took place in Ottawa under the auspices of the Canadian Partnership Branch of CIDA to explore interests and identify priorities in development programming for Canadians in Cuba. In all, ninety representatives from NGOs, universities, and businesses attended, surprising Canadian officials by the depth of interest. There are clearly several sectors interested in pursuing development projects in Cuba, and the government has taken notice.

Canadian universities have also helped to foster interest in Cuba. In all, fifteen universities have formalized agreements with their Cuban counterparts. The most important connection is Carleton University in Ottawa, which has been active in a variety of projects ranging from sugarcane research to language teaching. In 1994, with financial support from the International Development Research Centre, it instituted a joint M.A. program in economics with the University of Havana, and $4.8 million was provided by CIDA in 1996 for the continuation of this program. In Atlantic Canada, the University of New Brunswick, Saint Mary's University, and Dalhousie University have pursued research interests, development projects (in fisheries, integrated coastal zone management, and business administration), while the latter two Halifax universities have also held field schools in Cuba, and faculty from Dalhousie and Mount St. Vincent University (also in Halifax) have provided managerial summer school programs for hotel managers representing the Cubanacán hotel management group. Also worth noting is that in the mid-1990s at universities in Havana and Matanzas, a chair in Canadian Studies was instituted, making available a variety of lectures on Canadian matters.

An organization with significant political clout in Canada that has also made its voice heard is the Canadian Labour Congress, the umbrella organization for some 60 percent of all trade unions in Canada, representing 2.3 million workers. Led by Bob White, the CLC has raised concerns about the Cuban question since 1994. In a letter to Prime Minister Chrétien on the eve of the arrival of President Clinton in Ottawa in February 1995, White officially requested Chrétien to protest the proposed Helms-Burton legislation, while offering suggestions on the role for Washington to follow:

> The proposed legislation entitled the "Cuban Liberty and Solidarity Act" not only intends to destroy Cuba's successful trading relations with the world, it also seeks to shift Washington's own problems with Cuba onto the international community. In so doing it will penalize Canadian companies lawfully engaged in business and might lead to the loss of significant government revenues and employment for several thousand Canadian workers. . . .
>
> What is particularly appalling is that it is intended to "punish" Canada for its continued, independent policy towards Cuba. I would reiterate that the Canadian Labour Congress supports Canada's policy of promoting the reintegration of Cuba in the international community as has been communicated previously to Canadian officials. Canada cannot have its international relations determined by another country.[23]

In April 1995, accompanied by two assistants, White left for an official CLC trip to Cuba, where he met with a number of government ministers, trade union leaders, human rights activists, Canadian embassy staff, NGOs, and Cuban workers. In a press release, issued by the CLC on April 10, 1995, he noted that "the CLC is in Cuba to strengthen our relationship with Cuban workers' organizations. . . . We want to engage constructively with the Central de Trabajadores Cubanos (CTC) and Cuban NGOs to explore ways to promote peaceful change." He also noted the continuing frustration within the Canadian labor movement with Washington's policy: "Canada has an important role to play in the hemisphere in supporting Cuban workers and in counteracting the destructive role the United States plays through its embargo and recent investment laws."[24] In addition, the CLC has implemented a variety of small projects with its Cuban counterpart, ranging from providing advice on foreign joint ventures to translating collective agreements into Spanish.

The Surge in Canadian Business Interest

The main reason for the dramatic warming of relations since the Chrétien government took power was the increasing Canadian business experience in Cuba. We suggested in the previous chapter that this was the main reason that the Mulroney government had pursued a policy of benign neglect. While Mulroney was keen to ignore Cuba, he was constantly made aware of the increasing interest in export possibilities by the Canadian business sector.

From the moment one arrives in Cuba, it is impossible not to be aware of Canada's key role as a trade and investment partner in this Caribbean island. Varadero's airport was built by a Quebec company, and the new terminal at Havana's airport is being built by an Ontario construction company. Sophisticated landing equipment at Cuban airports and hotel reservation systems are also being supplied by Ontario businesses. Beach umbrellas advertising Labatt's beer are found poolside. McCain's french fries are standard fare in hotel kitchens. President's Choice cola and other food items (private-label products of the Loblaw supermarket chain) can be found in many dollar stores. Most of the sound equipment in Cuba's discotheques is imported from Canada. The compact discs of top Cuban music artists purchased by tourists are recorded in Canada, and many of the postcards are printed there too. Auto parts are shipped southward in large numbers. The first shipment to Canada of Cuban winter vegetables grown on a joint venue farm occurred in March 1997. Canadian franchised pizza restaurants of the Pizza Nova chain offer an alternative to Canadian-managed hotel restaurants. The Delta hotel chain manages nine hotels in Cuba, mainly in the eastern half of the country. Even Hatuey and Cristal beer have been brewed to Cuban specifications in Nova Scotia by a Labatt's subsidiary, while Canadian equipment has been introduced into Holguín breweries. A number of Canadian trading companies are supplying everything from foodstuffs to paper products, engineering equipment, paint, high-tech goods, and a variety of goods for the tourist market. The number of joint ventures between Canadian companies and the Cuban state has also skyrocketed, mainly in the mining sector, where Canadian companies dominate. And Canadians are keen to continue investing in Cuba: a debenture issue of Sherritt International raised $675 million in just one day in late 1996.

It was not always that way, however. The first Canadian joint venture (to make egg trays from recycled newsprint in 1988) was a failure. The demise of the Soviet Union and the dramatic impact that this has had on

Cuba—reducing Cuban purchasing power to a quarter of what it had been in 1989 and forcing Havana to find a new source for imports and a new market for its products—has proved a boon for Canadian entrepreneurs and investors. From the sprawling interests of Sherritt International, a nickel and cobalt mining operation valued at more than a billion dollars, to numerous small businesses specializing in exports of Canadian produce, it is clear that Canada is now a major player in Cuba.

The case of the small province of Nova Scotia (pop. 960,000) is instructive in this regard, for it illustrates the potential afforded by the Cuban market. In January 1994, and again in February 1996, Premier John Savage led two large business delegations from the province (twenty-five and fifty, respectively) to Cuba to investigate potential trade opportunities. Significant inroads into the Cuban market have since been made by a number of small businesses, leading one tourist consultant to comment with enthusiasm: "Doing business in Cuba is a license to print money for Canadians."[25] The evidence certainly points to a fair degree of local interest: Carlos Salsamendi, president of the Cuban Chamber of Commerce, visited Halifax in September 1994 to sign a memorandum of understanding with the Atlantic Provinces Chamber of Commerce; ships sail from Halifax for Havana every nine days (every twenty-one days just a year ago), with another shipping company set to compete with the established service; there are direct flights from Halifax to Varadero during the tourist season; Nova Scotia universities send students to field school in Cuba every year; and a new cadre of local companies have started to export their goods and services to the Cuban market. In all, some thirty companies are exporting local products to Cuba, and three joint ventures have been instituted. In many ways this represents a microcosm of the larger Canadian business approach to Cuba in recent years. It shows how a traditionally conservative, small province like Nova Scotia can create several hundred jobs when a dozen or so small companies step outside their traditional markets and venture to Cuba.

Canadian companies, together with European and Latin American counterparts, have been pressing ahead with some vigor in recent years. The end of the socialist bloc, the potential to use cheap, skilled labor, the absence of U.S. competition, and the opportunity to tap Cuba's commercial potential are understandable reasons for a close study of Cuba. In all, some thirty Canadian joint ventures have been set up either in Havana or through tax shelters in other parts of the Caribbean.

The tourist sector is one of the most visible examples of the Canadian commercial role. The 1995–96 season, saw 160,000 Canadians flocking to Cuba's beaches, usually on Canadian charter lines, and often staying at

Canadian-run hotels. The largest Canadian company involved in the Cuban tourist industry is Delta Hotels and Resorts, based in Toronto, which manages but does not own nine hotels, resorts, and lodges in Cuba (it was the first North American hotel company invited to do business in Cuba). These properties include three resorts and five ecolodges (all located in Santiago de Cuba and Holguín), as well as the Old Man and the Sea hotel at the Hemingway Marina in Havana. The Delta chain has significant business clout in Canada, being the country's largest privately owned hotel company (with thirty-seven hotels and resorts). This increasing role in the Cuban hotel trade is meaningful because Delta initiated operations only in late 1993 but has made considerable progress since then.

The sector of the Cuban economy that has been most aggressively developed by Canadian investors is the mining industry. According to Marc Henderson, president of one company that was active in mining in Cuba in recent years, Cuba's vast mineral resources are rivaled only by those of Chile.[26] Despite the fear of pressure from Washington, there is abundant evidence to point to the extensive Canadian role in this sector. The Miramar Mining Corporation of North Vancouver, for example, has agreed to develop an open-pit copper mine in Pinar del Río. There are an estimated 3–9 million metric tonnes grading 3.5 percent copper at the site, and approximately $1 million has been spent to date on studies. In addition Miramar is reported to be considering a potential gold-mine site on the Isle of Youth, with estimated gold deposits of 1.7 million ounces.

Three Toronto-based companies have also become involved in gold-mining projects in Cuba. Republic Goldfields, Inc., has obtained the rights to two potential goldfields in central and eastern Cuba. In addition, MacDonald Mines Exploration Ltd. has signed an agreement to exploit gold reserves in Camagüey. Apparently the mine contains 279,000 tons of gold ore, with a grade of 7.6 ounces per ton. In June 1994, MacDonald's president was cited as claiming that Cuba was "the newest, most exciting gold-mining frontier in North America."[27] A third Toronto company, CaribGold Resources, has also acquired rights to seven concessions on the island covering some 1.5 million acres.

Since August 1993 Joutel Resources Ltd. has held exploration and development rights to 4,662 square kilometers in central and eastern Cuba, where it is seeking gold, copper, zinc, lead, and silver. Joutel recently raised $4 million from European investors, partly on the strength of the sheer size of the exploration and development concessions of 1.2 million acres provided it by the Cuban government, making it the largest foreign landholder in Cuba. Joutel's CEO, Hugh Harbinson, was quoted in June 1993 as saying that some 25 to 30 percent of the company's shares were in American hands. He explained this recent development as being due to "the potential for high yields in the company's Cuban prospecting."[28] As in the case of the hotel industry, it is worth noting that these investments have all taken place in the last five years.

As a footnote to the wave of investment in the mining sector where more than 90 percent of all joint ventures are Canadian, it is worth noting that there are also a number of companies in auxiliary roles, such as supply vessels for oil rigs, laboratories that assess ore samples, geophysical surveyors, and others supplying a variety of smaller spin-off goods and services. In sum they show just how pervasive is the mining presence of Canadian companies.

One of the Canadian companies with the greatest commercial potential resulting from its role in Cuba is York Medical Inc., a Toronto-based company that was established to license medical technology from Cuba. It is a subsidiary of Yorkton Securities Inc., a Canadian investment banker. After extensive evaluation of the estimated 3,000 products being researched in Cuba's ninety-two scientific centers (funded in part by CIDA), it licensed five specific products for worldwide development and commercialization, and has been awarded rights of refusal for a variety of other products. The five products selected by Yorkton (already in an advanced state of development) are EGFr-MAb (biotech diagnostic/therapeutic for cancer), C-Kure (wound-healing antibacterial), Diramic (antibiotic sensitivity test system for use as a hospital diagnostic device), Dermofurol G1 (biotech antibacterial/antifungal/antiviral), and Herberkinase (recombinant streptokinase).

According to York, they have a combined market potential of nearly $3 billion. Licensing agreements for these products were signed in May 1995, and the company is now seeking initial private funding and potential development partners. When the U.S. embargo is lifted, given both the high quality of biotechnology products from Cuba and their low cost of production, Yorkton Medical Inc. will understandably be in an excellent position to market their connections with Cuba.

In the final analysis, the commercial bottom line has been the driving force in the bilateral relationship. In the mid-1980s, bilateral trade decreased rapidly, reflecting Cuba's lack of purchasing capacity and idle plant. Table 6.1 illustrates that Canadian exports to Cuba fell from $170 million in 1990 to just $113 million in 1992. As the Cuban economy has improved, so too have the trade figures, with bilateral trade increasing from $216 million in 1990 to $595 million in 1995. In 1995, Canada was Cuba's major trading partner. Data for 1996 showed a slight decrease in Canadian exports and a strong increase in Cuban exports over 1995. Canadian companies have come to appreciate the potential of the Cuban market, particularly because of the lack of U.S. competition, and are keen to establish their niche before a normalization of relations between Washington and Havana occurs.

The Sherritt Case Study

While the number of Canadian companies developing an interest in Cuba continues to grow (their executives can be spotted on the weekly flights to Havana from Montreal and Toronto), all are dwarfed by a company from Fort Saskatchewan, Alberta, whose corporate offices are in Toronto, Sherritt International. In Cuba it has two large interests, in nickel and cobalt extraction and refining and in oil exploration through its subsidiary Canada Northwest Energy, although it is also involved in market gardening (through Sherritt Green) and tourism. It is headed by Ian Delaney, who has steadily increased his investment in both fields and in the process has become close friends with Fidel Castro. He clearly has a soft spot for Cuba: "The Cubans are terrific people to do business with. . . . For one thing, they're totally incorruptible. We do business all over the world, but there's no place we like better to negotiate deals than Havana. They're trying to develop a system that has few parallels. Perhaps Canada, which is really a social democracy, comes closest."[29] In 1990 Delaney waged a proxy fight to win control of Sherritt, which was "near insolvency because its metals refinery had closed and it had no nickel to refine,"[30] and in 1991 he entered the Cuban market.

Canada Northwest Energy (CNW) first opened its office in March 1992, and since then has been heavily involved in the Cuban oil production scene, where it is drilling in three areas: Block 10, Block 23, and Block 9. Currently it has been working on three major projects: improving the productivity of existing wells, exploring for oil in Block 23 (Sancti Spiritus), and evaluating the discovery of oil (made in 1994) in the Bay of Cárdenas. The enhanced recovery program is important, since CNW is working on the majority of existing oil wells and is producing a further 8,000 barrels of oil a day, approximately 27 percent of the entire national production. These operations take place in the six fields, known as the Varadero Periféricos, around the Varadero area, the Boca de Jaruco field—30 km. east of Havana—and the Piña field in central Cuba. Also important is the discovery of oil in Cárdenas Bay, which is producing some 3,750 barrels a day.

Even more important is the unique joint venture agreement of December 1994 between Sherritt and the Compañía General de Niquel S.A. of Cuba, which has led to the creation of three companies that mine, refine, and market nickel and cobalt. The Cuban state now owns 50 percent of

Table 6.1. Canada-Cuba merchandise trade: exports and imports, 1985–95 (in thousands of $Canadian)

	Exports to Cuba	Imports from Cuba	Total two-way trade
1985*	330,327	44,345	374,672
1986*	368,019	72,614	440,633
1987*	274,459	51,472	325,931
1988*	230,613	87,117	317,730
1989	154,600	62,100	216,700
1990	170,500	130,200	300,700
1991	127,900	152,800	280,700
1992	113,000	256,100	369,100
1993	133,758	171,491	305,249
1994	114,600	194,400	319,000
1995	274,500	320,900	595,400
1996	240,387	401,163	641,550

Sources: Caribbean and Central American Relations Division, External Affairs and International Trade Canada; International
Trade Division, Statistics Canada.

*includes reexport

Table 6.2. Cuban economic association with foreign capital, by country and year

	1988	1990	1991	1992	1993	1994	1995
Spain	1	—	3	9	10	14	10
Mexico	—	—	2	3	3	4	113
Canada	—	—	—	2	8	16	26
Italy	—	—	—	1	5	4	717
France	—	1	—	3	5	2	213
Holland	—	—	—	1	2	3	39
Off-Shore	—	1	3	10	5	12	31
Latin America	—	—	2	3	11	9	429
Other	—	—	1	1	11	10	427
Total	1	2	11	33	60	74	31

Source: CONAS, *Cuba, Investment and Business.*

Sherritt's metal refining facilities in Alberta, as well as 50 percent of its marketing capabilities and corporate offices. In addition, $150 million is to be invested to upgrade the plant in Moa, in northeastern Cuba. For Sherritt, one of the main advantages of the agreement is that it now owns secure mineral resources, in effect, on its own property. The joint venture thus has a guaranteed supply to feed ore to its huge Alberta refining facilities. In all, the resources include more than 60 million tons with proven reserves of 80 percent. For Cuba, the deal represents a major change too, since it is no longer just a supplier of raw materials; instead it is a full partner in the refining and marketing process. Havana is understandably pleased at the importance of this venture, which government representatives point to as the desired prototype of economic joint ventures, while supporters of the Helms-Burton law indicate that Sherritt is the principal target of their ideological venom.

Sherritt has accomplished a fair amount since the company signed the joint agreement. The industrial accident rate, for example, has dropped to about one-half of its earlier rate, largely because the Canadian company shipped in free safety equipment (boots, hard hats, and acid-proof gear), items that previously the workers had been obliged to buy from the Cuban state. Moreover, production has improved dramatically, from an annualized production rate of 14,000 tonnes in December 1994 to more than 26,000 tonnes two years later. Indeed, finished nickel and cobalt production levels in 1996 were the highest in the Fort Saskatchewan refinery's forty-three-year history. This was due to a combination of Canadian management style (since the Cuban managers now have far greater say in running the plant) and a sliding scale of bonus payments in dollars. There are still problems facing the Moa plant: there are environmental concerns that result from an extremely lax approach to pollution control under the previous ownership; the equipment is outdated, and in some places is falling apart because of a lack of proper maintenance; and the workforce will need to be downsized to maintain its competitive edge. It is also evident, however, that the plant, which produces a mixed sulphide containing cobalt and nickel that is then shipped back to the refining plant in Alberta, can be enormously productive, and has already given indication of its potential, particularly if linked with the refining capacity and technology of a Canadian company like Sherritt.

Under Delaney the company has done extremely well financially. Mining, as well as oil and gas, remain its main interests. Sherritt has also invested in the tourism and market gardening sectors ("Sherritt Green") and is planning to expand its investments particularly in power generation, communications, transportation, real estate, and sugar. In a press conference in December 1994, for instance, Ian Delaney told reporters that it would cost about $4,200 a ton of metal to mine, but that, based on current metal prices, a ton would be worth $12,000).[31] As *Business Week* pointed out in June 1995, sales in Sherritt's metals unit rose 76 percent in 1994, with metals earnings producing U.S.$32.5 million (following a loss in 1993).[32] The Cuban joint venture, according to the same article, earned U.S.$14.3 million on sales of $131 million in its first quarter of operation. Canadian sources note that, after a loss of $41.4 million in 1993, Sherritt International realized a profit of $80 million in 1994, while its revenues more than doubled to $920 million. Moreover, despite Washington's pressure to punish Sherritt because of its investments in Cuba (the *Business Week* article cited above referred to the solid working relationship with Fidel Castro enjoyed by Delaney: "Meet Fidel's favorite capitalist"),[33] some 30 percent of its stocks and most of its bonds are held by U.S. investors.

Under the audacious leadership of Delaney, who was chosen as one of the top ten CEOs in Canada in 1994 by the *Financial Times,* the joint venture has thrived. There are political risks, of course, not the least of which is the Helms-Burton law, which threatens to punish foreign investments in Cuba that "traffick" in property that previously belonged to U.S. owners (the property in Moa had been expropriated by the Cuban government from a predecessor of Freeport McMoran Inc. of New Orleans). That said, Sherritt's involvement in the fertilizer business, its successful diversification of markets (in light of U.S. pressure, it now exports mainly to Europe and Japan), and the very real example of solid profits on its joint venture have made its activities in Cuba a risk that is worth taking. The decision in 1995 to separate completely Sherritt International, now involved solely in Cuban activities, from the parent company, was clearly taken as a means of deflecting mounting criticism from Washington.

In late June 1995, as debate on the proposed Helms-Burton Bill heated up in Washington, the name of Sherritt became increasingly prominent. As one of the largest investors in Cuba, with a clear profit record, a CEO who had struck up a friendship with Fidel Castro, and all this on land that had been owned by a U.S. company in the early 1950s, it understandably grated on the nerves of opponents of the revolutionary government in Washington. By attacking Sherritt, therefore, members of the U.S. Congress hoped to intimidate potential foreign investors by their degree of opposition to such ventures and deter them from seeking business in Cuba. One of the most outspoken opponents of foreign investment in Castro's Cuba, which he termed "one of the cruelest dictatorships in the world," was Lincoln Díaz-Balart, a Florida Republican who denounced all forms of foreign investment in Cuba: "I think investors who go over there and provide dollars to Castro knowing it is a slave economy . . . are part of a brutal, tacit coalition against the Cuban people."[34]

The war of words against Sherritt became quite nasty in the summer of 1995. Díaz-Balart went so far as to call Fidel Castro an "environmental prostitute" and accused Sherritt of shipping chemical waste from the nickel processing back to Cuba. No evidence was provided, and Sherritt Vice-President Patrice Merrin Best emphatically denied the charges of dumping chemical waste in Cuba: "Zero goes outside the border; not one speck."[35] But the pressure on foreign investment, and in particular on Sherritt, continued. The 1917 Trading with the Enemy Act, designed to prohibit U.S. dealings with enemies in World War I and amended in the 1940s, revolved around the publication of a list of corporations that are prohibited from all trade and investment with the United States. The office of Foreign Assets Control in the Treasury Department thus placed Sherritt's Cuban companies on a U.S. blacklist, along with corporations connected with Libya, Iraq, North Korea, and Serbia, and individuals such as Iraqi leader Saddam Hussein, Libyan president Mu'ammar Gadhafi, Bosnian Serb leader Rado-van Karadzic, Panama's Manuel Noriega, Palestinian leaders Abu Abass and George Habash, and leaders of various fundamentalist Moslem and Israeli organizations.

Sherritt's three companies dealing with Cuba: Moa Nickel S.A., which operates the mining plant in Cuba, Cobalt Refinery Co., Inc., which operates the actual refinery in Fort Saskatchewan, and International Cobalt Co. Inc., the marketing and sales agency, were placed on this blacklist. The reason for this one foreign company to be singled out was that it was the largest foreign investor in Cuba, and it was thus desirable to send a message to the scores of other, smaller companies with investments in Cuba, as well as the many other companies that were considering investing there. Lost in the ideological shuffle too was the fact that, in the wake of the breakup of the Soviet Union when conservative U.S. policymakers had also predicted the end of the Castro government, the rapid growth of joint ventures in Cuba had become the economic lifeline for Havana. By "squeezing" this lifeline, it was suggested, the Cuban revolution would be choked— hence the fury with which conservative U.S. politicians attacked Sherritt.

The Helms-Burton Act and Canadian-Cuban Relations

The opening of an article by Jeff Sallot, Parliamentary Bureau correspondent of the Toronto *Globe and Mail,* gave some indication of the tension that would arise between Washington and Ottawa over Cuba in 1995:

> Foreign Affairs Minister André Ouellet is such an admirer of Jean-Bertrand Aristide that he keeps a picture of himself with the Haitian president in his office.
>
> U.S. Senator Jesse Helms, on the other hand, hates Father Aristide with a passion, once describing him as a "psychopath."[36]

The foreign policy views of the senator from North Carolina and Canadian policymakers were obviously on vastly different wavelengths. Helms, for instance, has little time for the United Nations, in which the Canadian government, which has provided troops for UN peacekeeping missions in numbers that are far greater than its proportional size, believes strongly. His approach to development assistance, to Haiti, to Canada (in 1982 he had courted René Lévesque, the separatist premier of Quebec), and to Cuba are also clear points of disagreement. The midterm Republican victory of November 1994 and the appointment of the 73-year-old senator as chairman of the powerful Senate Foreign Relations Committee, meant that a strongly conservative approach to foreign policy was inevitable. In terms of Canada-U.S. relations, tensions would reach a peak with the introduction in early February 1995 of the "Cuban Liberty and Democratic Solidarity (LIBERTAD) Act of 1995," which was signed into law on March 12, 1996.[37]

The Helms-Burton legislation affects Canadians in several ways. In broad terms it seeks to internationalize the U.S. conflict with Havana by bringing in penalties for companies that rent or own property in Cuba that had been expropriated from U.S. citizens, whether they were citizens at that time or Cubans who later took out U.S. papers. According to Title III of the legislation, these foreign companies (working on property that was nationalized nearly forty years ago) can now be sued in U.S. court by the original owners, and their attachments in the United States can be obtained legally as compensation. Such a practice goes directly against international law, the norms of international economic exchange, and Canadian domestic law, since the normal dispute resolution mechanism is through U.S. and Cuban channels. Moreover, according to Title IV of the legislation, Canadians who are executives/principals in, or major shareholders of, companies that benefited from such properties, as well as their family members, are to be banned from entering the United States. In fact, on July 10, 1996, seven members of Sherritt International received official letters from the U.S. government informing them that they and their family members cannot legally enter the United States.

The Canadian government's response to Helms-Burton was and continues to be strongly critical and surprisingly robust. Prior to President Clinton's signing this bill into law, Canada vigorously opposed the legislation and lobbied hard against its passage. This active opposition included the intervention of Canada's ambassador to the United States, Raymond Chrétien. Foreign Affairs Minister Lloyd Axworthy was especially concerned about the extraterritorial application of the law. Simply put, Ottawa could ill afford to allow the United States to establish such a precedent, namely, legitimizing the reach of U.S. domestic laws into Canada.

The Canadian embassy in Washington made these very points in a succinct letter to the U.S. State Department. The letter argued that Helms-Burton represented "an objectionable attempt to extend U.S. measures against Cuba beyond U.S. jurisdiction and would constitute an illegitimate intrusion upon third countries."[38] On the issue of barring Canadian business-people from the United States, the embassy statement noted that since "the imposition of such punitive measures on those who are not parties to the original claims dispute is inconsistent with the principles of international law which recognizes the right of sovereign states to determine matters such as the ownership of property pursuant to the law of their own territory . . . Resolution of the claims should be limited to those who are parties of the original dispute." The basic thrust of the Canadian position was that it was wrong for third countries to "regulate companies incorporated under Canadian jurisdiction and engaged in commercial relations and activities that take place in, and that are wholly in accordance with, Canadian law."

The Canadian strategy in response to the legislation was to meet with like-minded opponents to form a coalition. Prime Minister Chrétien, speaking to a clutch of reporters at a gathering of Caribbean leaders, noted: "We condemn the action of the government of Cuba in shooting down the two planes, but we never accept the notion of extraterritorial application of American laws. We have to respect the jurisdiction of every country and I said so to the President of the United States."[39] Perhaps more significant, however, were Canadian efforts to gain support from members of the European Union (EU). In a March 19, 1996, meeting between Chrétien and EU Trade Commissioner Sir Leon Brittan, both Canada and the EU indicated their support for lodging a formal complaint against the law before the World Trade Organization (WTO).[40]

By late March Canada was still continuing its sharp and vocal attack on the Helms-Burton law.[41] On a visit to Washington, Foreign Minister Axworthy criticized the United States for what he described as a "disturbing trend" to "act unilaterally without regard for the legitimate interests of others." He continued: "If the world's only superpower is allowed to do this with impunity, what stops others from saying they can do the same thing, with chaotic consequences for governments and business interests alike?"[42] In his meetings with Secretary of State Warren Christopher, Axworthy pressed for Washington to seek a waiver on Canada's behalf from key provisions of the law.

The campaign was continued by Canada's International Trade Minister Arthur Eggleton in May 1996, when he attacked the U.S. government for its protectionist-minded behavior: "It would be ironic if the United States or Canada or any other country, which had helped to establish the rules-based system of trade now in ascendancy, should now act in ways that would threaten to unravel the very tapestry we have sewn."[43] More important, however, was the minister's veiled threat about possible retaliatory action against the United States. Indeed, in early 1997, the Canadian government introduced a number of retaliatory measures, including legislation that would "mirror" Helms-Burton and thus presumably allow Canadian citizens to sue for damages against U.S. corporate assets in Canada, as well as impose a visa requirement for U.S. citizens entering Canada.

By June 1996 Ottawa's offensive against Helms-Burton was continuing to gather momentum. At the OAS General Assembly in Panama held that month, the Canadian delegation, along with the Mexicans, drafted a resolution challenging the legal integrity of the legislation. In a vote of 33 to 1 the OAS backed the Canada-inspired resolution, which instructed the Inter-American Juridical Committee (IAJC) "to examine and decide upon the validity under international law of the Helms-Burton Act at its next regular session, as a matter of priority, and to present its findings to the Permanent Council."[44] Later the IAJC concluded that Helms-Burton did in fact violate international law.

Furthermore, in a joint press conference with Mexican president Ernesto Zedillo, Prime Minister Chrétien pledged to challenge the law under the terms of the NAFTA. Shortly afterward, Ottawa made known its plans to counter the act by applying the 1985 Foreign Extraterritorial Measures Act (FEMA). In addition to using "blocking orders" (declaring that judgments handed down by U.S. courts will not be enforced in Canada), the proposed legislation permits "Canadians to recover in Canadian courts any amounts awarded under those foreign rulings, along with their court costs in Canada and the foreign country."[45]

By early July 1996, Canada's strategy for countering the act was clear. Throughout June and July Ottawa sought to work in concert with its allies in the WTO, the Organization for Economic Cooperation and Development, the EU, the OAS, and the G–7. Within all of these fora, the Canadian government sought successfully to build a coalition of forces firmly aligned against the provisions of Helms-Burton. Senator Helms, meanwhile, unleashed a bitter attack against Canada. He noted that the legislation was successful in persuading businesses to leave Cuba and condemned Canada for "selfishly engaging in irresponsible business transactions." With a blatant disregard for history, he continued: "It's painful to note the hypocrisy of these countries. After all, the United States has rescued every one of them from tyranny at one time or another."[46]

Notwithstanding Helms's hyperbole, President Clinton chose what one *Washington Post* columnist described as "Clintonism: Split, Waffle and Wait."[47] Rather than waive or affirm Title III, the president chose to delay or suspend the provision for six months and has done so twice (most recently in January 1997). The important point from Ottawa's perspective, however, was that Clinton recognized the validity of the law. While the suspension of Title III was welcomed in Ottawa, it was not the decision that Canadian policymakers had been hoping for. As a result, Canada vowed to continue its campaign, along with like-minded countries, to fight against what it regards as the illegal application of the concept of extraterritoriality. In essence, Ottawa feels that Washington's incapacity to resolve its own problems with Havana should not be passed on to its allies.

The Helms-Burton law is in essence the continuation of the earlier Mack amendments and the 1992 Torricelli Bill. Not surprisingly, then, Canada's response, although admittedly far more concerted, amounts to a variation on the same theme. At the heart of these anti-Cuba measures lies the issue of extraterritoriality and the sanctity of international trade rules. It certainly did not hurt the Chrétien government that Canadian public opinion, along with the business community, the NGOs, parliamentarians, and the media, were all strongly opposed to Helms-Burton. A public opinion survey published in April 1996 showed that 71 percent of Canadians polled wanted Ottawa to ignore the U.S. legislation. In the end, however, it was the precedent-setting nature of the act that compelled the political leadership in Ottawa to respond in such a forthright fashion. In so doing, it is fair to say that virtually the entire international community agrees with the Canadian position, largely because of the extraterritorial measures contained in the U.S. legislation.

Helms-Burton also highlighted the seeming inability to divorce Canadian-Cuban relations from the larger Canadian-U.S. dynamic. And, like

other instances in the past, Canada's cordial relations with Cuba compli-
cated its relationship with Washington, just as they had thirty-seven years
earlier. Canadian officials, however, went out of their way to point out to
their U.S. counterparts that in fact Canada's response had little to do with
Castro's Cuba. Indeed, Ottawa would probably have reacted in a similar
fashion if Mexico had been singled out instead. But by the summer of 1996
the die was cast. Once again Canada adhered to its longstanding policy of
maintaining political and commercial linkages with Cuba, and yet again
Washington was on the offensive, seeking to cut or reduce those ties.

Not unexpectedly, Canada's strong opposition to the anti-Cuba law continued into 1997. Upon hearing of Clinton's low-risk decision to suspend
Title III for another six months, International Trade Minister Arthur Eggleton indicted that this was "unacceptable" and mused out loud about the
possibility of challenging the law under the terms of the North American
Free Trade Agreement (NAFTA) by invoking the provisions for a dispute
settlement panel. By early February, however, Mr. Eggleton, in an apparent
shift in strategy or retreat, decided to await the ruling of a European-spon-
sored challenge of Helms-Burton at the World Trade Organization (WTO)
before Canada proceeds with a NAFTA challenge.[48] He was quoted as saying, "Before I go further on the NAFTA challenge, I'd like to have a look at
how it unfolds before the WTO."[49]

Perhaps the most significant development in the Canadian-Cuban dynamic during the Chrétien period was the visit to Havana on 22–23 January 1997 by Foreign Minister Lloyd Axworthy—the first time that a senior
Canadian political figure has stepped foot on Cuban soil since Trudeau's
1976 visit. Not only did the visit generate a great deal of media coverage in
Canada—much of it negative in tone—but it also engendered a fair amount
of critical media and political attention in Washington.[50] U.S. State Department spokesperson Nicholas Burns criticized the trip bluntly: "It doesn't
make sense to reward a dictator in our hemisphere who is completely behind the times. You reward him by sending your foreign minister down to
visit, by having visits as usual, by trading. And we think that's wrong."[51]
In an effort to tame the rhetoric, President Clinton noted, "I'm skeptical,
frankly, that . . . the recent discussions between the Canadians and the
Cubans will lead to advances. I believe that our policy is the proper one,
but I'm glad that the Canadians are trying to make something good happen in Cuba." In contrast, Senator Jesse Helms was irate about the visit
and returned once again to his analogy of Canada's dealings with Cuba
being the equivalent of Chamberlain's appeasement of Adolf Hitler in 1938:
"You had someone named Neville Chamberlain, he went over and sat down
with Hitler and came back and said, 'We can do business with this guy,'

and you saw what happened. Now, if we're going to forget all principle and let Fidel Castro get by with all of his atrocities, then we [had] better look at the status of our principles and Canada certainly should look at hers."[52]

Notwithstanding Helms' ridiculous comments and President Clinton's skepticism, the Canadian government hailed the visit as a breakthrough. According to Foreign Affairs Minister Axworthy, "The reality is that I think we've gone further than anything they have been able to accomplish, by building those bridges."[53] The construction of those bridges began with a series of meetings between Axworthy and Cuban Foreign Minister Roberto Robaina and dinner with President Castro himself. The Canadian Press quoted Castro as saying, "Canada has a lot of prestige. What it says and what it thinks has great meaning for us."[54] The discussions touched upon a number of issues, including economic cooperation and foreign investment, agricultural and environmental matters, drug interdiction, and terrorism. (Reference was also made to the fact that Canada would continue to maintain a modest aid program in Cuba.) Much was made, however, of a joint Canada-Cuba statement on human rights, later touted by Ottawa as a major accomplishment, which had been in the works for more than a year. Among other things, both sides agreed to hold seminars and reciprocal visits of judges, legislators, academics, and other professionals. But there was no specific agreement on improving Cuba's political freedoms, the release of political prisoners, or the introduction of a multiparty system—other than the Cuban commitment to discuss these and other concerns. Still, this commitment on the part of the Cubans should not be dismissed as "meaningless crumbs," as the **Globe and Mail** editorial believes. As Axworthy noted, "What have the Americans accomplished?"[55]

The more important question, though, is how to explain why Axworthy undertook this visit to Cuba in the first place. Interestingly, the answer lies in the forces that have driven the bilateral relationship since 1959. Foremost, of course, is the trade-commercial factor, a key item from the Canadian standpoint. It was important for Canada to solidify political relations at the top as a means of further cementing economic linkages between the countries. The visit, then, was designed in part to shore up Canadian business connections with the island and any market niche that Canadians may have carved out for themselves. Recognizing that the U.S. embargo is likely to be rescinded sooner rather than later—and anticipating intense competition from the Americans—Ottawa wants to ensure that Canadian companies are not squeezed out of the Cuban market by any future onslaught by U.S. businesses. Politically speaking, the visit was consistent with the views of previous Canadian governments in the sense that it was about political symbolism or "optics." It signaled to Washington Ottawa's displeasure with the Helms-Burton law and to the Canadian public that Canada's approach to Cuba differs from that of the United States. For electoral reasons, it is important for Canadian governments to exercise the "Cuba card" whenever they can in order to score some political points at home. (This was pertinent because of a federal election called for June 1997.)Canadians generally prefer a government that is prepared to stand up to the Americans, or at least not to fear adopting a different position. This trip, then, was more about domestic political and economic concerns in Canada than about improving the human rights situation in Castro's Cuba.[56]

In Synthesis

"There's a forgotten Caribbean island called Cuba which, despite the fuss about Mexico and Chile, is going through its own dramatic revolution — and Canada has emerged as one of the key catalysts."[57] Although he exaggerated Canada's importance, Peter C. Newman, one of Canada's key business journalists, is correct in his article when he emphasizes the increasing role played by Canadian companies. The interest has been growing by leaps and bounds in recent years because Canadian companies have built on the steady rate of successful investments that have been made.

Buoyed by a supportive government climate under Prime Minister Jean Chrétien, Canadian commercial interests have increasingly turned to Cuba both as a market for their products and as a place to investigate joint investments. It was thus no surprise that Canadian-Cuban trade increased more than 80 percent between 1994 and 1995, and that Canada became Cuba's major trading partner that year. This new phenomenon is still in the exploratory stage. Nevertheless it is important, since it represents the driving force behind the rapidly evolving Canadian policy. The NGO sector is often overlooked as a major influence too, but as was the case in Central America during the 1980s, it is also an important actor in the Cuban scenario. Finally one should mention the Canadian cultural factor, since Canadians do not fear or reject the Cuban revolutionary process in the same way that mainstream America does. The increasing number of Canadians traveling to Cuba (more than 160,000 in the 1995–96 winter season) illustrates this fact.

The result is that Canadian policy toward Cuba has rediscovered the thread of the early Trudeau policy, with the major difference that the business community, eager to "make hay while the sun shines," is now particularly keen to encourage Ottawa to maintain that policy. Under Brian Mulroney this sector had begun to make its voice heard, but the Liberal agenda of consistently downplaying (although not completely ignoring) human rights concerns as a factor in Canadian foreign policy, while seeking to improve exports (seen most clearly in the China policy), has touched a resounding chord in the Cuban case. In addition, the enhanced policy provides yet another occasion for the new government to distance itself from the extremely pro-Washington policy of Mulroney. It is this fortuitous mixture of appeasing the NGO community, harnessing the initiatives of the business sector, creating employment in Canada, enhancing the image of an independent and balanced foreign policy (always useful as a factor in domestic politics, especially when it is at the expense of the United States), and respecting the rules of international commerce that has predominated during the Chrétien years.

A key issue in Canadian-Cuban relations has been U.S. policy, with Canada wanting to take commercial advantage of the absence of U.S. competition and encouraging Washington to "turn the page" on the Cuban impasse. To Ottawa, Bill Clinton's words on recognizing Vietnam, moving beyond "the haunting and painful past to find common ground for the future"[58] are equally pertinent to the Cuban case, since "this moment offers us the opportunity to bind up our own wounds that have resisted time for too long. We can now move on to common ground." If this occurs in a relationship with a country where some 58,000 U.S. personnel lost their lives, argues Ottawa, why can this not be done with Cuba, where it is also clear that there are substantial financial gains for U.S. corporations to make? Most countries in the world community desire this change in policy, as can be seen from the November 1996 condemnation of the U.S. embargo in the UN General Assembly by a 137 to 3 vote.

Since 1993, the commercial and political profile of Canadian-Cuban relations again rose. While nowhere near the high point of the early 1980s, they did regain both the government interest and commercial respectability that had been missing during the Mulroney years. In light of the abundant evidence to demonstrate the value of closer bilateral ties, one wonders why it took Ottawa so long to realize the commercial potential in the first place.

Conclusion

Followers of Canada's renewed interests in Cuba, seeing the high profile role of Canadian business there or hearing the prime minister speak about U.S.-Cuban relations or perhaps seeing the increased NGO interest, can well be excused for speculating that Canada is pursuing a major foreign policy initiative in Cuba. They are wrong, however.

It is important to recognize that, despite the strong commercial interest in Cuba, the large and increasing number of tourists who travel there, and even the strong statements of Canadian politicians on the controversial points of the Helms-Burton law, this process does not constitute a fresh approach toward Cuba. The businesspeople are simply doing what they would in Mexico or Chile, namely, pursuing solid commercial opportunities while their larger competition from the United States is out of the picture. Vacationers continue to travel to Cuba, not because of any fundamental ideological affinity but because, compared to southern Florida, it is safer and cheaper. And Canadian legislators have spoken out in defense of Canadian policy because they are furious at the Helms-Burton law, which they see as discriminatory and harmful. For example, the extension of U.S. protection to new, post-expropriation nationals goes directly against standard international legal practices. In addition, they see it as an approach that seeks to bully Canada, preaching deference in a most unsubtle fashion.

What Canada is seeking in its relationship with Cuba and also with the United States is a level playing field in both commercial and political terms. It wants to be able to trade with Havana in the same way that Great Britain or Japan can. It recognizes the weak points in the U.S. policy toward the Castro government, since most Canadian politicians believe that nearly four decades of that approach constitute a major failure in U.S. foreign policy. It believes that the 1990s are not the 1960s and that it is time for clearer minds to prevail.

There is nothing earth-shattering in that approach, nothing radical or particularly innovative. Rather, it seeks to recognize some self-evident truths: that Cuba does not represent a threat to any nation in the Americas; that

Havana has shown every desire to leave behind its policies of exporting revolution and now is struggling to maintain the core of its social policies in the face of harsh, post-Soviet realities; that the policy employed by Washington these past decades has been clearly unsuccessful; and that the solution afforded by legislation such as the Torricelli and the Helms-Burton laws, namely, to internationalize the conflict and co-opt other nations to support U.S. goals, is wrong, immoral, and impractical. Finally Canada believes that the best way to influence Cuban behavior is through a policy of constructive engagement and dialogue, not isolation and harassment, especially when U.S. allies are also being punished. In recognizing these realities, it is also important to recognize that the international community at large also holds these truths to be self-evident.

Canada has not "gone soft" on Cuba. Nor is it seeking to make a "fast buck." Rather, following the government of Brian Mulroney that was extremely pro-Reagan and pro-Bush to the point where that support was one of the main reasons that he became the most unpopular prime minister in Canadian history, the Chrétien government is merely swinging back to pursue the fundamental tenets of Canadian foreign policy. Undoubtedly there are good business opportunities in Cuba (as many U.S. interests know since allegedly more than 100 have signed letters of intent to invest in Cuba once normalization of relations takes place), and it would be foolish for Canadian companies not to pursue them. Without a doubt their U.S. counterparts would be doing exactly the same if government policy were to permit this.

It is significant to emphasize too that Canadian politicians are not "closet socialists" who are living out a vicarious ideological pleasure by supporting the Castro regime. On the contrary, on several occasions the Canadian government has vigorously protested the human rights record of the Castro government and cosponsored motions to this effect at the UN Human Rights Commission. Even the commercial ties between Canada and Cuba are not without flaws. Indeed, despite much fanfare, the amount of development assistance to Cuba has been limited—far less than that to Haiti or the anglophone Caribbean, or even right-wing countries such as Indonesia. It is especially significant that there is sufficient doubt and bureaucratic lethargy in Ottawa that official trade credits did not increase when other countries, most noticeably France or Spain, were increasing theirs. Finally, government literature points out to potential Canadian investors that political and commercial risks are high in Cuba and that Canada does not have an investment protection agreement (as do some European countries). In short, the Canadian government's approach to Cuba is not as exceptional as critics of its policy appear to believe.

In pursuing this policy toward Cuba, Ottawa is doing precisely what it did in the eighteenth century, namely, pursuing promising trade possibilities. Salt cod, lumber, and potatoes have now been replaced by spare parts, food, and tourists, but the fundamental underpinnings of the relationship are very much the same. Both nations depend on exporting to survive, and ideology plays, and traditionally has played, an extremely unimportant role in the development of the bilateral relationship. Since Canada has few political empire-building pretensions and is a minor player in the major leagues of international politics, it is much easier for Ottawa to develop relations with nations regardless of official likes and dislikes about their ideological affiliation. In sum, Canadian policy toward Cuba is normal, pursuing similar approaches as it does toward Mexico or Italy, Japan or Chile. It is not a "special" relationship at all; it has been made to appear so because of the atypical manner in which U.S. policy has been formulated. Ottawa's policy toward Cuba is not unlike that of dozens of nations around the globe, and Washington's approach is badly out of step with that of the international community.

There are thus two key words in seeking to summarize three centuries of this Canadian-Cuban relationship: "pragmatic" and "normal." The pragmatic nature of the relationship is seen most clearly in the trading focus that has dominated bilateral ties. Canada exported produce to Cuba when it was a Spanish colony and throughout the twentieth century when it became independent of Madrid. Whether under Machado or Batista, as well as under the government of Fidel Castro, the political label really has not been that important. Both countries have also sought to pursue a normal diplomatic relationship. Understandably, this was more difficult in the wake of the October 1962 Missile Crisis and as Havana became more dependent on the Soviet camp. There is still a residue of suspicion among the intelligence-gathering community in Canada about Cuba's "real goals" in Canada, and visas are often denied as a result of pressure from these groups, who still keep a watchful eye on supporters of Cuba in Canada, and Cuba remains a "scheduled country" for CSIS, Canada's counterespionage agency, which remains mired in a Cold War mindset. However, not being weighed down by the responsibilities of being a superpower but respecting the aspirations and successes of revolutionary Cuba, Ottawa never came close to severing diplomatic ties with Havana, despite pressure from Washington to do so. Instead, relations were as normal as they could be during a time of Cold War tension and disagreement with Cuba's role in international affairs. With the demise of the Soviet Union, the root of much of this disagreement simply disappeared, and Ottawa has swung back to the "business as normal" approach that has traditionally dominated the relationship.

That is not to say that Ottawa has completely overcome the security concerns that permeated the relationship for much of the last three decades nor that it is in agreement with many of the policies currently employed by Havana. Rather, its position is largely that differences of opinion are to be expected in all international relationships, as is the case between Canada and the United States (over what Washington perceives to be unfair grain and lumber subsidies), France (over nuclear testing in the South Pacific), and Spain (over excessive fishing in the North Atlantic). The important point is to see whether there are more salient characteristics that foster a cooperative rather than a disjunctive approach and that can be used as a basis for negotiation. Ottawa does not agree with many aspects of Indonesian policy, for example, but it has not cut off relations with Jakarta or prohibited Canadian companies from trading there. The Canadian approach, therefore, is pragmatic, as it is in its approach to Havana.

Despite the image projected by conservative sectors in the United States, Canada does not ignore the negative aspects of Cuba; the abuses of human rights, for example, are closely monitored by Canadian embassy staff in Havana, and there have been several formal protests at the Cuban government's treatment of dissidents. The views expressed are clear and well argued:

> On the other hand, the Cuban government has given no indication that it intends to move towards multi-party democracy. There has been limited reform of the National Assembly. Canada and other countries continue to have serious concerns on the government's human rights performance, especially in the area of civil and political rights (freedom of assembly, freedom of speech and freedom from arbitrary detention). At the same time, Canada recognizes Cuba's achievements in economic and social rights.[1]

The position on human rights is important because it shows that Canada is not guilty of simply ignoring these in favor of chasing commercial possibilities in Cuba.[2] Ottawa congratulated Cuba on inviting José Ayala Lasso, the UN high commissioner on human rights, to Cuba in November 1994 and indeed arranged for Ayala Lasso to meet with Cuban Foreign Relations Minister Roberto Robaina in Ottawa in March 1995.

At the official luncheon given in honor of Robaina by his Canadian counterpart André Ouellet, the latter noted that he had deliberately sat Robaina next to Canada's chief electoral officer as a means of stimulating a conversation on political reform in Cuba and offered Canadian assistance in any aspects of electoral or political reform that Havana might wish to pursue. That said, he made perfectly clear that this was a decision for Cubans to make, since their political traditions and culture were vastly different from those of North America. In his reply and later in a press conference, Robaina emphasized that the Canadian government had shown itself to be knowledgeable of conditions in Cuba. Disagreements had been expressed with frankness and clarity. Yet the key word in the Cuban minister's remarks was "respect," a term that Robaina used on half a dozen occasions. Ottawa at all times, even when there was no common ground on certain topics, had shown respect for the Cuban position, which was obviously appreciated by Havana.

The essence of the Canadian government's stand on Cuba is that, despite disagreements with Havana, there is far more on which both governments agree. Instead of concentrating on the negative, it seems more constructive to focus on areas where confidence-building measures can be introduced, bringing both countries closer together and exerting influence in a nonthreatening fashion. Canada, the government has stated clearly, has four basic objectives in Cuba:

> Support for positive, peaceful change in Cuba, both political and economic, in order that Cuba can become a more pluralistic society. Canada seeks to do so through engagement and dialogue rather than isolation.
>
> The promotion of concrete Canadian interests, especially to build on commercial activities. Encouragement of Cuba's full, constructive participation in international affairs. Support of Canadian organizations and individuals pursuing their development activities and exchanges with Cubans.[3]

The main difference between the position espoused by Ottawa and that of Washington is the concept of seeking to bring change in Cuba "through engagement and dialogue rather than isolation." It can be argued that under the Chrétien government a more active pursuit of these goals is being developed, and that commercial ties have become far more important than under his predecessor. It is also clear, however, that none of this constitutes a departure from the traditional Canadian position: Ottawa's policy, after the manifest pro-Washington proclivities of the Mulroney government, which were an aberration in Canadian foreign policy, is now back on course.

This strategy is far different (apart from the issues of human rights and domestic political change) from Washington's approach to Cuba. The independent, essentially pragmatic approach can be seen in a recent government document. In August 1995 the Standing Committee on Foreign Affairs of the Canadian Senate issued a report entitled "Free Trade in the Americas."

This committee, the Canadian equivalent of that chaired by Senator Jesse Helms, devoted significant attention to Cuba. Among its findings:

> The Committee believes that the Helms-Burton bills and the Administration proposals are unacceptable: no country ought to try to impose its own boycott against Cuba, or any other country, in an extraterritorial fashion.[4]

The standard position on the human rights record of Cuba is expressed:

> Vigorous opposition to any U.S.-imposed secondary boycott of Cuba does not mean that Canada should ignore Cuba's human rights record, which still falls far short of internationally acceptable standards. (61)

On trade with Cuba, the government was urged to "fast-track" its approach and was congratulated on its initiatives of the past year:

> The Committee believes that the Canadian government should not delay beginning to build closer trade and investment ties with Cuba. The evidence we received indicates that other countries are pursuing business opportunities in Cuba aggressively. Furthermore, when, and if, U.S. restrictions on trade with Cuba are lifted, as ultimately they were in the case of Vietnam, U.S. investors will not be slow in trying to seize the best opportunities. We commend the Canadian Government for the decision announced last year to give more weight to Canada's relationship with Cuba. (61–62)

This is the essence of Canada's pragmatic foreign policy toward Cuba. While it is displeased with the human rights situation, it is aware of many socioeconomic advances that place Cuba at the head of most social indices for the developing world. Canada also recognizes that the free market reforms taken by Cuba since 1993 are important and, instead of browbeating the government for not doing more, limits itself to constructive suggestions.[5] Canadian policy is firmly based on Cuba's current realities and supports the process of change toward open markets taking place in Cuba, encourages the establishment of a more pluralistic society, and urges all participants to seek a peaceful transition through a process of dialogue, engagement, and trade. Unlike Washington's position on Cuba, Canadian policy suggests that the isolationist approach is not helpful, and as a result, Canada has supported Cuba's return to the OAS, even offering to facilitate dialogue between Washington and Havana, if both parties so desire. And in this policy, as has traditionally been the case for

Ottawa, Canada will pursue its own interests. In sum, it is a *normal* foreign policy—nothing more and nothing less.

For Cuba, the relationship with Canada represents an economic lifeline at a time of great financial difficulties, as well as a potential ally (to a minor degree) on the world stage. There are vast differences between the large, wealthy North American country and the comparatively small Caribbean island. But as Fidel Castro noted, waxing eloquent on Canada in a private meeting with a Nova Scotian trade delegation in January 1994:

> Yet despite these differences they have been our best friends—the most firm and loyal, the most independent. . . . I have always given Canadian-Cuban relations as an example to follow. What a pity that, instead of having the United States so close by, and Canada so far away, it wasn't the other way around. . . . And I often ask myself, just what are these Canadians? Are they English? Or Europeans? Are they French? Or Indians and Inuit? What are they anyway? And I can find only one answer: they are good people.
>
> In this world in which there have been so many colonialists—the Canadians have colonialized nobody.
>
> In this world where rich nations have intervened everywhere—especially in Africa and Latin America—the Canadians have not intervened anywhere. So what are the Canadians? And I say that they are good people, wonderful people. And for all these reasons we Cubans are proud to be their friends.[6]

Since the eighteenth century, Canada and Cuba have developed a fairly solid trading relationship, one that continues to this day. It was based on commerce that was mutually beneficial. The Cuban revolutionary process brought new challenges to the relationship, and in general each country approached the other with respect and cooperation. It is not an exceptional working relationship, since there are clear differences of opinion on a variety of matters. There is also a commercial imbalance, given Canada's status as Cuba's largest trading partner, whereas Cuba is relatively insignificant to Ottawa from a commercial standpoint.

The troubled Washington-Havana axis serves as a useful contrast to the Canadian-Cuban dynamic and has led these past four decades to some U.S. politicians criticizing Ottawa's approach to what it perceives as the "Cuba problem." The fact is, however, that there is no problem. Indeed, the only country in the world which still has significant differences with Cuba is the United States. It clearly is time for Washington to exorcise the demons of the 1960s, since with the new millennium fast approaching it is clearer than ever that its policy is an anachronism as well as a failure. Perhaps Washington officialdom should consider the Canadian approach.

Notes

Chapter 1

1. See the letter to Dr. Coleman from the Department of External Affairs, Ottawa, March 11, 1949, 7, National Archives, Ottawa (file no. unknown).

2. For a detailed discussion of this report, see Boyer, 5.

3. Cited ibid., 7.

4. Ibid., 11.

5. McFarlane, 25.

6. McFarlane suggests that the influential Americans deliberately sought out Van Horne's cooperation, in part because of his Canadian citizenship: "The problem for the general [Alger] and the secretary of war [Root] was that the U.S. military administration in Cuba, fearful of a Cuban nationalist backlash at the wave of U.S. speculators then devouring the island, was reluctant to allow non-Cuban nationals to control the island's railways. Van Horne, as a Canadian, might be able to succeed in bending the rules where U.S. promoters had failed." See ibid., 27.

7. For information in this brief section we are indebted to Professor Jack Ogelsby, who has pioneered work on Canadian-Latin American relations.

8. See Boyer, 24.

9. Much of the information in this analysis of the role of Canadian banks in Cuba is taken from McDowall, 169–201.

10. Figures cited in this section are from Boyer, 32.

11. For a detailed discussion of these trends see ibid., 77–80.

12. See "Annual report of the Havana Office," National Archives of Canada, RG 20, vol. 1459, file 18–1–13–1948, 3.

13. See R. G. C. Smith, "Conditions in Cuba," May 28, 1948, National Archives of Canada, RG 20, vol. 1459, file 18–1–13–1948, 4.

14. See the "Annual Report of the Havana Office: 1952," National Archives of Canada, RG 20, vol. 1459, file 18–1–13 (1952), 3.

15. See Ambassador Scott's letter to the secretary of state for external affairs, April 2, 1953. National Archives of Canada, RG 25, vol. 2750, file 513–40 (20–20), 2–3. He further noted that "the friendly dominance" of the United States was "best illustrated by the position of Mr. Beaulac, U.S. Ambassador. His every action is news, and it is an unusual day on which his picture does not appear in the press" (3).

16. See Ogelsby, 58.

17. See letter from Mariano Brull to Rafael P. González Muñoz, minister of state, Sept. 12, 1947, Archives, Ministry of External Relations, Havana.

18. See Mariano Brull's letter to Carlos Hevia, minister of state, Feb. 16, 1949, Archives, Ministry of External Relations, Havana.

19. See Mariano Brull to Carlos Hevia, minister of state, Jan. 21, 1949, Archives, Ministry of External Relations, Havana. Following the departure of Brull in August of that year, two chargés d'affaires took over until 1952, when D. H. Pupo y Proenza arrived in Ottawa as ambassador, to be replaced in 1955 by Dr. Juan A. Vázquez Bello.

20. See the Letter of Instructions sent to the Canadian ambassador by the secretary of state for external affairs, January 31, 1953, National Archives, Ottawa, File no. 4900–B–4–40, 10.

21. See his report, "Current Events in Cuba for the Period December 11, 1955–January 31, 1956," February 1, 1956, 1, National Archives, Ottawa, RG 25, vol. 2750, file 513–40.

22. See his review of current events, to cover the period March 1–27, 1956, and sent to the secretary of state for external affairs, March 28, 1956, National Archives, Ottawa, RG 25, vol. 2750, file 513–40, 4.

23. See his report to the secretary of state for external affairs, "Political Situation in Cuba," March 26, 1957, 3, National Archives, Ottawa, RG 25, Acc 86–87/414, vol. 5, file 10224–40, pt. 4.

24. See Browne's report, "Current Events in Cuba, Nov. 1–Dec. 8, 1956," submitted to External Affairs on December 9, 1956, National Archives, Ottawa, RG 25, vol. 2750, file 513–40, 2.

25. See G. A. Browne, "Political Situation in Cuba," July 29, 1957 (no. D-283), National Archives, Ottawa, file 10224–40, 2.

26. See Ambassador Allard's numbered dispatch (D-172) of May 9, 1958 to the secretary of state for external affairs, National Archives, Ottawa, file 10224–40, 1–2.

27. See the "Annual Report on the Work of the Havana Office for the Year 1958," National Archives, Ottawa, RG 20, vol. 1459, file 18–1–13–1958, 2.

28. See the Department of External Affairs (American Division) report, "Memorandum for the Governor General," June 21, 1957, National Archives, Ottawa, file 10224–40, 2–4.

29. Later Canadian diplomats would seek to excuse their misinterpreting Cuban reality: "We have come to the conclusion that the reporting was very good. Indeed the adequacy of the reporting may be considered remarkable when one realizes the very trying circumstances in which the mission had to operate. . . . The two factors, one civilian and the other military, which turned the tide of events in favour of Castro were extremely difficult to predict accurately in the conditions existing in Cuba during 1958." See numbered letter 246 to the under-secretary of state for external affairs, entitled "Situation in Cuba," February 13, 1959, National Archives, Ottawa, RG 25 ACC 86–87/414, vol. 5, file 10224–40, pt. 5, 1.

Chapter 2

1. Nash, "Public Opinion," 2.

2. McIntosh, *Ottawa Unbuttoned,* 101.

3. Cited in Newman, *Renegade in Power,* 252.

4. Cited in Nash, *Kennedy and Diefenbaker,* 56.

5. In his memoirs, Charles Ritchie, appointed Canadian ambassador to the United States in January 1962, recounts his meetings with Diefenbaker and the incumbent ambassador, Arnold Heeney: "Not only are there substantive differences of policy involved, but the atmosphere is poisoned by the mutual aversion of the Prime Minister for the President and the President for the Prime Minister. President Kennedy seems to regard Mr. Diefenbaker as a mischief-making old man who cannot be trusted, whereas Mr. Diefenbaker sees the President as an arrogant young man and a political enemy." See Ritchie, *Diplomatic Passport,* 185–86.

6. Robinson, *Diefenbaker's World,* 168.

7. See Nash, *Kennedy and Diefenbaker,* 121.

8. Robinson, *Diefenbaker's World,* 206–7.

9. Nash, *Kennedy and Diefenbaker,* 160.

10. The Kennedy White House was also displeased with Secretary of State for External Affairs Howard Green's opaque criticism of U.S. conduct in the Bay of Pigs fiasco. It was even more disdainful of Green's suggestion that Canada, perhaps with the assistance of both Mexico and Brazil, could conceivably play the role of mediator between Washington and Havana.

11. Ritchie, *Storm Signals,* 16–17.

12. It is worth noting, however, that the Diefenbaker government, though unwilling to support an embargo against Cuba, did adhere to some of the embargo's provisions, including those on shipping strategic materials to Cuba and using Canada as a transshipping route for third country goods.

13. McNaught, 7.

14. Ibid., 8.

15. Cited in Newman, *Renegade in Power,* 263.

16. Ambassador Américo Cruz to Raúl Roa, January 16, 1961, 1, Archives, Ministry of External Relations, Havana.

17. Nash, *Kennedy and Diefenbaker,* 150.

18. Cited in Robinson, *Diefenbaker's World,* 147.

19. Cited in Morley, *Imperial State and Revolution,* 194.

20. Ambassador Allan Anderson to the secretary of state for external affairs, November 4, 1960, 2, RG 25 90–91/001, vol. 66, file 4568–40, pt. 2, National Archives, Ottawa.

21. Allan Anderson to the secretary of state for external affairs, October 18, 1960, 1–2, file 4568–40, sec. 70, National Archives, Ottawa.

22. Memo from Luis Molina Parrado to Benito Besada Ramos, head of the Legal Department (Departamento de Consultoria Legal), November 18, 1960, 4, Archives, Ministry of External Relations, Havana.

23. See the diplomatic note from the Canadian embassy in Havana to the Ministry of External Relations, October 8, 1963, and the reply, dated June 23, 1964 (both in the archives of the Ministry of External Relations, Havana).

24. Note from the Canadian embassy in Washington to the under-secretary of

state for external affairs, January 10, 1961, RG 25, Acc 90–91/001, file 4568–40, pt. 4, Archives of the Department of External Affairs, Ottawa.

25. A. E. Ritchie to R. A. Farquharson, minister-counselor at the Canadian embassy, Washington, February 10, 1961, 1, RG 25, Acc. 90–91/001, file 4568–40, pt. 4, Archives of the Department of External Affairs, Ottawa.

26. See the letter from the Canadian ambassador to the under-secretary of state for external affairs, October 25, 1960, 1, RG 25, 90–91/001, vol. 66, file 4568–40, pt. 2, Archives of the Department of External Affairs, Ottawa. The ambassador continued with a summary of their talk: "But Bonsal does not like our neutral position. He believes that the threat is not only to Cuba, not only to Latin America, but to the United States and Canada, and to NATO. And he believes that the threat is imminent" (p. 2).

27. See the letter from the Canadian chargé d'affaires to the under-secretary of state for external affairs, November 4, 1960, 1, RG 25, 90–91-001, vol. 52, file 2444–40, pt. 5, National Archives, Ottawa.

28. Robinson, *Diefenbaker's World*, 146.

29. See the ambassador's report to the under-secretary of state for external affairs, January 24, 1961, RG 25, 90–91/001, vol. 67, file 4568–40, pt. 4, National Archives, Ottawa. Comments from Mr. Parlour were an appendix to this dispatch.

30. Robinson, *Diefenbaker's World*, 166.

31. See the appendix to Ambassador Anderson's letter to the under-secretary of state for external affairs, January 18, 1961, RG 25, 90–91/001, vol. 67, file 4568–40, pt. 4, National Archives, Ottawa.

32. Nash, *Kennedy and Diefenbaker*, 104.

33. See the letter from Ambassador Américo Cruz to Dr. Carlos Olivares Sánchez, April 27, 1961, 1, Archives, Ministry of External Relations, Havana. (All quotations in this paragraph are from the same letter.)

34. Letter from Cmdte. Guillermo Jiménez to Cuban Ambassador Américo Cruz, June 8, 1961, 3, Archives, Ministry of External Relations, Havana.

35. "[Diefenbaker] told me that Canada looked very favourably upon the Cuban Revolution, and understood that to a large degree the U.S. press had covered Cuba with great irresponsibility and sensationalism." Significantly, though, the prime minister, "informed me that the only thing which concerned Canada was Cuba's foreign policy, and he asked me what there was of truth to the rumours about communist infiltration in our government." See the letter from Ambassador Luis A. Baralt to Marcelo Fernández Font, interim minister of external relations, 1, Archives, Ministry of External Relations, Havana.

36. Letter of Américo Cruz to Dr. Carlos Olivares Sánchez, Havana, June 6, 1961, 1, Archives, Ministry of External Relations, Havana.

37. Américo Cruz to Raúl Roa, minister of external relations, May 15, 1961, 1, Archives, Ministry of External Relations, Havana.

38. Américo Cruz to Dr. Carlos Olivares Sánchez, January 24, 1961, 1, Archives, Ministry of External Relations, Havana.

39. Américo Cruz to Dr. Carlos Olivares Sánchez, April 25, 1961, 1, Archives, Ministry of External Relations, Havana.

40. Ibid.

41. Américo Cruz to Raúl Roa, August 29, 1962, 1, Archives, Ministry of External Relations, Havana.

42. Hector Allard to the secretary of state for external affairs, April 30, 1959, 4, file no. 5670-40, 31, National Archives, Ottawa.

43. Hector Allard to the secretary of state for external affairs, D–154, April 2, 1959, 5, 10224-40, 54, 30, National Archives, Ottawa. Ambassador Allard ends his dispatch by noting: "In the circumstances, there can only be one reply to the question raised at the beginning of this letter as to whether or not Castro could be the leader of a government—and it is a most emphatic 'No'" (6).

44. Allan Anderson to the secretary of state for external affairs, January 13, 1960, 2, RG 25, vol. 2750, file 51340, National Archives, Ottawa.

45. Allan Anderson to the under-secretary of state for external affairs, November 20, 1959, 2, RG 25, vol. 2750, file 51340, National Archives, Ottawa.

46. Allan Anderson to the secretary of state for external affairs, November 10, 1959, 1, RG 251, vol. 2750, file 51340, National Archives, Ottawa.

47. Allan Anderson to the secretary of state for external affairs, November 10, 1959, 3, RG 25, vol. 2750, file 51340, National Archives, Ottawa.

48. Allan Anderson to the under-secretary of state for external affairs, December 28, 1960, 1, RG 25, 90–91/001, vol. 223, file 10224-40, pt. 10, National Archives, Ottawa.

49. Allan Anderson to the under-secretary of state for external affairs, October 18, 1960, 1, RG 25, 90–91/001, vol. 223, file 10224-40, pt. 9, National Archives, Ottawa.

50. Américo Cruz to Raúl Roa, August 29, 1962, 1, Archives, Ministry of External Relations, Havana.

51. Allan Anderson to the under-secretary of state for external affairs, October 25, 1960, 2, RG 25, 90–91/001, vol. 66, file 4568-40, pt. 2, National Archives, Ottawa.

52. Allan Anderson to the under-secretary of state for external affairs, November 14, 1960, 2, RG 25, 90–91/001, vol. 66, file 4568-40, pt. 2, National Archives, Ottawa.

53. Allan Anderson to the under-secretary of state for external affairs, October 25, 1960, 2, RG 25, 90–91/001, vol. 66, file 4568-40, pt. 2, National Archives, Ottawa (emphasis added).

54. Diefenbaker, *One Canada,* 79–80.

55. Again sounding a note of defiant nationalism, Secretary of State for External Affairs Howard Green pleaded in Cabinet for an independent position by Canada: "'If we go along with the Americans now,' he said, 'we'll be their vassals forever.'" Cited in Newman, *Renegade in Power,* 337.

56. Américo Cruz to Raúl Roa, September 5, 1962, 1, Archives, Ministry of External Relations, Havana.

57. Américo Cruz to Raúl Roa, October 29, 1962, 1, Archives, Ministry of External Relations, Havana.

58. Ibid.

59. "He insisted time and time again that Cuba simply had to consent to the bases being inspected. . . . It appears that the Canadian government does not want to make any commitment towards Cuba, and is trying to follow the U.S. line." Américo Cruz to Raúl Roa, November 6, 1962, 1, Archives, Ministry of External Relations, Havana.

60. Cited in Morley, *Imperial State and Revolution,* 191.

61. Américo Cruz to Raúl Roa, May 26, 1963, 1, Archives, Ministry of External Relations, Havana.

62. Ibid.

63. Américo Cruz to Raúl Roa, May 17, 1961, 1, Archives, Ministry of External Relations, Havana.

64. M. N. Bow to the under-secretary of state for external affairs, June 15, 1961, 4, RG 25, 90–91/001, vol. 224, file 10224–40, pt. 1, National Archives, Ottawa.

Chapter 3

1. Pearson, *Peace in the Family of Man,* 19–20.

2. Pearson, *Words and Occasions,* 188.

3. Ibid., 98.

4. Ibid., 88.

5. "Canada must continue the closest possible co-operation with the United States and with her friends in NATO. . . . The Cuban crisis showed up some of the gaps in our partnership," ibid., 205.

6. Ibid., 199.

7. "It was the Cuban thing, more than anything else, that changed my mind. It was the thought that here we were, a part of continental defence, on the eve of this possible great tragedy, and we were completely impotent allies." Cited in Thordarson, *Lester Pearson, Diplomat and Politician,* 121–22.

8. Ibid., 123.

9. Pearson, *Mike,* 128.

10. Ibid., 120–21.

11. See his diary entry in *Mike,* 139–40.

12. Cited in Nash, *Kennedy and Diefenbaker,* 314.

13. Letter to George M. Schuther, assistant director, Trade Services Branch of the Department of Trade and Commerce from O. G. Stoner, Economic Division, Department of External Affairs, October 24, 1963, RG 25, 80–81 (22) box 3, 20–1–2–Cuba, vol. 2, Archives of the Department of External Affairs, Ottawa.

14. Américo Cruz to Raúl Roa, July 29, 1963, 2–3, Archives, Ministry of External Relations, Havana.

15. Roberto Márquez to Raúl Roa, October 21, 1967, 1, Archives, Ministry of External Relations, Havana.

16. Roberto Márquez to Raúl Roa, October 10, 1967, 1, Archives, Ministry of External Relations, Havana.

17. Américo Cruz to Raúl Roa, June 1, 1967, 1, Archives, Ministry of External Relations, Havana.

18. Américo Cruz to Raúl Roa, August 18, 1967, 1, Archives, Ministry of External Relations, Havana.

19. Américo Cruz to Raúl Roa, September 11, 1967, 1, Archives, Ministry of External Relations, Havana.

20. Américo Cruz to Raúl Roa, February 7, 1964, 1, Archives, Ministry of External Relations, Havana.

21. Américo Cruz to Raúl Roa, March 23, 1965, 1, Archives, Ministry of External Relations, Havana.

22. Américo Cruz to Raúl Roa, August 4, 1967, 1, Archives, Ministry of External Relations, Havana.

23. Américo Cruz to Raúl Roa, July 31, 1964, Archives, Ministry of External Relations, Havana.

24. Américo Cruz to Raúl Roa, October 7, 1966, 1, Archives, Ministry of External Relations, Havana.

25. Carlos A. Neira García to Américo Cruz, September 14, 1967, 1, Archives, Ministry of External Relations, Havana.

26. "NATO Ministerial Meeting, December 1963. The Situation in Latin America and Cuba: Talking Points," 20–1–1–13, vol. 1, 2, Archives of the Department of External Affairs, Ottawa.

27. See "Papers for the Meeting between Prime Minister Pearson and President Johnson," January 13, 1964, 3, 20–1–2–Cuba ("Political Affairs-Policy and Background-Global Trend-Latin American Situation"), Archives of the Department of External Affairs, Ottawa.

28. Ibid., 7.

29. Ibid., 9–10, emphasis added.

30. Ibid., 10.

31. Ibid., 11.

32. Ibid., 10.

Chapter 4

1. Cited in Stewart, *Shrug,* 107–8.

2. Cited in Granatstein and Bothwell, *Pirouette,* 195.

3. See Latin American Working Group, "Canadian Investment," 1.

4. Ibid., 24.

5. Ibid., 23.

6. All figures taken from ibid., 25.

7. P. A. Bridle, Latin American Division memo on the prime minister's interview with the Cuban ambassador, December 31, 1968, file 20–1–2–Cuba, vol. 8 (May 1968–April 1969), Archives of the Department of External Affairs, Ottawa.

8. See "Talking Points for Dinner Given by the Ambassador of Cuba in Honour of the SSEA," February 13, 1974, file 20–1–2–Cuba, vol. 27 (73–10–01 to 74–09–31), Archives of the Department of External Affairs, Ottawa.

9. See the memo from Canadian embassy, Havana, to under-secretary of state for external affairs, July 28, 1969, 20–1–2–Cuba, vol. 10 (June 21, 1969–December 31, 1969), 1–2.

10. Letter from ambassador to Cuba León Mayrand to under-secretary of state for external affairs, January 15, 1969, 20–1–2–CUBA, vol. 8 (May 1968–April 1969), 1. Archives of the Department of External Affairs, Ottawa.

11. "Trade with Cuba: The Question of Export Credit Insurance," draft memorandum for the prime minister prepared by M.S. of the Department of External Affairs, April 17, 1969, 20–1–2–Cuba, vol. 9, 1, Archives of the Department of External Affairs, Ottawa.

12. See the memo of J. C. Langley prepared for the under-secretary of state for external relations, and sent on April 29, 1969, to the Canadian embassy in Washington, 20–1–2–Cuba, 2, Archives of the Department of External Affairs, Ottawa.

13. "Confidential Notes for Meeting of Prime Minister with President Nixon, March 24–25, 1969," 20–1–2–CUBA, vol. 8 (May 1968–April 1969), 2, Archives of the Department of External Affairs, Ottawa.

14. Charles E. Stedman, Caribbean Branch, "Canada-Cuba Relations," November 15, 1971, 20–1–2–Cuba, 19, 10, 1, Archives of the Department of External Affairs, Ottawa.

15. See Trudeau's remarks, reported in the *CIIA Monthly Report on Canadian External Relations*, vol. 8, no. 3 (March 1969), 84.

16. See the confidential memo from F. M. Tovell to P. A. Bridle of the Latin American Division, December 22, 1969, 20–1–2–Cuba, Archives of the Department of External Affairs, Ottawa.

17. Cited in *International Canada*, vol. 5 (1974), December 1974, 231.

18. *International Canada*, vol. 6 (February 1975), 31–32.

19. *International Canada*, vol. 6 (July/August 1975), 202.

20. *Canadian News Facts (1975)*, 1365–66.

21. *International Canada*, vol. 6 (February 1975), 29.

22. See the unpublished report by Baldomero Alvarez Ríos, Agustín Calzada Fuentes, and Armando López Moosman on behalf of the directors of Radio Habana Cuba (October 1967), Archives, Ministry of External Relations, Havana.

23. Confidential note from the office of Raúl Roa, minister of external relations to vice-minister and Departamento Política II, December 25, 1968, Archives, Ministry of External Relations, Havana.

24. The actual letter, dated December 14, 1970, from Pierre Trudeau to Fidel Castro thanking the Cuban leader, was short and to the point:

Dear Mr. Prime Minister,

On behalf of the Government of Canada I wish to express to you our sincere thanks for the co-operation extended by your Government in the arrangements leading to the safe release of Mr. James Cross.

The co-operation of your officials in Havana and in Canada proved to be a vital element in the early stages of working out the details of the safe conduct offer, as well as in the subsequent lengthy period waiting and on the day when these plans finally bore fruit.

The Canadian Government greatly appreciates the helpful attitude shown by the Cuban Government throughout this situation. I also understand that, in keeping with the good relations between our two countries, the individuals who have been given safe-conduct will not while in Cuba undertake any activity directed against Canada.

I am most grateful for your personal interest in the matter and for the effective part played by your Ambassador and his staff in making this humanitarian gesture possible.

See file 20–1–2–Cuba, vol. 12 (December 1, 1970–April 30, 1971), Archives of the Department of External Affairs, Ottawa.

25. See the dispatch of Serge April to the under-secretary of state for external affairs, January 19, 1977, 2, file 20–1–2–Cuba, vol. 28 (October 1, 1974–December 15, 1977), Archives of the Department of External Affairs, Ottawa.

26. See William Mader's detailed cover story, "A Very Special Chemistry," *Time* (Canada), February 9, 1976, 10.

27. Ibid., 6.

28. Ibid.

29. *International Canada*, vol. 7 (January 1976), 5.

30. *International Canada*, vol. 7 (February 1976), 29.

31. Ibid.

32. Four Cubans (including two diplomats) were expelled, while a fifth, who was already out of the country, was not allowed to return. Apparently they had used the Montreal consulate of Cuba to train a mercenary to undertake acts of espionage in what was then Rhodesia.

33. *International Canada*, vol. 8 (January 1977), 18.

34. See CIDA, *Canadians in the Third World*, 19.

35. In the summer of 1976, Canadian ambassador James Hyndman passed along to Fidel Castro a personal letter from Trudeau, in which he noted his difference of opinion with his Cuban counterpart, while encouraging Castro to disengage from Angola: "I have continued to watch with considerable interest the passage of events in Southern Africa and congratulate you on your program of troop withdrawals from Angola. I continue to be of the opinion, as I expressed to you in Cuba, that the resolution of the basic political problems of that country, and the achievement of permanent stability, will be hastened by the removal of all elements of foreign involvement. Your commitment to a military disengagement is accordingly welcomed by the Canadian government." Letter of August 10, 1976, file 20–1–2–Cuba, vol. 28 (October 1, 1974–December 12, 1977), Archives of the Department of External Affairs, Ottawa.

36. Sawatsky, *Men in the Shadows*, 4.

37. See the note from Diego R. Rivero, Cuban consul in Montreal, to Ambassador Américo Cruz, April 13, 1967, accompanying the letter from the exile group, Archives, Ministry of Foreign Relations, Havana.

38. Sawatsky, *Men in the Shadows*, 6. In his book the author emphasizes that Canadian and U.S. security forces regularly traded information on Cuban activities

in Canada. Specifically, he notes: "The CIA received complete access to security service files on Cubans in Canada, including surveillance results—information that only a host government could effectively provide," ibid.

39. See "Memo for the Minister. Subject: 'Cuban request for a Courtesy Call,'" June 25, 1981, file 20–1–2–Cuba, vol. 32 (November 1, 1980–August 31, 1982), Archives of the Department of External Affairs, Ottawa.

40. See J. R. Morden, acting director general, Bureau of Development, Industry and Science Relations, memo for the minister ("Canada/Cuba Relations paper"), May 13, 1980, 1, file 37–16–1–Cuba, vol. 12 (March 1, 1980–October 10, 1982), Archives of the Department of External Affairs, Ottawa.

41. See the telegram from the Department of External Affairs to Canadian Ambassador Bartleman on the topic "Meeting with José Arbesú, 26 May," file 20–1–2–Cuba, vol. 32 (November 1, 1980–August 31, 1982), 1–2, Archives of the Department of External Affairs, Ottawa.

42. See the letter from Pierre E. Trudeau to Fidel Castro of April 3, 1981, file 20–1–2–Cuba, vol. 32 (November 1, 1980–August 31, 1982), Archives, Department of External Affairs, Ottawa.

43. Ibid.

44. Trudeau, *Memoirs*, 301.

45. See his dispatch ("Farewell interview of Ambassador Léon Mayrand with Raúl Roa," June 3, 1970, 5, file 20–1–2–Cuba, vol. 11 (January 1, 1970–November 30, 1970), Archives, Department of External Affairs, Ottawa.

46. See the dispatch of Ambassador Bow to the under-secretary of state for external affairs, April 4, 1974, 2, file 20–1–2–Cuba, vol. 27 (October 1, 1973–September 31, 1974).

47. See the memo of H. R. Rousseau, Cuba Desk officer, "Possible Invitation to Ramón Castro," March 17, 1983, 1–2, file 20–1–2–Cuba, vol. 33 (September 1, 1982–December 12, 1983), Archives, Department of External Affairs, Ottawa.

48. Draft memo for the minister of external affairs, "The Future Course of Canadian Relations with Cuba," September 13, 1974, 4, file 20–1–2–Cuba, vol. 27 (October 1, 1973–September 31, 1974), Archives, Department of External Affairs.

49. Cited in the dispatch of Ambassador Mac Bow, reporting on his meeting with Fidel Castro, January 9, 1974, 1, file 20–1–2–Cuba, vol. 27 (October 1, 1973–September 31, 1974), Archives, Department of External Affairs.

50. See the memo, "Le règlement municipal contre les incendies et la chancellerie de Cuba," May 27, 1969, file 20–1–2–Cuba, 2, Archives, Department of External Affairs, Ottawa.

51. See the memo from the Department of Agriculture to the Canadian embassy in Havana ("Cable re: Karsh"), October 22, 1971, file 20–1–2–Cuba, vol. 14 (Oct. 1, 1971–November 30, 1971), Archives, Department of External Affairs, Ottawa.

Chapter 5

1. See "More help after the Storm of the Century from Argentina, Venezuela, Chile and Canada," *Granma International,* April 18, 1993, 1.

2. In all 20,000 tons of potatoes were acquired. The first 5,000 tons were a gift from the federal and New Brunswick governments, while Cuba paid for packaging, cleaning, and sorting of the other 15,000 tons, at a cost of $1,300,000.

3. Dave Todd, "Federal Government's Dithering Stalls Aid to Cuba, Critics Say," *Ottawa Citizen*, May 22, 1993, A6.

4. Cited in Alan Freeman, "Major economic reform Mulroney legacy," *Globe and Mail*, February 25, 1993, A8.

5. Lawrence Martin, *Pledge of Allegiance*, 273.

6. Cited in ibid., 41.

7. Cited in ibid., 61.

8. Jeffrey Simpson, "Mr. Mulroney's Farewell Tour of U.S. Ex-Presidents and Millionaires," *Globe and Mail*, April 8, 1993, A14.

9. Dosman, "Canada and Latin America," 529.

10. Ibid.

11. Rochlin, *Discovering the Americas*, 149.

12. "Canada's joining of the OAS represents not so much a decision to become a member of an organization as it does a decision to become a partner in this hemisphere. For too long, Canadians have seen this hemisphere as our house; it is now time to make it our home." See Joe Clark, "Notes for the Remarks," 1.

13. Eric Margolis, "We're Helping Castro Hang On," *Toronto Sun*, October 15, 1992, A6.

14. Slinger, "Fidel Would Make a Fine Father of Confederation," *Toronto Star*, February 18, 1992, A2.

15. Gorham, "Canada-Cuba Relations," 203–4.

16. Clark, "Notes for a Speech," 8.

17. Cited in Rochlin, *Discovering the Americas*, 199.

18. See Charlotte Montgomery, "Canada Seeks to Thaw Frost in U.S.-Cuban Relationship," *Globe and Mail*, April 14, 1990, A7.

19. "Canada Seeking Better Cuban Ties," *Globe and Mail*, April 27, 1990, A4.

20. D.G.T., "Cuba y Canadá," 9.

21. The first time that the ambassador used this metaphor was at a meeting held at the Canadian embassy in Washington and organized by the Forum on Canada and Latin America (FOCAL) of Ottawa to assess Canada's first year at the OAS, and was in response to a question put to him by the authors. The second time that he used the image was at the annual conference of the Canadian Association of Latin American and Caribbean Studies, held at Laval University in Quebec City.

22. See Department of External Affairs, "Canada Expresses Concern."

23. Larry Luxner, "U.S. Embargo Aids Canadian Ventures," *Toronto Star*, May 3, 1994, C1.

24. Cited in Scott White, "Bush Expected to Veto U.S. Export Bill," *Globe and Mail*, November 30, 1990, A7.

25. Cited in Government of Canada, "Canada Issues Order," 1.

26. Cited in "Canada Could Penalize," 1.

27. See "Canada Confronts a Big Mack Attack" (editorial), *Globe and Mail*, November 30, 1990, D6.

28. "Last year, this resolution focused solely on the legal issue of extraterritorial jurisdiction of national legislation. Canada has experienced the effects of inappropriate attempts to assert extraterritorial jurisdiction and strongly believed, and continues to believe, that the legal principles embodied in the resolution must be respected. We therefore voted in favour. This year Canada abstained. The resolution contained additional elements to the primary embargo by the United States on Cuba, something Canada has never commented upon." Personal letter from Louise Fréchette to the authors, November 15, 1993.

29. Jeff Sallot, "Don't Let Washington Call the Shots," *Globe and Mail*, July 16, 1993, A17. The opening paragraph of his column summarized well the growing corporate anxiety at Ottawa's lack of initiative: "Who's in charge here? The Canadian Parliament? Or the U.S. Congress? Some Canadian subsidiaries of U.S.-based firms are turning away business deals with Cuba despite Canadian free-trade laws."

30. See "Jays Watch White House Signals," *Ottawa Citizen*, February 5, 1993, A6.

31. Letter from Rev. Dr. Howard M. Mills, general secretary, United Church of Canada, to the Hon. Barbara McDougall, secretary of state for external affairs, October 14, 1992.

32. Smillie, *The Land of the Lost Continent*, 151.

33. Letter of John Foster, national secretary, OXFAM-Canada, to the Hon. Perrin Beatty, secretary of state for external affairs. Significantly, the letter concluded: "We urge you to continue Canada's opposition to the American embargo on Cuba. . . . We believe Canada's position would carry much more weight, however, were we to set a better example with our own policies regarding the humanitarian needs of the Cuban people."

34. Unclassified telex from the Canadian embassy to External Affairs, April 11, 1991, 1, 6.

Chapter 6

1. Sallot, "Liberals Seek Elbow Room from U.S.," *Globe and Mail*, November 13, 1995, A4.

2. Cited in Giles Gherson, "In Mexico and China, Trade and Gentle Persuasion Are Ottawa's Way," *Globe and Mail*, March 25, 1994, A18.

3. Cited in Ross Howard, "Canada Puts Trade before Rights," *Globe and Mail*, May 12, 1995, A1.

4. Cited in Sallot, "Liberals Seek Trade Ties with China," *Globe and Mail*, November 29, 1993, A4.

5. Cited in Jonathan Manthorpe, "Ottawa's Human Rights Tradeoff," *Moncton Telegraph Journal*, July 24, 1995, A9.

6. Cited in Rod Mickleburgh, "Beijing Gives Chrétien a Boost," *Globe and Mail*, November 7, 1994, A4/A7.

7. Cited in Sallot, "PM Calls for United Front with Mexico," *Globe and Mail*, March 26, 1996, A1.

8. Cited in Bob Cox, "Chrétien Veers Away from U.S. in Foreign Policy," *Halifax Mail-Star,* November 26, 1994, B7.

9. Cited in Mimi Whitefield, "Saying 'the Cold War Is Over,' Canada Restores Aid to Cuba," *Miami Herald,* June 21, 1994. The citations in this paragraph attributed to Christine Stewart and Douglas Campbell are from the same article.

10. Cited in Isabel Vincent, "Canada Calls for an End to Cuban Isolation," *Globe and Mail,* June 8, 1994, A8.

11. Cited in Sallot, "Congress worries Chrétien, Zedillo," *Globe and Mail,* November 23, 1995, A3.

12. "Cuba's absence at Americas Summit," 3.

13. Ibid., 3–4.

14. Ibid, p. 4.

15. Letter from André Ouellet to Edgar Dosman, May 31, 1994.

16. Cited in Gord McIntosh, "Canada, Mexico Oppose U.S. Bill," *Halifax Mail-Star,* April 28, 1995, B16.

17. Cited in "Renew Ties, U.S. Told," *Globe and Mail,* April 19, 1995, A2.

18. Ibid.

19. Letter to the authors from Perrin Beatty, then secretary of state for external affairs, September 7, 1993, 2.

20. Government of Canada, "Cuba becomes eligible."

21. See Cuba-Canada Interagency Project, *Dossiers, 1.*

22. According to a June 1996 report on CIDA's 1995 activities, several projects in Cuba were being funded. Its Partnership Program administered 14 projects in Cuba worth Can.$1,272,293, the Industrial Cooperation division had provided Can.$661,114 in seed money for eight projects, the NGO division had provided Can.$547,179 for four projects, and the Institutional Cooperation division had allocated a further Can.$64,000. See CIDA, *Equity for Sustainable Growth,* 47.

23. Letter from Robert White, president, Canadian Labour Congress, to Prime Minister Chrétien, February 23, 1995, 1.

24. See Canadian Labour Congress, "White to strengthen," 1.

25. Jim McAuley, director of the tourism and hospitality management program at Mount St. Vincent University in Halifax, cited in Ward, "Cuba can do," 1.

26. See "Mining: Canadians See Gold," 3.

27. Cited in Rosanna Tamburri, "More Mining Companies from Canada Explore for Gold, Other Minerals in Cuba," *Wall Street Journal,* June 21, 1994.

28. "Canadian Mining Concern," 9.

29. Cited in Newman, "Going Capitalist on the Canbuck," 45.

30. Symonds, "Meet Fidel's Favorite Capitalist," 58.

31. Allan Robinson, "Sherritt to Mine Nickel and Cobalt in Cuba," *Globe and Mail,* December 3, 1994, B3.

32. Symonds, "Meet Fidel's favorite capitalist," 58.

33. In June of 1995, Sherritt's chairman Ian Delaney attempted to give an alternative view of Fidel Castro, with whom he has established a good personal relationship: "You don't keep his job by being a repressive dictator . . . he's charismatic, charming, a terrific listener whose depth of knowledge is very good." See Mathew

Ingram, "Sherritt Unfazed by Cuban Crisis," *Globe and Mail,* June 16, 1995, B7.

34. Cited in Drew Fagan, "Sherritt Assailed for Cuban Ties," *Globe and Mail,* June 15, 1995, B1.

35. Cited in ibid.

36. Sallot, "Canadian Officials Cringe as Helms Set to Resurface," *Globe and Mail,* November 28, 1994, A3.

37. Initially, President Clinton stated bluntly that he would veto the bill should it receive the blessing of both houses of the U.S. Congress. But after the tragic events of February 24, 1996, when two Cessna aircraft belonging to the Cuban exile group Brothers to the Rescue were shot down by Cuban fighter jets in an area straddling international waters and Cuba's 12-mile territorial limits, he changed his mind and signed the bill into law.

38. All quotations are from a copy of the letter, undated, provided by a senior Canadian diplomat who has requested anonymity.

39. Cited in Susan Delacourt, "PM Denounces U.S. Cuba Bill," *Globe and Mail,* March 4, 1996, A1.

40. Barrie McKenna, "EU Shares Canada's Dismay over U.S. Anti-Cuba Bill," *Globe and Mail,* March 19, 1996, B2.

41. Just hours after President Clinton signed the bill into law, Canada requested consultations with the United States before initiating a formal dispute settlement challenge of the law under the terms of the North American Free Trade Agreement (NAFTA).

42. Cited in Fagan, "U.S. Steps 'Beyond Rules' with Unilateral Actions," *Globe and Mail,* March 28, 1996, A8.

43. Cited in Fagan, "Eggleton Warns U.S. about Trade Bill," *Globe and Mail,* May 7, 1996, A1.

44. Organization of American States, *Resolutions,* 11.

45. Department of Foreign Affairs, "Government Announces," 2. In late August, Foreign Affairs Minister Lloyd Axworthy and International Trade Minister Arthus Eggleton met with U.S. special envoy on Cuba Stuart Eizenstat to discuss Canada's policy toward Cuba and the controversial Helms-Burton law. Both Axworthy and Eggleton made it known that they would not be coerced into changing Canada's policy of constructive engagement, nor would Canada desist from demanding the removal of the most offensive provisions of the anti-Cuba law. The *Globe and Mail* read on August 31, 1996, "Canada won't be coerced, U.S. told" (p. A4). The Liberal government also made known its intentions to introduce legislation in the fall sitting of Parliament to diminish the impact of the law through a series of amendments to FEMA. Drew Fagan, "Ottawa launching attack against U.S. law," *Globe and Mail,* September 13, 1996, p. B10.

46. Cited in Fagan, "Canada 'Selfish' to Oppose Cuban Law," *Globe and Mail,* July 10, 1996, A1. When the legislation was first making its way through the Senate (where it was approved in a 72 to 22 vote), Helms was just as outspoken. He sought to lecture Canadians on history: "Let me say to our friends in Canada: you have become a part of what you condone. . . . By their very advocacy in this matter and

by their opposition to this bill, they are condoning Fidel Castro. I suggest that they should be ashamed of themselves." Cited in Fagan, "Canada Assailed as Cuba Bill Passes," *Globe and Mail,* March 6, 1996, A1.

47. Charles Krauthammer, "Clintonism: Split, Waffle and Wait," *Washington Post,* July 19, 1996, A27.

48. The European Union request for a WTO panel was made in early February, with Canada and Mexico being third-party intervenors in the complaint.

49. Laura Eggertson, "Eggleton Delays Challenge of Helms-Burton," *Globe and Mail,* February 7, 1997, B1. Curiously, in a late January letter to the *Globe and Mail,* he wrote: "It is clearly premature to declare victory." He went on to say that Canada and its allies "are fighting hard against the law." Arthur C. Eggleton, "Canada and Cuba," *Globe and Mail,* January 30, 1997, A18.

50. See, for example, a particularly over-the-top editorial on January 23 by the *Globe and Mail,* "Canada's Gift to Mr. Castro," and Drew Fagan, "Our Man in Havana Wakes Up Washington," *Globe and Mail,* January 25, 1997, D1.

51. Laura Eggertson and Paul Knox, "Cuba Law Swaying Canada, U.S. Says," *Globe and Mail,* January 22, 1997, A1.

52. "Cuba Visit Likened to Appeasing Hitler," *Globe and Mail,* January 24, 1997, A8.

53. Ibid.

54. Paul Knox, "Canada, Cuba Agree on Trade, Aid," *Globe and Mail,* January 23, 1997, A1.

55. "Cuba Visit Likened to Appeasing Hitler." Prime Minister Chrétien, on a state visit to France, was quick to react to U.S. criticism of the Axworthy visit. He noted: "They're just making it possible for Castro to stay in power, because he has an excuse, he can blame the Americans. Let them normalize the situation between Cuba and the United States and I don't think Mr. Castro will have it easier." Madelaine Drohan, "Chrétien fuels fight by blaming U.S. for helping Castro," *Globe and Mail,* January 23, 1997, A11.

56. One could also take into account a number of other ancillary factors: Axworthy's personal interest in Cuba; this visit as a response to previous visits to Canada by Foreign Minister Robaini, National Assembly President Ricardo Alarcón, and Cuban Vice-President Carlos Lage; and the fact that the Canadian business community has been urging the government to strengthen linkages with Cuba.

57. Newman, "Going capitalist," 45.

58. Cited in "Clinton States Position on Vietnam," *Globe and Mail,* July 12, 1995, A5.

Conclusion

1. See the general summary of bilateral relations issued by the Caribbean and Central America Relations Division (LCR), "Cuba: Political and Economic Situation," issued in 1995, 1.

2. The summary continues: "In the area of human rights, Canada has encouraged Cuba to improve its record on civil and political rights. Canada has co-spon-

sored resolutions in the UN on Cuba's human rights performance and regularly raises human rights concerns directly with the Cuban government, both in Ottawa with the Cuban embassy and in Havana through our ambassador. We have encouraged Cuba to cooperate with the Inter-American Commission on Human Rights." Ibid., 2.

3. Ibid.

4. The Senate of Canada, Report of the Standing Committee on Foreign Affairs, "Free Trade in the Americas: Interim Report," August 1995, 60.

5. "The Canadian Government should continue to use every opportunity to raise its concerns about Cuba's human rights record. . . . In addition to bilateral action, we recommend that the Canadian Government continue to support multilateral efforts, such as those of the UN Commission on Human Rights, to persuade the Cuban Government to show greater respect for human rights." Ibid., 62.

6. Fidel Castro in a private address to the Nova Scotia business delegation that visited Cuba in January 1994.

Bibliography

Barry, Donald, ed. *Toward a North American Community?* Boulder, Colo.: Westview Press, 1995.

Bothwell, Robert. *Canada and the United States: The Politics of Partnership.* Toronto: University of Toronto Press, 1992.

Boyer, Harold. "Canada and Cuba: A Study in International Relations." Ph.D. dissertation, Simon Fraser University, 1972.

Brenner, Philip. *From Confrontation to Negotiation: U.S. Relations with Cuba.* Boulder, Colo.: Westview Press, 1988.

Campbell, Beverly. "Cuba-Nova Scotia Trade Growing." *Cubanews* 4, no. 5 (May 1996): 7.

"Canada Aiding Embargo?" *Cubanews* 4, no. 5 (May 1996): 7.

"Canada Could Penalize Subsidiaries that Observe Torricelli Bill." *Granma Weekly Review,* October 4, 1992: 1.

Canadian Conference of Catholic Bishops. "Notes on a CCCB Visit to the Cuban Bishops," April 26, 1995, unpublished mimeo.

Canadian International Development Agency. *Equity for Sustainable Growth.* Ottawa: CIDA, June 1996.

———. *Canadians in the Third World: CIDA's Year in Review, 1980–81.* Ottawa: Ministry of Supplies and Services, 1982.

Canadian Labour Congress. "A Report of the CLC Mission to Cuba, April 8–12, 1995."

———. "White to Strengthen Ties to Cuban Workers," CLC Communiqué, April 10, 1995.

"Canadian Mining Concern to Sign Joint Venture Contract." *CubaINFO* 5, no. 9 (July 16, 1993): 9

Chrétien, Jean. *Straight from the Heart.* Toronto: Key Porter Books, 1985.

Clark, Joe. "Notes for the Remarks by the Rt. Hon. Joe Clark, P.C., M.P., Secretary of State for External Affairs at the Meeting of the General Assembly of the Organization of American States, November 13, 1988."

———. "Notes for a Speech by the Secretary of State for External Affairs, the Rt. Hon. Joe Clark, to the University of Calgary on Canadian Policy towards Latin America." 90/08, Calgary, Alberta, February 1, 1990.

Clarkson, Stephen. *Canada and the Reagan Challenge.* Toronto: James Lorimer, 1982.

Clarkson, Stephen, and Christina McCall. *Trudeau and Our Times: The Magnificent Obsession.* Toronto: McClelland and Stewart, 1990.

CONAS, *Cuba: Investment and Business.* Havana: CONAS, 1994.

———. *Cuba: Investment and Business, 1995–1996.* Havana: CONAS, 1995.

Cuba-Canada Interagency Project. *Dossiers.* Ottawa: CCIP, mimeo, April 1995.

"Cuba's Absence at Americas Summit Skirts Formal Agenda." *CubaINFO* 6, no. 16 (1994): 3.

Department of External Affairs. "Canada Expresses Concern about Human Rights Situation in Cuba." *Communiqué* 237, December 17, 1992.

———. *Foreign Policy for Canadians.* Ottawa: Queen's Printer, 1970.

Department of Foreign Affairs and International Trade Canada. "Canada Encouraged by U.S. President's Decision on Helms-Burton Act." *News Release* 127. July 16, 1996.

———. "Cuba: Political and Economic Situation," April 1995.

———. "Government Announces Measures to Oppose U.S. Helms-Burton Act." *News Release* 115, June 17, 1996.

D.G.T. "Cuba y Canadá por el camino de mayor entendimiento." *Granma Resumen Internacional,* May 6, 1990: 9.

Diefenbaker, John G. *One Canada: The Memoirs of the Right Honourable John G. Diefenbaker.* 3 vols. Toronto: Macmillan, 1975–77.

Domínguez, Jorge. *To Make a World Safe for Revolution: Cuba's Foreign Policy.* Cambridge, Mass.: Harvard University Press, 1989.

Dosman, Edgar J. "Canada and Latin America: The New Look." *International Journal* 47, no. 2 (Summer 1992): 529–54.

———. "Hemispheric Relations in the 1980s: A Perspective from Canada." *Journal of Canadian Studies* 19, no. 4 (Winter 1984–85): 42–60.

Erisman, H. Michael. *Cuba's International Relations: The Anatomy of a Nationalistic Foreign Policy.* Boulder, Colo.: Westview, 1985.

Erisman, H. Michael, and John M. Kirk, eds. *Cuban Foreign Policy Confronts a New International Order.* Boulder, Colo.: Lynne Rienner, 1991.

Feinsilver, Julie. *Healing the Masses: Cuban Health Politics at Home and Abroad.* Berkeley: University of California Press, 1993.

Ghent-Mallet, Jocelyn, and Don Munton. "Confronting Kennedy and the Missiles in Cuba, 1962." In *Canadian Foreign Policy: Selected Cases,* edited by Don Munton and John Kirton, 78–100. Scarborough, Ont.: Prentice-Hall Canada, 1992.

González, Edward. *Cuba Adrift in a Post-Communist World.* Santa Monica, Calif.: RAND, 1992.

———. *Cuba: Clearing Perilous Waters?* Santa Monica, Calif.: RAND, 1996.

Gorham, Richard V. "Canada-Cuba Relations: A Brief Overview." In *Cuban Foreign Policy Confronts A New International Order,* edited by H. Michael Erisman and John M. Kirk, 203–5. Boulder, Colo.: Lynne Rienner, 1992.

Government of Canada. "Canada Issues Order Blocking U.S. Trade Restrictions." *Communiqué* 199, October 13, 1992.

———. "Cuba Becomes Eligible for Canadian Development Assistance." *Communiqué* 94–23, June 20, 1994.

Granatstein, Jack L., and Robert Bothwell. *Pirouette: Pierre Trudeau and Canadian Foreign Policy.* Toronto: University of Toronto Press, 1991.

Haar, Jerry, and Edgar J. Dosman, eds. *A Dynamic Relationship: Canada's Changing Role in the Americas.* New Brunswick, N.J.: Transaction, 1993.

Haydon, Peter. "The RCN and the Cuban Missile Crisis." In *Canadian Military History: Selected Readings,* edited by Marc Miller, 349–67. Toronto: Copp Clark Pitman, 1993.

Hennessy, Alistair, and George Lambie, eds. *The Fractured Blockade: West European-Cuban Relations during the Revolution.* London: Macmillan, 1993.

Hernández, Rafael, and Jorge Domínguez, eds. *U.S.-Cuban Relations in the Nineties.* Boulder, Colo.: Westview Press, 1992.

House of Commons, "Private Members' Business," February 20, 1995, *Hansard* (Debate on U.S. embargo of Cuba): 9791–800.

Instituto de Relaciones Europeo-Latinoamericanas (IRELA). *Cuba: Apertura económica y relaciones con Europa.* Madrid: IRELA, 1994.

Jeffrey, Brooke. *Breaking Faith: The Mulroney Legacy of Deceit, Destruction and Disunity.* Toronto: Key Porter Books, 1992.

Kingston, Anne. "Our Manager in Havana." *Report on Business Magazine* (December 1995): 51–61.

Kirk, John M. "Descifrando la paradoja: La posición del Canadá respecto de Cuba" (Deciphering the Paradox: Canada's Position Concerning Cuba). *Estudios Internacionales* 27, no. 107–8 (July/September–October/December 1994): 570–85.

———. "In Search of a Canadian Foreign Policy towards Cuba." *Canadian Foreign Policy* 2, no. 2 (Fall 1994): 73–84.

Kirk, John M., Peter McKenna, and Julia Sagebien. "Back in Business: Canada-Cuba Relations after 50 Years." The FOCAL Papers, Ottawa, 1995.

Klepak, H. P., ed. *Canada and Latin American Security.* Laval, Que.: Méridien, 1993.

Latin American Working Group (LAWG). "Canadian Investment, Trade and Aid in Latin America," *LAWG Letter* 7, no. 1–2 (May–August 1981).

Mader, William, "A Very Special Chemistry." *Time* (Canadian edition) (February 9, 1976): 8–11.

Martin, Lawrence. *Pledge of Allegiance: The Americanization of Canada in the Mulroney Years.* Toronto: McClelland and Stewart, 1993.

McDowall, Duncan. *Quick to the Frontier: Canada's Royal Bank.* Toronto: McClelland and Stewart, 1993.

McFarlane, Peter. *Northern Shadows: Canadians and Central America.* Toronto: Between the Lines, 1989.

McIntosh, Dave. *Ottawa Unbuttoned.* Toronto: Stoddart Publishing, 1987.

McKenna, Peter. *Canada and the OAS: From Dilettante to Full Partner.* Ottawa: Carleton University Press, 1995.

———. "Canada's Policy towards Latin America: A Statist Interpretation." *International Journal* 49, no. 4 (Autumn 1994): 929–53.

———. "Needed: A Policy for Latin America." *Policy Options* 14, no. 4 (May 1993): 27–28.

McNaught, Kenneth. "Castro's Cuba, Ottawa and Washington." *Saturday Night* 76 (January 21, 1961): 7–8.

Miller, Tom. *Trading with the Enemy: A Yankee Travels through Castro's Cuba.* New York: Atheneum, 1992.

"Mining: Canadians See gold." *Cubanews* 1, no. 3 (November 1993): 3.

Morley, Morris. *Imperial State and Revolution: The United States and Cuba, 1952–1986.* Cambridge: Cambridge University Press, 1987.

———. "The United States and the Global Economic Blockade of Cuba: A Study in Political Pressures on America's Allies." *Canadian Journal of Political Science* 17, no. 1 (March 1984): 25–48.

Murray, David. "The Bilateral Road: Canada and Latin America in the 1980s." *International Journal* 37, no. 1 (March 1984): 108–31.

Nash, Knowlton. *Kennedy and Diefenbaker: The Feud That Helped Topple a Government.* Toronto: McLelland and Stewart, 1991.

———. "Public Opinion in Cuba: Diefenbaker Si! Pearson No!" *Maclean's* (April 6, 1963): 2–3.

Nef, Jorge. *Canada and the Latin American Challenge.* Guelph, Ont.: Cooperative Programme in Caribbean and Latin American Studies, 1978.

Newman, Peter C. "Going Capitalist on the Canbuck." *Maclean's* (February 13, 1995): 45.

———. *Renegade in Power: The Diefenbaker Years.* Toronto: McClelland and Stewart, 1963.

Ogelsby, Jack. *Gringos from the Far North: Essays in the History of Canadian-Latin American Relations, 1866–1968.* Toronto: Macmillan, 1976.

———. "A Trudeau Decade: Canadian-Latin American Relations, 1968–1978." *Journal of InterAmerican Studies and World Affairs* 21 (May 1979): 187–208.

Organization of American States (OAS). *Resolutions Adopted by the General Assembly at Its Twenty-Sixth Regular Session.* Panama: OAS, June 3, 1996.

Parent, Gilbert. "Speaking Notes for the Honourable Gilbert Parent, M.P. Speaker of the House of Commons. Dinner in Honour of the President of the Cuban National Assembly. April 24, 1995."

Pearson, Lester B. *Mike: The Memories of the Right Honourable Lester B. Pearson.* Volume 3: 1957–1968. Toronto: University of Toronto Press, 1975.

———. *Peace in the Family of Man: The Reith Lectures, 1968.* London: British Broadcasting Corporation, 1969.

———. *Words and Occasions: An Anthology of Speeches and Articles Selected from His Papers by the Right Honourable L. B. Pearson.* Cambridge: Harvard University Press, 1970.

Pérez, Louis A. *Cuba and the United States: Ties of Singular Intimacy.* Athens: University of Georgia Press, 1990.

Pratt, Cranford, ed. *Middle Power Internationalism: The North-South Dimension.* Montreal: McGill-Queen's University Press, 1990.

Rich Kaplowitz, Donna, ed. *Cuba's Ties to a Changing World.* Boulder, Colo.: Lynne Rienner, 1993.

Ritchie, Charles. *Diplomatic Passport: More Undiplomatic Diaries, 1946–1962.* Toronto: Macmillan, 1981.

———. *Storm Signals: More Undiplomatic Memories, 1962–1971.* Toronto: Macmillan, 1983.

Ritter, Archibald R. M., and John M. Kirk, eds. *Cuba in the International System: Normalization and Integration.* Basingstoke, U.K.: Macmillan, 1995.

Robinson, H. Basil. *Diefenbaker's World: A Populist in Foreign Affairs.* Toronto: University of Toronto Press, 1969.

Rochlin, James. *Discovering the Americas: The Evolution of Canadian Foreign Policy towards Latin America.* Vancouver: University of British Columbia Press, 1994.

———. "The Evolution of Canada as an Actor in Inter-American Affairs." *Millennium* 19, no. 2 (1990): 229–48.

Sagebien, Julia. "Canada-Cuba Diplomatic and Trade Relations from 1959 to Mid-1995." Centre for International Business Studies, Dalhousie University. Discussion Papers in International Business No. 148 (October 1995).

Sawatsky, John. *Men in the Shadows: The RCMP Security Service.* Toronto: Doubleday, 1980.

Schuyler, George. "Canada and Cuba: A New Policy for the 1990's." Toronto, Canada-Caribbean-Central America Policy Alternatives: A CAPA Occasional Paper, February 1994.

Senate of Canada. Report of the Standing Committee on Foreign Affairs, "Free Trade in the Americas: Interim Report," August 1995.

Smillie, Ian. *The Land of the Lost Continent: A History of CUSO.* Toronto: Deneau Publishers, 1985.

Smith, Wayne. *The Closest of Enemies.* New York: W. W. Norton, 1987.

———. "Shackled to the Past: The United States and Cuba." *Current History* 95, no. 598 (February 1996): 49–54.

Smith, Wayne, and Esteban Morales Domínguez, eds. *Subject to Solution: Problems in Cuba-U.S. Relations.* Boulder, Colo.: Lynne Rienner, 1988.

Stewart, Christine. "Address by the Honourable Christine Stewart, Secretary of State for Latin America and Africa, to the *Economist* Conference's Second Roundtable with the Government of Cuba, June 20, 1994."

———. "Notes for an Address by the Honourable Christine Stewart, Secretary of State (Latin America and Africa), to the Symposium on the Helms-Burton and International Business Sponsored by the Canadian Foundation for the Americas and the Center for International Policy." May 16, 1996.

Stewart, Walter. *Shrug: Trudeau in Power.* Toronto: New Press, 1971.

Stursberg, Peter. *Lester Pearson and the American Dilemma.* Toronto: Doubleday Canada, 1980.

Symonds, William C. "Meet Fidel's Favorite Capitalist," *Business Week* (June 26, 1995): 58.

Thordarson, Bruce. *Lester Pearson, Diplomat and Politician.* Toronto: Oxford University Press, 1974.

———. *Trudeau and Foreign Policy: A Study in Decision-Making.* Toronto: Oxford University Press, 1972.

Trudeau, Pierre Elliot. *Conversations with Canadians.* Toronto: University of Toronto Press, 1972.

———. *Memoirs.* Toronto: McClelland and Stewart, 1993.

Ward, Joanne. "Cuba Can Do." *North American Policy Newsletter* (Halifax) 1, no. 2 (July 1994): 1.

Index